# GIVING WAY

# GIVING WAY

*Thoughts on Unappreciated Dispositions*

Steven Connor

Stanford University Press
Stanford, California

Stanford University Press
Stanford, California

© 2019 by the Board of Trustees of the Leland Stanford Junior University. All rights reserved.

No part of this book may be reproduced or transmitted in any form or by any means, electronic or mechanical, including photocopying and recording, or in any information storage or retrieval system without the prior written permission of Stanford University Press.

Printed in the United States of America on acid-free, archival-quality paper

Library of Congress Cataloging-in-Publication Data

Names: Connor, Steven, 1955– author.
Title: Giving way : thoughts on unappreciated dispositions / Steven Connor.
Description: Stanford, California : Stanford University Press, 2019. | Includes bibliographical references and index.
Identifiers: LCCN 2019007913 | ISBN 9781503610248 (cloth : alk. paper) | ISBN 9781503610835 (pbk. : alk. paper) | ISBN 9781503610842 (e-book)
Subjects: LCSH: Courtesy. | Inhibition. | Social ethics.
Classification: LCC BJ1533.C9 C66 2019 | DDC 177—dc23
LC record available at https://lccn.loc.gov/2019007913

Cover design: Rob Ehle

# Contents

1. Modulating — 1
2. Minding Your Tongue — 34
3. Backing Down — 64
4. Refraining — 94
5. Apologizing — 121
6. Losing Well — 148
7. Taking Care — 174
   Conclusion: Ministering — 205
   Works Cited — 219
   Index — 235

# 1 Modulating

SILENCE, RESERVE, SHYNESS, reticence, restraint, inhibition, forbearance, acquiescence, eschewal, withdrawal, detachment, discipline, distance, deference, repression, resignation, renunciation, concession, abstinence, abstention, holding back, humility, hesitancy, compliance, passivity, docility, succumbing, surrender, submission. None of these qualities can very easily be thought of as positive these days, and much of the time they will tend to be marked with disapproval, sympathy, or revulsion and to be regarded as failings rather than qualities. At least two of them, shyness and reticence, have been characterized as a mental disorder, in the form of social anxiety or social phobia. There are many interesting things to be said about the nature, appearances, and functions of shyness, but very few of them can be said in a literature that is concerned with identifying the causes and treating the effects of shyness (G. Phillips 1965; Crozier 1990; Lane 2007; Daly and McCroskey 2009). Allied qualities like patience and forbearance and self-sacrifice may not necessarily be thought of as negative, and may even on occasion provoke admiration, but can also seem to give off a sickly, saintly glow. What has happened to our sense of these comportments, which might once have been thought of as indispensable virtues, or at least indispensable to virtue, and why?

We might attribute our dislike of such terms to the alleged waning of religion, especially Christianity, which Nietzsche saw as a weak, petulant turning inward of the will on itself, and have done with it. But that old sociological assumption is hard to sustain these days, in the face of such various and vigorous forms of religious resurgence, even if those resurgences tend in fact to be expressed in much more aggressively assertive forms than in previous eras when the authority of religion might have been more established. Perhaps it is the effect of the wide acceptance of the value of what is called "agency," which makes everything that does not allow for or might require the restraining of agency, along with everything that might suggest the moderation of power rather than empowerment, puzzling or provoking. So we might cheerfully recommend people for "assertiveness training" (oddly oxymoronic idea though it may seem, to make people obedient to the imperative to assert themselves) but would shudder at the notion of, say, "acquiescence discipline"; we might prefer to call that "anger management," which has a stronger suggestion of taking charge rather than giving way. Some of the forms of restraint and refraining I have it in mind to explore can be represented as "self-control," which positivizes in a similar way. Much might be said in this respect about "willpower," a phrase recorded in print for the first time only in 1874, the meaning of which seems to flicker between the power of the will and power exercised (but by what?) over the will.

Even the word *virtue*, despite its virile beginnings and earlier associations, has come to seem rather feeble. This may have something to do with the fact that what we call virtues have tended to be identified with the specific virtues demanded of females, the virtues, for example, of chastity, modesty, continence, and patience in adversity. The revulsion toward this history of asymmetrical moral subjugation via the ideal of female virtue makes virtue itself, as opposed to more conventionally masculine qualities like strength, toughness, and courage, difficult to stomach or take seriously. So while we might allow for certain actions and outlooks to have virtue (but then that would probably just mean that they had a certain kind of utility) or be virtues, to call people "virtuous" would probably be to suggest something rather goody-goody about them or even that they are a little bit too concerned with cultivating their reputation. Merely being virtuous seems, despite what the word itself announces, insufficiently, well, virile, for our present taste, in which a generalized will-to-virility, or autonomized androgen, separated from its privatively masculine associations, holds uncontested sway.

There is no word for the countervailing values and actions that I set out to discuss here. That is, there is no one word. In fact, there are many words for what I would like to talk you into regarding as aspects and avatars and expressions of my subject, and some of them provide the titles of the chapters that follow. But I have not been able to find an existing word that would satisfactorily encompass them all, no zero-degree term of which *apology, politeness, reservation, resignation, submission*, and so on could be regarded as the inflected forms. At a time when dispositions of this kind dare not speak their name, and are rarely themselves spoken of except in regret, repulsion, or deprecation, it seems telling too that there should apparently be no inclusive name *for* them, no general term, to counterpose with *agency* or *empowerment* that might indicate that complex and internally variable end of the spectrum of attitudes and behavior in which one does not display agency or aggressively advance one's cause but is rather, to revive a folkish bit of nonsense I grew up hearing people say, "backward in coming forward." I have thought of naming the subject of this book "negative virtue," but that sounds more negative than I want to be, besides leaving all the work to be done by a not very specific adjective. If there were a nongerundive way of referring to different kinds of refraining, that might do—though I doubt that an invention like *refraint* is going to be up to the job. The antique-sounding *yieldance* was suggested to me by a friend who is rarely wrong about such things, and it certainly has an attractively courtly feel to it. Many of the terms we use to describe these forms of outlook and behavior—the blend that the word *comportment* seems to give—do indeed come in the form of negatives, even when they are used approvingly—as when, for instance, we say that someone is "unassuming." So one could also imagine a coinage like *undignation* exerting a certain amount of force. But what I want to try to come at is the positive force of such retractions and subtractions, such holdings back and standings aside. They may be regarded as positive, not just in their effects but also in the sense that there may be a positive impulse toward them. For I want to show that the mitigation of assertion and the attenuation of agency are indeed often powerfully affirmative and require skilled and attentive application. They are not just ways of not doing things, either with words or with actions, because the ways in which we hold back from doing things are themselves substantive actions.

In a sense, Giorgio Agamben's *impotentiality*, as a word for the capacity to decline to do things or the action of not acting, might cover many of the kinds of cases that interest me (1999, 182). In Agamben's explication, Aristotle distinguishes between a general potentiality, exemplified in the child who, through being able to be transformed by growth or education, may have a potential to become an architect or a poet, and the specific potentiality possessed by the one who is already possessed of the knowledge necessary to make buildings or poems:

> Whoever already possesses knowledge . . . is not obliged to suffer an alteration: he is instead potential, Aristotle says, thanks to a *hexis*, a "having," on the basis of which he can also not bring his knowledge into actuality (*mē energein*) by *not* making a work, for example. Thus the architect is potential insofar as he has the potential to not-build, the poet the potential to not-write poems. (179)

The capacity Agamben calls "impotential," translating Aristotle's *adynamia*, does not mean impotence, or lack of a power, but the power, so to speak, to lack or hold back. This is Agamben's explanation:

> In its originary structure, *dynamis*, potentiality, maintains itself in relation to its own privation, its own *sterēsis*, its own non-Being. This relation constitutes the essence of potentiality. To be potential means: to be own's own lack, *to be in relation to one's own incapacity*. Beings that exit in the mode of potentiality *are capable of their own impotentiality*; and only in this way do they become potential. They *can be* because they are in relation to their own non-Being. (182)

To be sure, the concept of impotential usefully points to the way in which the positive and the negative may be intermingled and the way in which the potential to do—which must be what is meant by power itself—implies and complies with the power to not do (and splitting the infinitive feels necessary for the positive action of nonperformance meant here). But in the end, impotential is still a form of potential rather than a way of actually doing things—except in the case where one conspicuously performs one action instead of another. What will preoccupy me in this book are the positive actions of avoidance, abstention, and forbearance, the performances, in other words, of nonperformance, that are nevertheless unmistakably actual to the point of forming the tissue and quick of social life.

I offer in the next few sections some remarks on some of the forms these positive abstainings and refrainings take: humility, resignation, mercy, and remission, all of which have operated as part of religious discourse but do not necessarily imply any relation to formalized religious belief, Christian or otherwise. All of them need to be seen as ways of withdrawing from action that nevertheless in themselves constitute positive actions—practices or delicate disciplines of stylized existence. We will see that the very fact that such practices seem like inflections of an absent or at least unnameable zero degree, for which I have so far been able to find no more clinchingly inclusive designation than "giving way," is part of the work of modulation or the civilizing deflection of violent absoluteness that they all do.

## Humility

We nowadays have no discourse on submission, which may suggest the tenacity of what we feel we should believe about it. Yet social life is nothing without and perhaps little but the willingness to submit and the skill in deploying submission. There is nothing we can do without submission, yet little we can do with it intellectually except instinctively, that is, unintellectually, to recoil from it. This tension suggests that there may be something to be inquired into.

The complexity of social demands and the mediated reach of social norms mean that we are perhaps more subject to forms of submission than ever before. More and more "experiences" are experiences of undergoing things, adventures of exposure, things to which we actively seek to submit ourselves.

The power of submission is indicated by how easily positive terms for politeness can start to imply dislike or disapproval for hypocritical displays of the quality in question. So nowadays being *suave* does not really suggest sweetness of disposition, while to be *unctuous* or *sanctimonious* is far from implying the genuine possession of religious grace or sanctity. We have lost or abandoned much of the language that allows us to express approval of withdrawal, reserve, or constraint. Politeness has become political, while meekness (*meek* has the same Germanic base as *muck*) now seems cloyingly unpleasant.

A similar movement seems to have occurred with the word *humiliate*, which, until the end of the seventeenth century, tended to be used reflexively, in expressions suggesting self-humbling, as in Robert Burton's injunction in 1621 that "we ought to feare our owne fickle estates, remember our miseries and vanities, examine and humiliate our selves, seek to God, and call to him for mercy" (1989–2000, 1.408). Over the next four centuries, *humiliate* gradually lost this reflexive sense and was extended to more transitive uses to signify the action of lowering or assaulting the dignity of others. By 1867, George Macdonald could write, "I think humiliation is a very different condition of mind from humility. Humiliation no man can desire: it is shame and torture. Humility is the true, right condition of humanity—peaceful, divine" (1867, 2.70). Humiliation is violation, effected by one on another, rather than a virtue practiced reflexively on oneself. Recent years have seen a growing acceptance of the idea that whole groups may be subject to forms of collective or "national humiliation." Here, too, the movement has been from reflexive to nonreflexive humiliation. Days of public fasting, humiliation, and prayer were proclaimed after disasters taken to signify the judgment of God or before undertaking some demanding collective endeavor, this happening as late as 1901 during the South African War.

We do not nowadays have a word for the action of self-humbling that used to be signaled by the word *humiliation*. The fact that the suspicion of hypocrisy or self-servingly strategic display can attach so easily to extravagant forms of self-abasement suggests that we might find a use for a term like *humilitation*, the aggressive, Uriah-Heep-like performance of humility. Not only can there be egotistical forms of self-abasement; one must suspect that all forms of self-abasement provide an opportunity for extreme ambivalence. There cannot but be the possibility of self-aggrandizement in the gesture by which one cuts oneself down to size, if only because, as the very word *human* implies, it is such a human speciality.

"The eternal silence of these infinite spaces terrifies me" (Pascal 1995, 73). There is indeed a terror in Blaise Pascal's contemplation, but in what exactly does it consist? Were I to say that the infinite silence numbed or silenced me, that might be the simplest acknowledgment of the disparity between me and the immensity of the It, for it would permit the It to enter into and inundate me. But my terror at the immensity of interstellar space is an insurgence in response to this immeasurability, a protest and protection against the enormity of its enormousness. And this insurgence pushes in two directions at once. To be sure, it compresses me inward, but it does so from some external vantage point, which gives me a picture of my immense littleness, allowing me an identification in imagination with the very immensity that diminishes me. This is a confirmation of the principle that every acceptance of a limit is an implicit transcendence of it.

There must always be a kind of magnificence in humility, if only because the condition of humility implies the action of humbling oneself or lowering oneself from some assumed state of grandeur, authority, or power. The combination of largeness and lowering in humility is indicated in the word *magnanimous*, which points to a largeness of mind that is expansive enough to encompass its own weakness, as in Wordsworth's sonnet "Great Men Have Been Among Us," in which the said great men "knew . . . / . . . what strength was, that would not bend / But in magnanimous meekness" (1954, 116). This dimensional duality is contained in the adjective *humble*, which since the thirteenth century has been used to mean both lowly (humble beginnings) and self-lowering (your humble servant). There is always the possibility of some minimal moral uplift in lowering oneself or restraining one's exaltation. This possibility seems to be recognized in the word *humility*, which could once be used to mean being humble in the first, unreflexive sense but can now signify being humble only in the second, reflexively self-lowering sense. So while it is still possible for objects to be described as humble, humility cannot now be ascribed to them, hence the oddity for modern readers of Charles Lamb's remark about a meager dinner that led him to "a sort of apology for the humility of the fare" (1913, 35). Humility must be performed or asserted in display, making it always liable to the suspicion of strategy. The suggestion of anthropomorphic humility does, however, persist in the idea of "unpretentious" dwellings, furnishings, or food. Humbleness and humility seem often to suggest an association with homeliness (welcome to my humble abode), though there is no etymological warrant for this, *humble* having a Latinate origin and *home* being Germanic. Despite appearances, wayfaring humans can often find something homely in humility.

The reflexiveness of humility echoes the reflexiveness that has accrued to the idea of "esteem." The earliest meaning of *esteem* was estimation. By the beginning of the seventeenth century, *esteem* was starting to be used without a qualifying adjective to mean good or favorable valuation, in particular in terms of reputation. *Self-esteem* tended before the nineteenth century to be used critically to indicate exaggerated self-regard, for example, in a 1619 attack:

> His wit being so shallow, and selfe esteeme of his owne worth and works so great, that as before he neuer more bragged thē wher he had least cause, and was most ouerthrowne . . . hauing passed the bounds of modesty by his . . . immoderate praysing of himselfe, without further reflection he rusheth forwards, and in lieu of this excuse and humble opinion of himselfe he cometh aloft with an *Iô triumphe*. (Coffin 1619, 353)

Gradually, through the nineteenth century, self-esteem itself came to seem estimable, as an equivalent to self-respect and, indeed, as an essential ingredient in the formation of a healthy and mentally secure individual subject, with "low self-esteem" becoming from the late twentieth century onward the target of systematic remedial effort.

Samuel Beckett may be regarded as a powerful exemplar of imperious humility or aggrandizingly low self-esteem. Though never showing serious signs of any kind of religious conviction, Beckett drew heavily on religious myths and language, especially to embody his sense of the humiliations of the flesh and the piteous arrogance of the intellect. He read Thomas à Kempis's *Of the Imitation of Christ*, a work dedicated to the virtue of humility, with approving attention in the early 1930s, and seems to have drawn repeatedly on it for his characterizations of the will-lessness he valued, or claimed to, given the logical trickiness of voluntarily seeking will-lessness (Ackerley 2000; Wimbush 2014). There is almost always a defiance in the forms of Beckett's submission, if only a defiant noncompliance with the values of expansiveness and willful self-assertion. Beckett's nonassertiveness is highly assertive, his quietistic giving way always grimly impenitent.

In fact, humility is always potentially paradoxical, precisely to the degree that it may be valued, and therefore itself the source of an approval and admiration that may unhumbly be internalized as gainful self-congratulation. It is for this reason that James S. Spiegel speaks of the "moral irony" of humility:

> Humility is a virtue, then, which turns the natural fallen moral condition of human beings on its head, introducing a different and more profound sort of moral irony. For in exhibiting this virtue, the humble person consequently increases in actual moral worth and is therefore deserving of greater moral credit than she otherwise would be and more than other persons who are not humble, other things being equal. (2003, 142)

There is a long tradition within Christianity of what may be called "sublime humility," a humility that identifies with the ultimate self-lowering or kenosis of the divine in the incarnation. In his "Letter to All the Friars," Saint Francis wrote rapturously of the Eucharist: "O admirable height and stupendous condescension! O humble sublimity! O sublime humility! That the Lord of the universe, God and the Son of God, so humbles Himself for our salvation that He hides Himself under a morsel of bread" (1906, 114–15). "Stupendous condescension" is nowadays readable only as a reproof rather than praise. Recalling the Petrine injunction "Humble yourselves therefore under the mighty hand of God, that he may exalt you in due time" (1 Peter: 6–7), Francis urges, "Consider, brothers, the humility of God and 'pour out your hearts before Him,' and be ye humbled that ye may be exalted by Him" (1906, 115).

But the possibility of calculating on exaltation in abasement may then seem to require a supplementary turning away from self—perhaps, given that *humiliation* has ceased to be available for reflexive uses, we might call such an act a "humiliance"—in order to disclaim the reward of approval that humility may garner:

> But—and this is the new, positive irony that supplants the irony of abject pride—the humble person refuses to act so as to affirm her greater moral worth (where "acting" may be taken in the broad sense, inclusive of speaking about or dwelling upon something). In fact, to consistently display humility and grow in it is to successfully resist the temptation to affirm one's increasing moral worth resulting from its demonstration. (Spiegel 2003, 142)

As I noted at the beginning of this chapter, cultural politics has been much taken up over the last few years with descrying and promoting the value of what is called "agency," which is usually taken to mean something like the power to act knowingly and affirmatively on own's own behalf. The primacy of agency seems to entail an understandable resistance to the condition of being without agency and a particular queasiness regarding the kind of voluntary curbing or surrender of agency involved in acts of submission.

Despite my rising irritation over the last few years with the unreflective parroting of the need for and value of "agency," agency is a complicated notion and, luckily for me, complicated in just the way that might be needed for an account, such as the one proposed here, of the modes of social holding back. *Agency* of course means the power to act and can sometimes seem to be used as a synonym for *action* itself. Human beings perform actions all the time—getting dressed, making cups of tea, walking to and from the bus stop—and they must necessarily and, for the most part, unremarkably, be the agents of those actions. But the word *agency* is used not to signify what is presumed and precipitated by action but what seems to make action possible in the future. The power to act, although it depends on and has all of its meaning by reference to the action toward which it is aimed, can be power only as long as it is not yet or in fact action. In other words, it can be the potential for action only as long as it holds back from it. Agency can have potency as the potential for action only as long as it is not in fact the potential for *action*.

In fact, in all its uses, the word *agency* indicates some indirectness, naming that by which, or through which, or on behalf of which, action is performed. Indeed, though agency suggests the power to act for yourself, the word itself always seems to stand back or aside from what we call direct action, especially, perhaps, through the phrase "acting for yourself": if you act for yourself, can you really be just acting? It is not just that the word *agency* must itself stand for an idea or projected intention of immediate or unimpeded action rather than be it; it is also that there is something substitutive or surrogatory in every kind of agency that looks less and less like what it is supposed to be the more closely one inspects it. Agency names a theory about the possibility of the kind of action I am able to perform. Wherever there can be agency, which sees and knows itself as such, it is something more or other than simple action. In knowing itself for what it is, and in being experienced as future possibility, agency must no longer be the elementary and unreflective doing of a thing that it is supposed to be. Of course, in most uses, agency tends to mean something like the power to perform valuable and significant forms of action, actions that are capable of emblematizing my status as a respected and freely choosing agent. Agency therefore signifies the power to perform actions that themselves signify my power to perform them. Agency has much more to do with a power to act, and therefore not to act, than with agency in the sense of simply doing things.

One effect, and so therefore sign, of this complex sense of reservation about action may be the flooding of erotic writing, especially by and putatively for women, by the idea of submission, and the reciprocal flooding of the idea of submission with the notion of the erotic: *Submission at the Tower*; *Maid for His Submission*; *Seducation and Submission*; *The Submissive Housewife*; *Spanked into Submission*; *Diary of a Submissive*; *The Submissive Deputy Head Teacher*; *Tracy Takes Control*; *Submissive Professors: Collared and Craving It*; *Submissive Sissy Short Stories*; *The Diary of an English Submissive*; and the fifteen-volume box set of Hannah Ford and Kelly Favor's *His Submissive*. If we are resistant to the idea of submission, submission is the resistance to this resistance. The strong identification of such writing with female authors and readers could easily be a cause for regret and moral reproof. That this does not happen more often may be the effect of the archness or self-protective performativity of such writing, which seems designed to keep ironically at a distance the submissiveness with which it plays. The reassuring sense of being prescribed would make ludicrously literalistic any suggestion that such submissive behaviors or dispositions might seriously be being prescribed.

## Resignation

Social life, like the inner lives of individuals, is made up as much of restrainings, withdrawals, reservations, and inhibitions, in all the forms of what Richard III vexedly calls "mannerly forbearance" (Shakespeare 2000, 179), as it is of projects, ventures, enterprises, and undertakings. One of the most striking forms is *resignation*, a term that, like *humility*, has come to seem like an unwholesome residue from a religious past, which schooled the poor and oppressed in salvation through resignation rather than resistance. In our boredom and impatience with the value accorded to resignation, we are all militant Nietzscheans, scorning the mustn't-grumble slave morality enforced by religions that urge their followers to suffer and be still.

But there are two sides to resignation, discernible in the prepositional flicker that makes all the difference between resignation to and resigning from. The first kind of resignation is reflexive, for it is oneself that one resigns, gives up or signs over, to suffering or irreparable contingency, whereas when one resigns one's occupation or office, one actively steps away from it, perhaps shedding or spurning it. In the course of counseling the first, approved kind of resignation in his poem *Resignation* (1762), enlarging the conventional sentiment found in his earlier, sensationally successful *Night Thoughts* (1742–45), that *"Patience*, and *Resignation*, are the Pillars / Of human Peace on Earth" (1989, 245), Edward Young comes close to articulating the relief that can come from the second, more active kind of resignation:

> *Resign*; and all the load of life
> that moment you remove,
> its heavy tax, ten thousand cares
> devolve on one above. (Young 1762, 21)

We can no longer use the word *resign* in the intransitive way Young does, to mean accept or accommodate yourself to; but our contemporary polarization of the passive and active modes of resigning may actually disguise their sinuous solidarity. There is more defection than acquiescence in this kind of active resignation. Indeed, in the active joining of one's will to that of God, there can be a divine kind of triumph:

> By closing with the skies we make
> *Omnipotence* our own;

that done, how formidable *ill*'s
whole army is o'erthrown. (34)

With that phrase "closing with the skies" Young means "coming close to" or means us to take him to mean that: but the appropriation of omnipotence that follows also suggests a kind of scrimmage with divinity, from which omnipotence is wrested.

What is resignation? *Resignation* can be used as a synonym for *despair* or the liquidation of the will, often as a way of coping with tensions that cannot otherwise be endured (Gourevitch 1980, 177–82). But like so many other ways of giving way, resignation should be understood as a complex blend of assertion and acquiescence. A resignation is the voluntary acceptance of a limitation of one's will. Abandonment is not resignation, for resignation maintains contact with the thing that one has lost. The Renaissance proverb "forbearance is no quittance," meaning that not enforcing payment of a debt does not amount to its cancellation, a proverb that Phebe in *As You Like It* brisks up to "omittance is no quittance" (Shakespeare 2006, 285), recognizes this continuing liability. Seeming resignation can in fact keep resentment at a sullen simmer. This is why you cannot in any simple way "resign yourself to your fate," because your resignation means that, in partially acceding to your fate, you imagine yourself partially as its author, thereby making of necessity a kind of choice and forcing a kind of freedom into fatality. In fact, just as it is not possible to live fully without being resigned to the fact of eventual death, so it is not possible to love, or live as a social being, without resigning a large proportion of our desires and what we may feel to be our entitlements.

To resign is to reassign, redesignate, or unsign, *signare* meaning to mark with one's seal. The primary meaning of Latin *resignare* is therefore to unseal, to open, disclose, release, or make available for others (though the word has on occasion been used transitively, as a synonym for *sack*, or force to resign). Resignation therefore has three axes: the person who resigns; that which the person resigns; and the one to whom it may be reassigned, or signed over. At the heart of this notion is the idea that to sign something is to make your mark on it, thereby making it your own. In the ritual gesture of making the sign of the cross on one's person known as *signation* (known also in earlier times as *consignation* and *obsignation*), one signs oneself over to another, effecting an identification with the crucified Christ, crucifixion itself being understandable as the reduction of the body to a mere sign. In use from around AD 150 among Christians, signation represents a kind of binding into a community, combined with an apotropaic warding off of evil, especially if combined with blowing and spitting (Vogel 1963, 40–41). Originally, signation involved making the sign of the cross on the forehead; the so-called grand signation associated with the Latin rather than the Greek church, which implicates forehead, chest, and shoulders, seems to have come into common use only from the beginning of the ninth century (50). Signation is itself a compromise between a sign and a corporeal wounding and so resembles a mobile, renewable tattoo. Tattoos, scarifications, and other bodily markings often indicate a kind of resignation, or reassignment, of the body; and it is telling that the physical remaking of the body to make it conform to the idea of a particular gender is nowadays named *gender reassignment*, the managerial-sounding term intimating a deeper, magico-theological force. In resignation, one gives oneself over to some other while, as it were, retaining custody of the act of giving. In giving myself away, I give myself to the act of giving, of which I retain custody and indeed can never be taken away from me. To sign myself is to make my self-dedication my own. This re-signing of the self is an elopement from the condition of having to be resigned to one's natural, which is to say, unchosen condition.

Early twentieth-century accounts of tattoos emphasized their prominence among outsiders, criminals, homosexuals, and those suffering from personality disorders (Ferguson-Rayport et al. 1955). The proliferation of tattooing, to signify membership in many different kinds of groups, may be a sign of a generalized wish for reassignment, a kind of mass need for identification, not as much with particular kinds of marginal or deviant group as with collectivized disidentification itself. G. K. Chesterton is said to have said that when one ceases to believe in God, one does not believe in nothing but rather in anything (I omit to supply a reference because he does not seem ever to have said any such thing). But we might articulate a similar principle with regard to this seeming need for or pleasure in self-dedication: as deference dissolves, it gives way to a devotion to voluntary devotedness, or a liquid system of solidarism.

Resignation therefore involves a tension with regard to action and agency. Resignation means a withdrawal or holding back from action. One allows whatever one is resigned to to take its course unopposed. But at the same time resignation names a very specific kind of action. Resignation requires an illocutionary act. One cannot properly be said to have resigned from something, as opposed to simply being resigned to something, unless an adequate performance of such an act has taken place. Not only must this act be performed; it must also in some circumstances be countersigned by the one who agrees or not to accept the resignation; as Thomas L. Dumm observes, a letter of resignation is "a collaborative act, undertaken by the resigner and those who are charged with the duty of accepting the resignation" (1999, 55).

The collaborative network required for resignation may be the reason that it is so difficult to resign from something experienced as a calling rather than an occupation. Edmund Bergler suggests that, in the case of writers, for example,

> *the megalomaniac pleasure of creation . . . produces a type of elation and pleasure which cannot be compared with that experienced by other mortals.* It is as near as one can come to infantile megalomania. A person who has tasted it even once (and even in fantasy, as is the case of writers who have never written a line) cannot be weaned from it. Once a writer, always a writer—at least in one's wishes. . . . It is impossible to resign from the writing profession, whatever the illusions of the person presenting the "letter of resignation." (1953, 42)

In this sense, resignation is the act of desisting from action, the enacting of one's impotential. This meta-act of asserting one's power to unact can be very important in circumstances in which there may be a suspicion that the resignation has in fact been forced, thereby undoing the agency of the act and turning a jump into a push:

> Maintaining a clear distinction between those responsible for forcing a resignation and the decision of the resigner to resign is often the goal not only of those who force the resignation but of the resigner as well. This distinction is important to the resigner because if others fail to distinguish the forces that cause the departure from the action of the person who resigns, they fail to acknowledge the agency of the resigner and hence implicitly denigrate his or her authority. (Dumm 1999, 55)

The necessity of a formal and performative dimension to the act of resignation—an "I hereby" kind of utterance often doubled by the magical act of forming a physical signature, or surrendering up one's name—indicates that a resignation is indeed a kind of re-signing, a performative unforming of a contractual bond that recapitulates the inaugural act of forming it.

Thomas L. Dumm's fine, intricate meditation on the meaning of resignation, whether formally announced or taking the form of the slow, locked condition of nonconsent to the conditions of one's life by those "resigned to not being able to resign" (1999, 65), or who have "failed to sign their resignations" (66), centers on the way in which resignation holds together public and private existence, in the making and breaking of promises, both in their way contractual:

> The character of a resignation, then, is potently public, a symbolic gathering together of those who had mutually promised by way of a formal address, in order to mark the breaking of the promise. And yet, because this public is being called together at the moment of its dissolution, simultaneously the act of resignation is potently private, dispersing the community of the contract that had been assumed to exist when the contract was being honored. (58)

If this leads to the conclusion that "anyone who is an individual is so by virtue of the fact that he or she has the capacity to resign" (61), then this is so because of the necessary knitting in of every individual to the kinds of contract that allow for resignation and to which one must resign oneself to qualify as an individual. I can resign *from* only on condition of this resignation *to*.

The ambivalence of resignation can sometimes manifest itself in humor: There can be comedy in resignation, and one can resign oneself to the comedy of circumstances. To resign oneself may bring about something like the economizing on affective investment that Sigmund Freud saw in jokes. However, Freud's 1927 essay "Humour" makes a distinction between resignation and the operations of humor, which he characterizes more as a triumph over circumstances than a succumbing to them:

> Like jokes and the comic, humour has something liberating about it; but it also has something of grandeur and elevation, which is lacking in the other two ways of obtaining pleasure from intellectual activity. The grandeur in it clearly lies in the triumph of narcissism, the victorious assertion of the ego's invulnerability. The ego refuses to be distressed by the provocations of reality, to let itself be compelled to suffer. It insists that it cannot be affected by the traumas of the external world; it shows in fact that such traumas are no more than occasions for it to gain pleasure. (1953–74, 21.162)

For this reason, Freud counterposes resignation and humor: "Humour is not resigned; it is rebellious. It signifies not only the triumph of the ego but also of the pleasure principle, which is able here to assert itself against the unkindness of the real circumstances" (21.163). But this surely takes too little account of the yield of pleasure to be had in resignation itself, which may have in it that element that Freud sees in humor of the superego looking down in indulgent superiority at the childish concerns of the ego: "In a certain situation the subject suddenly hypercathects his super-ego and then, proceeding from it, alters the reactions of the ego" (21.165). "Humour . . . means 'Look! here is the world, which seems so dangerous! It is nothing but a game for children—just worth making a jest about!'" (21.166). In distinguishing between resignation and humor, Freud effaced the humorous elements of resignation, the distance and uplift that make it different from despair or surrender. It is not that suffering is made negligible or ridiculous, for in that case there would no longer be anything to be resigned to; it is that a path is opened to a perspective from which it might seem so. Resignation does not convert the given to the chosen, exactly, but does at least seem to make it choosable. What relieves in resignation is not the change of sign but the opening of the possibility of reassignment. What we call the "significance" of suffering is changed from something that has significance to something that does not, and it is changed by a resignation that is also a resignification, as something chosen, which is precisely to say given its significance for me by choice or the consent that comes from choosing not to resent. To be resigned to something is to reassign oneself as a being capable of re-signing. Resignation is itself a form of rebellion: it may appear like a surrender to the given, but it is a resignation from givenness.

## Mercy

Resignation and humiliation have historically been modes of self-limitation exercised mostly by individual beings, either as specific codes of self-discipline or as ethical horizons of action. But there are also modes of self-curbing exercised by the bearers of collective power. Among the most important and powerful of these modes of self-limiting power is the exercise of mercy.

*Mercy* shares a root with *merchant* and *mercantile*, implying relations of transaction and exchange. When we say *merci* in French, we are making recompense by offering gratitude for some gift or service given. But this is probably why there is no one word in French for what in English is called mercy. For in English mercy signifies something that cannot be, to use Portia's word, "strained" (Shakespeare 2010a, 347), that is, expected, guaranteed, or claimed of right. You can sue for mercy, but you cannot count on it or bargain for it without destroying its claim to be mercy. Mercy is therefore a kind of grace and indeed is largely identical with divine grace. From a modern viewpoint that assumes the primacy of deserving and reward, it is one of the many mad and monstrous astonishments of Calvinism that salvation should be a matter of such complete arbitrariness, viewed from an ethical point of view. If grace is an arbitrary tempering of, or divergence from, the rule of law, then Calvinism may be regarded as a promotion of this arbitrariness itself to the condition of a law. Only mortals are subject to the slavish requirements of fairness; the proof of divinity is that it can destine what it likes. The force of this law is to be found in the fact that grace becomes a kind of force rather than a gift, in the doctrine of *grata irresistibilis*, or irresistible grace, which holds that it is not possible for the subject of divine grace to resist the call to salvation.

This leads to a strange and unexpected judgment. Liberal democracies like to imagine themselves as tender, tolerant, and forgiving and, therefore, more merciful in contrast to tyrannies, dictatorships, autocracies, or other kinds of totalitarian rule. Dominic Erdozain sees the beginnings of religious nonconformism in the radicalism of Gerald Winstanley and others in the seventeenth century as part of a "metaphysics of mercy" that rejected the idea of a distant and transcendent God: "Mercy pointed to pantheism," he concludes (2016, 83). But mercy is possible only as the mitigation, and therefore simultaneously the expression, of a sovereign and irresistible power. Mercy is therefore, a little unnervingly, the prerogative of tyrants. Mercy is not possible, or, if it is possible, can never be just in a just society that has set its face against all forms of arbitrary power. This is why it is not possible for individual judges to *pardon* criminals, a word that says they are given mercy *par don*, by means of a gift; judges who do so in effect, by imposing the most lenient of penalties, are rightly suspected of irresponsibly exceeding their power. As Jeffrie Murphy neatly explains, "If mercy requires a tempering of justice, then there is a sense in which mercy may require a departure from justice. (Temperings are tamperings.)" (1988, 167). Pardons are the prerogative of those who have, or at least are bearers of the idea of, sovereignty.

Mercy is not only, in Portia's words, "mightiest in the mightiest" (Shakespeare 2010a, 347); it is in fact really available only to the mightiest. We can certainly be kind, forbearing, and charitable even if we are not among the mighty, but our capacity to be merciful must always be directly proportional to our might. I can be merciful to a fly because I have so much power over it. But if I decide in the final round of a grueling but evenly matched boxing match to ease off my battered opponent out of mercy, then my mercy will be at the very least disrespectful, in that it will involve an assumption that I actually have the power to be merciful, an assumption that may be both false and foolhardy. Mercy is for this reason grandiose, though we are accustomed to think of it as a mark of gentle modesty.

Partly for this reason, mercy must always also be unnecessary and gratuitous: you can be merciful only in the absence of any absolute requirement that you do so and, often, in fact when the odds are dead against it. And this is why, under some circumstances, the guard in a concentration camp, say, sparing an inmate simply to show she can, the exercise of mercy can be indistinguishable from a sadistic expression of power. The gap in standing and worth that is always required for the exercise of mercy can often be secured by the deliberate submission of the one who sues for it: people do not on the whole "apply for" or "request," and can certainly never "demand," mercy; rather, they "throw themselves on the mercy" of the one from whom it is sought, since they have no chance of being shown mercy if they display any sign of thinking they have a right to it. Pious people who trust to the mercy of God, on the grounds perhaps that mercy can be counted on from such a source at least, must be concealing from themselves what they otherwise know about mercy. If a merciful God were constrained always to be merciful, then it could neither be merciful nor a God.

During his first term, Donald Trump exercised his instinct for outraging people by issuing pardons to persons whose claim to it seemed dubious—even though that is exactly the point about mercy, that you are eligible for it only if you do not in fact deserve it. In June 2018, speaking on ABC's *This Week* with presenter George Stephanopoulos, Trump's legal adviser Rudy Giuliani delivered himself of the view that there was nothing in the US Constitution to prevent the president from pardoning himself if he were summoned by the investigation of special counsel Robert Mueller concerning whether he may have colluded with Russia's interference in the 2016 election ("*This Week* Transcript 6-3-18" 2018). Though the articulation of this view caused astonishment, I think it has to be admitted that the US president probably does have the power arbitrarily to set aside legal judgments on himself just as he has on others. This is precisely not because this power must be regarded as part of the web of rationally consistent democratic commitments of the US Constitution but rather because the president's right to pardon is a right to set aside considerations of justice, since arbitrariness is of the essence in exercising mercy.

Every time we exercise mercy, no matter what station we may occupy, whether president or pauper, we thereby empower ourselves in the exertion of a limit on our own powers.

## Remission

Our understanding of values and virtues tends to be simplistically bipolar, focusing on simple positives and the forces that act contrary to them, which we often mistake for their negations (a contrary is directly opposed to a primary meaning, but a negation may have no relation with it). We are particularly liable to this kind of psychomechanical dreamwork when our thoughts turn to questions of power. But most composite situations and events have more complex and angular relations of contrariety. Power has many different kinds of contrary: acquiescence is not, for instance, the same as submission, and having power, as seen in the discussion of agency earlier, is not the same as using it, even if it is not exactly its contrary either. It always partially weakens a government to put tanks on the street, because it encourages the insurgency to start totting up how many they have got. I will be interested throughout this book in the complicated forces and stresses involved in actions that a bipolar way of thinking might see as a simple absence of agency: the many forms of not-doing that we all know are nevertheless not ways of doing nothing at all.

This is particularly the case with the complicated way of doing things involved in the act of communication. The phantasm attaching to communicative media is of a hungry positivity, without shadow or contrary. It is impelled by a principle of absolute productivity, always aimed at overcoming resistance to itself. An online search for the phrase "Internet free zone" results in news of lots of zones of free, that is, unrestricted Internet: free to, therefore, rather than free from. Similarly, what are known as "data shields" are shields for data, not from it. When we think of what are sometimes rather exasperatedly known as no-fi zones, on the analogy perhaps with no-fly zones, we think of areas or periods in which access to media is inadequately provided or actively prohibited.

But there are also forms of voluntary sequestering from media. Software packages that help users keep themselves free from Internet contact include SelfControl, AntiSocial, Freedom, and Cold Turkey. There are also socially sanctioned places of retreat or quiet zones amid the hubbub of contemporary communications. British intercity trains are often equipped with a Quiet Coach, in which the use of mobile phones is strongly deprecated. We know that one of the reasons that overhearing people on mobile phones can be so disturbing is that people tend to speak more loudly and at a higher pitch on telephones, even though this is less necessary than in ordinary face-to-face conversation: my mother always stood up to perform the act known as "telephoning," in the intransitive usage that once held sway, as though to give her voice greater carrying power. In fact, though, the disturbance caused by somebody speaking on a mobile phone also seems to have something to do with the fact that the person is betraying or subtracting himself or herself from the present-at-hand social space, thereby in a sense not merely ignoring it, as one lost in reverie might, but somehow draining and derealizing it.

There are other kinds of quiet zones. Nearly all networked devices allow you to enable Flight Mode, which many use on the ground when traveling to protect themselves from large roaming data charges. Hospitals sometimes impose restrictions on cell-phone use in order to avoid interference with sensitive medical equipment. Telephone calls are often interrupted on the 91 bus in London as it passes through what appears to be an area of inhibited signal around HM Prison Pentonville on London's Caledonian Road. Perhaps the earliest and still the most extensive Quiet Zone was set up around the National Radio Astronomy Observatory in Green Bank, West Virginia, which was built in a valley that already did a good job of keeping out electromagnetic signals. In 1958, the National Radio Quiet Zone was established, forbidding all radio and electromagnetic transmissions. Residents in an area of thirteen thousand square miles sign an agreement that they will forgo the use of microwave ovens, Wi-Fi, cordless telephones, and even, because of the interference produced by spark plugs, gasoline-powered cars. Restrictions of varying degrees of specificity apply to the areas around radio telescopes in other countries, but there are as a minimum restrictions on motorized traffic and the erection of radio transmitters: for example, in Ondrejov in the Czech Republic, Metsähovi in Finland, Penc in Hungary, and Medicina in Italy. In these cases, the zone is much smaller than in the United States, typically of a radius of around one and a quarter miles ("Radio Quiet Zones Around Observatories" 2018).

Surprisingly, perhaps, the imposition of the Quiet Zone has not produced widespread protests, or suspicions of nefarious military research, but has rather become a site of pilgrimage for people believing themselves to suffer from the condition of electromagnetic hypersensitivity, who attribute their headaches, nausea, debility, weight loss, and other conditions to the proximity of cell-phone towers, power lines, lawnmowers, and other electrical devices. One sufferer, Diane Schou, explained that "the electricity became so painful that when a neighbour ran their coffee-maker I was in such pain, with such a headache" ("Why Does This U.S. Town Ban WiFi and Cell Phones?" 2016). In 2015, two filmmakers, Karl Lemieux and David Bryant (guitarist with the band God Speed You Black Emperor!), produced *The Quiet Zone*, a film that explored and attempted to convey the symptoms of those who sought safe haven from electromagnetic persecution in the National Quiet Zone. This is all the more remarkable since part of the work of the national radio telescope in Green Bank is scanning the skies for signs of extraterrestrial intelligence. It seems that the electromagnetic refugees who have settled in the region are more sanguine about the possibility of alien transmissions than they are about the effects of the interior alienation of terrestrial media. It does not in fact appear that sufferers from electromagnetic hypersensitivity can reliably detect the presence or, similarly, the absence, of electromagnetic fields.

Predictably, there is a community, mediated, of course, through websites and Internet videos, that aims to spread understanding of, and offers expertise and training in, the dangers of "electrosmog" and ways of taking refuge from it. There are claims that the danger of electrosmog is dramatically on the increase. Two contributors to the journal *Electromagnetic Biology and Medicine* asserted dramatically that

> the group of electrosensitive people around the world, including Sweden, is not just a small fraction that deviates from the rest of the healthy population. Instead, it points at the possibility that electrosensitivity will be more widespread in the near future. The extrapolated trend indicates that 50% of the population can be expected to become electrosensitive by the year 2017. (Hallberg and Oberfeld 2006, 189)

Some of the persecution feelings relating to information overload can come close to the "influencing machine" delusions described by Viktor Tausk (1933). But those who seek relief from contemporary media and information seem to see media not as invasion but as solicitation—though we might recall that Daniel Paul Schreber's invasive and emasculating rays produced "a greatly increased feeling of voluptuousness" as well as torment (2000, 59). Today's form of the "technical delusion," as the "influencing machine" psychosis is sometimes called, is likely to be experienced not as taking over your thoughts but as operationalizing your own interior monologue, making it appear not as an alienating machine but as an immanenting machine, a machine that pirates you with yourself.

Ever since *The Parasite* (1980, 1982b) and most recently in *Le mal propre* (2008b, 2011), Michel Serres has linked communication not only to joy, blessing, and invention but also to dirt, death, and the violent appropriation of space. You can occupy space by physical force, but it is much cheaper and more durable to occupy space through media—through making a subject people communicate in your language rather than in theirs, for example, or by drowning out the possibility of communication in noise, hubbub, racket, or, in electronic terms, what has become known in English since the beginning of World War 1 as "jamming." *Le dur ne dure pas, seul dure le doux* is Serres's motto for this (2008a, 115): the hard does not endure, only the soft. Serres followed his book *The Parasite*, which ends in a paradoxical overload of interferences, with his book *Detachment*, which is an exploration of the saving grace of gaps, remissions, and spaces of suspension. The book begins with a nightmarish evocation of intensive cultivation in China and evokes the necessity for spaces apart from such enclosing exposure:

> I can breathe freely and fully only in a field because it is bordered by brushwood full of quarrelling birds, because that field lies at the outskirts of a forest, marked by deserted areas, by spaces left fallow, badly tilled. (Serres 1989, 7)

David Jay Bolter and Richard Grusin use the term *remediation* to signify "the formal logic by which new media fashion prior media forms" (1999, 273). If *remediation* is the word for the self-propagation of media, media mediating themselves, then media remission might be regarded as a kind of remedy for media. Indeed, the word *remediation*, translating Latin *remediatio*, was in use in English from the late eighteenth century to mean remedy or therapy, and the word is still used to mean mitigation or abatement of a wrong or danger. This makes the word *remediation* something of a pharmakon, at once toxin and auto-antidote. There is an economy of dilation and deterrence in all media, meaning that every medium or mode of mediation must at some point need to be subject to moderation. Indeed, *media* and *moderation* share the root meaning of think, weigh, take account of, as in Greek μέδο μαι, to think, be concerned with (Ernout and Meillet 2001, 392). Émile Benveniste speculates interestingly on the relation between words that unfold from the Indo-European root *med-* and *medicus*, a physician, the parallel between Latin *medeor* and Avestan *vī-mad*, to treat or care for the sick, suggesting that the shared conception may be the idea of treating in a measured or appropriate manner. Benveniste finds in the word *modus* the idea of "a measure imposed on things, which supposes knowledge, reflection, authority: not a measure of mensuration (as in *mensis*, month), but a measure of *moderation* (cf. *modus: moderor*), applied to that which ignore or violates rule" ("une mesure *imposée* aux choses et qui suppose connaissance, réflexion, autorité; non une mesure de mensuration [comme dans *mensis*], mais une mesure de *modération* [cf. *modus: moderor*], appliquée à ce qui viole ou ignore la règle") (1945, 5). The mediation of medicine involves careful reflection, as attested by the related term *meditation*. There are very few, if any, groups of humans who do not conceive of health in terms of the equilibrium of quantities, whether of humors, or elements, or chi, or other forms of magic energy, implying that there may be quite a dense entanglement between medicine, moderation, and media, which goes far beyond familiar notions like music therapy. Calvin Watkins has similarly explored the networks of association in Indo-European languages between poetry, the magical convergence between word and measure, and medicine (1995, 537–45).

Every phase of intensified mediation, every net increase in transmissive capacity, seems to prompt the apprehension of overload and the countervailing necessity for remission, or medical media modification. The problem of overcoming limits is always liable to flip into, or be shadowed by, the problem of resisting limitlessness or tempering saturation. The mass producibility and reproducibility of texts is remarked on perhaps twenty-five hundred years ago as one of the forms of human vanity and weariness in Ecclesiastes: "Of making many books there is no end; and much study is a weariness of the flesh" (12:12). Mediation always both impels and imperils propriety (property, appropriateness), allowing for the enlargement of territory and threatening the self-possession of others. The need to keep your data safe increases in parallel with the need to keep yourself safe from data, even, perhaps, your own. This is classically a problem of sound: the increase in the volume, in both senses, of sound transmissions creates the pressure for noise abatement. But sound typically provides the register in which to discuss the pressure of mediation itself.

Communication is necessary for human social existence, but the more extensively socialized, and therefore the more intensively mediated, human existence becomes, so the more necessary the principles of distance, spacing, or suspension are to maintain peaceful coexistence. The moderation or modulation of media is an important part of the codes of politeness that Norbert Elias (1978) saw as necessary to the cooling of aggression and violence in what he called the "civilizing process." Walter Ong is often considered to be the proponent of oral forms of human communication, with their capacity to enact presence and the sense of pleasurably shared being, but he also warned that oral cultures are often anxious, unstable, and violent, precisely because there is nothing within immediate communication to hold back the communication of violent impulse (1967, 132–33). For Ong, orality is, as he puts it, "adversative" (1989, 35), and writing is an abatement of the unquestionable immediacy of voice, helping scoop out the subject in the fine and private place of the mind (1967, 135). This accords with Jacques Derrida's offhand but far-reaching remark, made in passing in the context of reflections on a tape-recorded interview, that "language, in the strict sense, oral discourse, is already, *almost* in its totality, a machine for undoing urgency" (1995, 34).

In fact, remission and transmission are interpenetrating opposites, meaning that transmission must depend on patterns of interior remission. In English, to remit means both to make a payment as required and to waive the requirement for the payment altogether, as in the remission of sin in religion. So one remits a payment that is due, but the one to whom it is due also has the option of remitting the debt, that is, canceling it, the idea being perhaps that the debt is being sent back.

Freud suggested in *Beyond the Pleasure Principle* that Eros is to connection and complexity as Thanatos is to dispersal and disconnection (1953–74, 18.55). Perhaps all media are impelled by, or at least amount to, a kind of death drive, aiming at their own abolition in the absolute immediacy of the perfect mediation. At the same time, there is the impulse to procrastination, or self-deterrence, in every medium, a reflexive self-tending or what Gilles Deleuze calls an "inclension" (1993, 3) that makes every medium in part an attempt to jam or interfere with its own work of mediation. This is in fact the real death drive inhabiting every medium that turns it inward on itself, progressively drowning every signal in the fiddle-faddle of its own circumstance. It is this deterrence of communication that Internet self-denial attempts to deter.

Data abatement, the remission of transmission, the moderation of mediation, is a kind of mercy as well as a mutilating prohibition. But we should not forget that mercy is a secondary effect of absolute power, precisely as its arbitrary or gracious suspension—as soon as mercy became an established part of a democratic system of justice, it would be unjust. As we have seen, that is why mercy and the remission of sin is in the hands of a deity who cannot be sued, only pleaded with.

In fact, media and media systems are not to be thought of as either positively present or, as it were, positively absent, since, to be effective, every code must be able to encode its own abeyance, transmit its own remission. Whether in music, language, or mathematics, mediation starts to do much more work as soon as there is a zero sign, a sign for the suspension of signification, or communication, as we say, in standby mode. Indeed, the word *zero* spawns the word *cipher*, which, deriving from Arabic *ṣifr*, the arithmetical symbol for naught, itself a translation of Sanskrit *śūnya*, empty, means both an empty sign and, from 1528, a secret code (an apparently empty sign that in fact has something to it). There must be what is called in French the *mesure pour rien*.

What is true of human actions is true of the communicative media they increasingly use to perform those actions; the capacity to be off must be part of how a medium proceeds or goes on. All media and all media systems have a dimension of self-inhibition intrinsic to them. George Spencer Brown pointed in *Laws of Form* to the essential principle of reflexivity that seems intrinsic to the universe: "We cannot escape the fact that the world we know is constructed in order (and thus in such a way as to be able) to see itself. This is indeed amazing" (1969, 105). Just as remarkable, though much less often remarked on, is the fact that the principal yield and leading purpose of the capacity of systems to refer to themselves is to figure and operationalize their own withheld functioning.

Media not only have ways of shutting down; they also have means of modulation, that is, quantitative and qualitative variation, whether in the volume control; or the verbal moods, indicative, imperative, subjunctive, with which many languages are provided; or through genres, musical keys, and so on. Media are capable not only of different forms of amplification, through repetition, propagation, and translation; they also include capacities of self-diminishment and self-inhibition. They possess what in the title of one of his texts Samuel Beckett calls "lessness" (1995, 197–201). Media multiply not only their own instances and occasions; they also multiply intermissions of remission, quasi spaces of the "off," whether offside, offstage, off-air, offscreen, offshore, off-line, or on and off message, all of them means of "standing by."

The social life of media is built around patterns of exhibition and inhibition. There are no human groups without the power of communication but equally, and as part of the same condition, no human groups without secrets, obscenities, and sacred ineffabilities, things kept incommunicado, all of them, of course, depending on media systems for their existence. The ability to suspend speech in an impulsively vocalizing creature like a primate, in which sound making is closely linked to the limbic system and so scarcely to be distinguished from the feeling of which it is the index, is largely identical with the capacity for mediation itself, understood as the capacity to be and remain at a distance from what one represents. Articulation perfectly matches the duality of mediation, in that it both connects and separates. One must be able to say no to the medium that itself permits and brings into being the possibility of naysaying. Every medium must have a way of communicating its own zero degree, transmitting its own breaks in transmission. Such a signification is found at the end of Beckett's *Krapp's Last Tape*, as the tape spools emptily away (1986, 223). It is in fact a characteristic of all media that being off is a modality of their being on.

Media are, like many forms of human vehicle—horses, perambulators, boats and trains, books, symphonies, films and phones—both vector and habitat, ways of moving and ways of abiding. To live out of contact in an unmediated space is still to have some connection to mediated or media-saturated space. Time tends to be made substantial in terms of space, or rather certain ethereal kinds of imaginary "space-substances," that allow us a material correlate for the idea of a tenuity: as when we say that a signal is "patchy": something that comes and goes is experienced as a fabric of latencies and potentials.

The immanent silence of a medium, or zone of mediatic autoremission, has often been thought to be the reservoir of danger—transmitting what is known as "dead air," an unmodulated carrier wave, is still an offense in the United Kingdom—and also sometimes of magical possibility. The "electronic voice phenomena" that Konstantine Raudive (1971) convinced himself he had detected on blank recordings of an inputless microphone have had a long and excitable career in the ears and minds of those willing to believe.

So a crucial part of the potential of media is their power not to be. "Radio silence" indicates the necessity for withholding or retraction as part of the apparatus of media communication. Early radio users adopted the principle of nonoverlap through the conventionalized use of the word *over* at the end of one party's transmission, a word that splices the idea that the utterance is, at least for the time being, over, with the suggestion that it may therefore be passed over to the interlocutor. Space travel, or the necessary delay that comes even with signals moving at the speed of light, fills the plenum of media communication with painful rents and suspensions, the most agonizing in recent human history being the wait for return of radio contact following the ionization blackout resulting from the frictional heat of reentry into the atmosphere. No silence is primary; all silence is a subtraction, or holding back, an impotentiating of something held to be primary but that can only really have potency if it includes the capacity for self-limitation. The abeyance of sense can also provide dangerous loopholes. One of the ways employed at Bletchley Park for breaking into the Enigma code was provided by the fact that German radio operators in unexciting locations tended dutifully to report that there was nothing to report—*keinen besonderen Ereignisse*. These yawning articulations of nothing-doing supplied one of the most important blind spots of redundancy that helped the cipher to be deciphered (Milner-Barry 1993, 93–94).

We inhabit an era, or more likely an interval, of recoil from the seemingly irresistible and omnidirectional propagation of media techniques and effects, of which the expansion of media studies and the very idea of what might possibly count as a medium are a cooperating part. Such recoils are part of the climatic fluctuations of media. The urgent need seems to be for regulation, on the one hand, and stoic self-restraint, on the other. How do we know of this recoil, this impulse to manumission from mediated life? In the same way we know everything else: because we can read, hear, and see it everywhere, without a pause. Whisper who dares: remission is in the air, and everywhere writ loud.

## Manners

I do not mean to compose a lament for the loss of gentler, more concessive outlooks in an age of aggressive self-aggrandizement. In fact, part of my motivation is to investigate the strange fact that what we say and what we do and expect others to do seem in this respect so strikingly ill aligned. For even if we speak much less about forms of the inhibition of behavior, there is probably more pressure and expectation than ever before on individuals and groups to develop non-assertive or even frankly self-restraining outlooks. When it comes to sexism, racism, and other kinds of hostile prejudice, we rightly tolerate little in the way of empowering self-assertion and, in this and other respects, probably require of ourselves and others higher and more continuously exercised levels of inhibitive self-monitoring than ever before. If we are disturbed by the apparent need among students to create "safe spaces," or spaces of remission of free speech, in universities on the grounds that universities ought to be places in which young people (and, for that matter, old ones) encounter intellectual and emotional challenges—and I certainly myself have felt some uneasiness on this score—it cannot reasonably be because we think that social life ought to carry more risk of hurt, offense, and psychological injury than it does. Rather, it is to follow the immunological logic that exposure in measured doses to forms of threat and aggression allows for the development of a kind of emotional and intellectual resilience that in the long run makes one safer, while fearful nonexposure puts one at greater risk of having no resources to absorb or deflect threat and aggression. If this can sometimes seem like a matter of policing rather than politics, our growing sensitivity and responsiveness to the need to mitigate social harm and our active and widely shared willingness to reduce levels of aggression is one of the many proofs that, in Peter Sloterdijk's hair-raisingly optimistic words (I *think*, perhaps too optimistically, they are optimistic), "the path of civilization is the only one that is still open" (2009a, 18).

All of the terms I have been discussing tend to combine two rather different kinds of idea. One idea is holding oneself apart from others (distance, detachment, reticence). The other is holding oneself apart *from oneself* (deference, humility). They are both ways of not asserting oneself, but obviously operate differently, and can sometimes seem like opposites. Silence and detachment can be, or seem, arrogant and aggressive (sometimes "passive-aggressive," that rather telling locution). Apparent deference can also seem undesirably self-demeaning or suspiciously self-serving.

Nevertheless, they deserve, taken all together, to be thought of, if not necessarily as civilizing, then certainly as essentially civil and essential to civility. They are comportments unimaginable in any conceivable "state of nature" and without which the sorts of complex, demanding collective existence that human beings currently have would scarcely be possible. I offer in this book to reflect on a range of them and the actions in which they may be embodied, seeing them as virtues in which we are more expert than we seem to know but about which we have lost the knack of being, or the motivation to be, morally articulate.

Yet this book is neither a history nor a philosophical defense of what is called civility. My subject is a diverse class of behaviors that, though they are prominent in many understandings of civility, are not simply interchangeable with it. The different ways in which the impulse to withdraw, hold back, or stand aside exerts its effects have a kind of coherence or at least form a conversation among themselves, albeit one that is difficult to apprehend in the absence of a single term encompassing them all. This makes the subject of this book both less and more than civility. It is less, because it is one ingredient among others in the blend of behaviors and institutions that, broadly since the Renaissance in Europe, has become known as civility or, as its mooted product, civil society. Yet it is more than civility, because it is an ingredient in many other kinds of behavior, arrangement, and outlook. The growth of cities produced a distinctive set of pressures on their citizens, but I doubt that any human collectivity is conceivable without some of the elements of civility. One of the distinctive features of the idea of civility is that it tends to be privative, that is, it provides a way for a particular human group to set itself apart, either from the natural world or from other groups of humans. I want to claim that the binding force of abstention is much greater in most human groups than any positive characteristics they might ascribe to themselves or characteristic actions they may perform. In the particular form taken by European civilization, that civility was caught up in a militant exercise of subjugation of other groups, who are taken to be less civilized and closer to a state of nature. The story of how the "civilizing process" has been caught up in an exercise of imperial and colonial dominion has been rehearsed often and persuasively enough for it to be merely pious to repeat it here. Many of the accounts of civility that have appeared in recent years have seen it less as a way of diminishing power than of dissimulating it. Their emphasis tends to be on an understanding of politesse as social policing and on the diffusion or deflection of aggression as the internalization of systems of discipline and control. There is no need for me to break with or beat back arguments of this kind, though I do not share the conviction that power may reasonably be regarded as a kind of universal equivalent or common denominator in human affairs. The idea that once one has read off a given phenomenon as an expression of power or provided an account of the power relations within which a given phenomenon acts or is fixed, one has said enough and may safely move to other topics, may come to be regarded as part of the common sense of our days, a common sense about which we are curiously and uncommonly incurious. But we should not be surprised to find that the remission of power should be able to become so powerful and so should often need to find ways of exercising power over itself.

Cultures are often thought of in terms of constitutions and institutions, ways of occupying spaces and positions. Humans, who seem, at least to themselves, to have occupied the earth and proclaim the fact in the earthen name they give themselves, may have developed, or at least be the vehicle for, another mode of occupying space. It is evoked well in Michel Serres's reflections in *Genesis* on dance as an action of systematic displacement, as the answer to or deflection of the military understanding of the occupation of place, the trench-whispered mondegreen of reinforcement for advance into three and fourpence for a dance:

> Whoever is nothing, whoever has nothing, passes and steps aside. From a bit of force, from any force, from any thing, from any decision, from any determination, the dancer, the dance step aside. The step is a step aside. Thus is movement born, thus is grace born. Grace is nothing, it is nothing but stepping aside.
> 
> Thus is movement born, thus, perhaps, is born time.
> 
> Not to touch the ground with one's force, not to leave any trace of one's weight, to leave no mark, to leave nothing, to yield, to step aside.
> 
> The dancer steps aside. Dance leaves the spot, it gives way to any other. Dance is Alba itself, it is its blank space. To dance is only to step aside and make room, to think is only to step aside and make room, give up one's place. (1995, 47)

Peace, and therefore survival and the capacity for invention and diversification in human life, depends almost entirely on varieties of turning aside, the actions of deflection or defection often signified by the prefix *apo-*, related to Latin *ab*—apostrophe, apotropaism, apostasy, apophasis, apophony (vowel variation), apoplexy (lit., being struck off), apoptosis (falling away, especially in cell death), aposiopesis, apostle (one who is sent away), apothesis (laying aside, the setting of a fractured limb), abstaining. Apology is "speaking away"—*apo-logos*: excusing, explanation, justification. In Greek an ἀπόλογος is a story, fable, or allegory, that is, an oblique turning aside of direct expression. Apostrophe is literally a "turning aside" and is defined by Quintilian as the action during a legal representation of turning away from the judge to address some other person or personified object (2001, 210–11), this gradually being extended to absent, deceased, or imaginary persons.

My aim is not principally to argue for the importance or amplification of such comportments (surprisingly, perhaps, an amplification of acquiescence is indeed possible), though such arguments may well be considered along the way. In this, my aim is different from that of Benet Davetian (2009), whose impressive history of civility is powerfully animated by the assumption that an understanding of the anatomy of civility and incivility can help prevent social cruelty. I repose no such confidence in whatever kinds of understanding might be provided by this book. My aim is rather to make out for giving way, standing aside, and other oblique cases of social action, what I have been calling since the late 1990s a cultural phenomenology, an articulation of the work that, whether or not we are articulate about and aware of them, these comportments may nevertheless be doing (Connor 1999). When I first began thinking about what a cultural phenomenology might be, I thought that it would have the advantage of enlarging the cultural dimensions of the kinds of topics that writers in the phenomenological tradition had tended to think of largely as matters of individual perception and experience, or characteristic of a kind of universal individuality. In the case of the inhibitive habits I have in view (*inhibition* in fact being almost the same word as *habit* and for good reasons), one might approach something like a phenomenological account of "culture" itself, in the general sense of a style of collective existence, or being in common, that would be formed just as much through these Polonian "assays of bias" (Shakespeare 2005, 232), the coordination of these directions and indirections, inflections and deflections, as through the positivity of institutions and their programs of action.

Part of the challenge of making out a history of these gestures, tendencies, attitudes, and potentials is to retain their quality of indirection. For they stand aside, not just from the positive occupation of positions but also from the negative inversions of such things. It is for this reason that this book is not a study of negativity, which has been a leading theme in much contemporary philosophy. The philosophical and political interest in negativity usually exhibits a tendency to precipitate into positive form through the celebration of pure or absolute forms of negativity, whether it be the principle of absolute loss or absolute eschewal of gain in the ethics of the gift relation or, more recently, through the investigation of sacrifice, for example, in Terry Eagleton's *Radical Sacrifice*, which argues that the most compelling version of sacrifice concerns the flourishing of the self, not its extinction. It involves a formidable release of energy, a transformation of the human subject and a turbulent transitus from death to new life. If sacrifice is a political act, it is not least because it concerns an accession to power. (2018, 7)

But sacrifice evacuates the self entirely, in a way that allows it to triumph. In the blaze of terminal consumption, the self is consummated. Suicide is not a giving way, because it leaves nothing left to be given at all. Giving way and standing aside need and mean a self deployed, not destroyed, so must decline the glorifying immolation of destitution.

When I have spoken about the social forms and actions described in this book, the response has tended to take one of two forms. Among certain readers and audiences, sometimes with strong religious or what are called "spiritual" convictions, I have been taken approvingly to be issuing a manifesto for acquiescence and "letting be." Among others, I have been taken to be setting my face against the need for struggle and opposition, to vanquish the ills and injustices wrought by capitalism, patriarchy, authoritarian government, and other forms of nastiness. The attention paid here to the modes of giving way is neither of those things, in that it does not represent a position or ideal of human conduct. In particular, the discourse I attempt to develop is not to be seen as a program of action or read off in terms of the great either/or of our time and perhaps of all human times, the struggle for possession and power, on the one hand, and the passive acquiescence to power, on the other. Giving way is as various and pervasive as it is because it is neither the opposite of power nor its simple abdication but rather its necessary modulation. So an understanding of the workings of giving way should not be expected to provide guidance or gratifying justification for any particular forms of political resistance, assertion, or aggression: it does not, for example, provide an argument for the superiority under all circumstances of nonviolent resistance over violent revolution, even if, as in the case of the political strike discussed in Chapter 4, it may well be a feature of many forms of collective action such as the withdrawal of labor. So giving way is not the name of a way of life, to be set alongside or against the military life; the consumerist life; the religious, academic, or bureaucratic life; and so on. It is a way of recognizing the styling of life as such. It is the principle of modulation that often demands a refraction into form of whatever the zero degree of "pure experience" or round unvarnished utterance might otherwise be thought to be. Form need not necessarily mean some established code or pattern, for form is just what arises from the forming of an action, performing it in a certain way that gives it an angle of incidence to the action as such. Declining, in the sense employed when one speaks of declining an invitation, thereby links importantly to declining in the grammatical sense, as in the declension of a noun through or across its different cases. Manners are modulations, and modulation is the whole work of social life.

## 2   Minding Your Tongue

THE ESSAY THAT inaugurates the serious study of politeness, Erving Goffman's "On Face-Work," opens with a small but indicative deflection:

> Every person lives in a world of social encounters, involving him either in face-to-face or mediated contact with other participants. In each of these contacts, he tends to act out what is sometimes called a line—that is, a pattern of verbal and nonverbal acts by which he expresses his view of the situation and through this his evaluation of the participants, especially himself. (1955, 213)

How, one might wonder, does a "face" become a "line"? This line gives the static and immediate image of the face a direction, tendency, or intent. The line is not a position but the implied taking of a position, and this implication is important because it is defined as much by the other participants in an interaction as by the one who seems to take it:

> Regardless of whether a person intends to take a line, he will find that he has done so in effect. The other participants will assume that he has more or less willfully taken a stand, so that if he is to deal with their response to him he must take into consideration the impression they have possibly formed of him. (213)

You take a particular line by taking the position you take others to take you to be taking, and it is this nested overlay that constitutes face: "The term *face* may be defined as the positive social value a person effectively claims for himself by the line others assume he has taken during a particular contact" (213). This is why the concept of face is a transactional principle rather than a personal property: one speaks of "losing face" but not of "losing one's face"—and Chinese allows one to speak of giving or gaining face—precisely because one's face in these circumstances is not in fact one's own. The principal respect in which the face, as *figura*, may be thought of as a vector is that it is the locus of speech, which is launched from and itself seems to launch the face into social motion. Precisely because speaking always involves the taking of a line, "face-work" is principally conservative and stabilizing: it typically consists of the production of dynamic compromises that deflect the force of what are known as face-threatening acts.

The growth of politeness research has tended to increase the stabilizing turn inward to questions of what politeness is and how it works rather the potentially destabilizing turn outward to questions of what politeness does. Disagreement regarding questions of the first kind is perfectly compatible with the extension and consolidation of the field of politeness studies. Disagreement regarding the function of politeness may lead away from politeness itself, as a branch of linguistic behavior, to other matters entirely. Politeness research focuses on the variable details of polite usage in order to understand how politeness and impoliteness work in different languages and circumstances. There is undoubtedly much to watch and wonder about here, but such investigations usually take it for granted that we know what the work of politeness actually is. Investigating what is and is not polite—whether American English speakers find "please" as polite as British English speakers, for example (M. Murphy 2016)—need not, and usually nowadays does not, tell you much about what politeness is. Knowing how things work is not the same as knowing what that work is or does.

Politeness does two kinds of work. First of all, it reduces or averts conflict; second, it binds both parties to the exchange into a pleasurable acknowledgment of their shared acquiescence to the work of polite acknowledgment. It rotates the said into the saying and substitutes the manner of the saying for its simple factuality. The existence of the many subtle modulations in politeness effects makes the shared knowledge of precisely how the modularity works, along with the implicit awareness that both parties are taking the necessary care with it, more enjoyably cohesive.

Much of the work that fills the flagship *Journal of Politeness Studies* is concerned with the question of what, if any, features or principles of politeness may be said to be universal. But the universal feature of politeness may be the fact that it exists, without exception though in different forms, in all languages and social systems. As Goffman argues, "Universal human nature is not a very human thing. By acquiring it, the person becomes a kind of construct, built up not from inner psychic propensities but from moral rules that are impressed upon him from without" (1955, 231). What is universal is differentiability or, more specifically, modality.

Modality is the means by which human beings inhabit their paradoxical condition of necessary conditionality. It is not only possible for humans to differ in ways that have significance; it is necessary to them that this conditionality should be marked as significant. Every time somebody testily falsifies a universalist claim that human beings must feel and act in certain ways, by objecting that "it is not like that for us" and so asserting the exception represented by the individual's own group, this response being particularly common in discussions of politeness, the objection verifies the more properly universal principle that everything that humans do must be done in some way or other, in some manner that matters. There is no mode of being human that is universal, precisely because of the modalism that is universal in human life. Rather than impose uniformity, as is often imagined, the universality of modality forbids it; modal anomalism rules out any exceptions.

Actions as well as utterances have their own distinct intonations, as indicated by the orienting parts of speech known as adverbs. Adverbs supply the quasi or quomodo of the what that verbs name. Politeness is not just a way of moderating behavior or utterance; it must itself be self-moderating, because too much politeness starts to seem impolite. There are no wholly neutral adverbs, since even adverbs like *neutrally, plainly, monotonously,* or *expressionlessly* point to specific modes among others of performing actions. I once participated during a departmental awayday in a game of "Adverbs" in which the subject is enjoined to mime certain actions in the manner of a specific adverb, ferociously, laboriously, cursorily, as it may be, that has to be guessed by the audience. The head of department, Barbara Hardy, performed a series of actions illustrating an adverb that nobody was able to guess, since, though the actions she was performing were perfectly recognizable, her performances seemed mysteriously unmarked by any distinguishable characteristics. Finally, we had to confess ourselves defeated, upon which she smugly revealed that she had been performing her actions (and in the process also playing the game) *well.*

It is for this reason that modality is the way in which individuals are blended with groups and groups incorporate individuals. The way in which a mode blends continuity with difference—a melody that remains recognizably the same even after undergoing modulation into a different key, for instance—allows for subtle and dynamic coordination of individual humans with ways of belonging to groups or collectively being-human, which always depend precisely on the fact that there are ways in which this is done. Perfect pitch is thought of as a rare accomplishment, but, to the degree that it impedes the appreciation of the capacity for a melody in C minor to be played in B minor, is in fact a disability. In social terms, perfect pitch would be the same as being tone deaf. Politeness asserts the social principle that manner matters and that there is no act without its accent.

Modality has the deflection of violence and the diffusion of conflict among its effects, but it is more than merely defensive. Though we do indeed call the work of deferring conflict "moderation," modality is ranged principally not against violence but against singularity. The work of modality is a qualification of definiteness and of the impoverishment of possibility that every absolute statement entails. Modulation normally implies a kind of muting, softening, or muffling. This is sometimes done through generalizing; often, what matters most about a particular form of politeness is precisely that, as a form, it connects the singular to the general, thereby lowering intensity and containing the dangerously formless force of individual events. It therefore blends the one with the plural.

Goffman's formulations provided the foundation for work in the pragmatics of politeness, which may be thought of as the specifically sociolinguistic dimension of face-work. The principal impetus for this work was provided by Penelope Brown and Stephen C. Levinson, who share Goffman's view that "people cooperate (and assume each other's cooperation) in maintaining face in cooperation, such cooperation being based on the mutual vulnerability of face" (1987, 61), and distinguish "negative face," meaning the assumption of freedom of movement, or freedom from imposition, from "positive face," meaning the desire to share or impose one's values or desires. To be polite is to allow people room to move, and it is to act as though to share or approve their projects.

Proposing a universal energy scale for physical and symbolic phenomena, Michel Serres proposed a thermodynamics of communication that would make communication equivalent to the request "keep me warm" (1982, 76).

In 1973, Robin Lakoff offered a helpful reformulation of the principles for mitigating face-threatening acts, offering three rules of politeness that suggest a slightly more complex principle, in that it balances "keep me warm" with "give me air." Rules 1 and 2 of her code, Don't Impose and Give Options, amount to the negative requirement not to infringe or constrain my space of action, while Rule 3, Be Friendly, suggests the need for approach, propinquity, and inclusion (298). The interesting thing to be accounted for is how politeness allows for coolness and warmth, distance and intimacy, at once. By opening up a space in which you can operate independently of me, I create a metaphorical bond of friendly respect between us, thereby creating closeness from a distance. We are thereby associated through our shared detachment, warmed by the amicable air between us.

So Lakoff's three principles of politeness amount to the need to maintain a productive tension between the two principles of nonencroachment and inclusion, or letting be and letting in. Insofar as it is hard to imagine any kind of human society—or any kind of animal grouping for that matter—that did not have to negotiate the balance between individuality and collectivity, identity and identification, it has a strong claim to represent something like a universal grammar of intraspecific relations. Politeness aims to ensure that one's interlocutor is both permitted the individual's own space and yet welcomed into that of the speaker. Don't Impose and Give Options amount to negative and positive aspects of nonencroachment, while Be Friendly involves offering a share of a space held in common.

The complexity of politeness conventions derives in large part from the fact that these two opposites must be held in balance, through constant small adjustments. Distance and intimacy can in fact become equivalent, through reflexive level switching. Observing the principle of nonencroachment, for example, itself becomes a kind of inclusiveness if it allows recognition of the fact that it is a convention shared between both parties, who are therefore included in a common space of presumed nonencroachment, or a publicly maintained privacy, in which one is both safe from and safe with one's interlocutor. (One might imagine a cooperation between this model and a psychoanalytic understanding of the relations between the Oedipal and the pre-Oedipal. Entry into the symbolic order of shared representations allows for the creation of a sustaining illusion of a we-intimacy that has had to be given up with the forming of separate subjectivity.)

The relation between levels is itself something that must be constantly in transaction. Increased levels of politeness can often be accompanied by accentuating codification ("That's very decent of you"); but the switch to a higher level of code awareness ("That's not a very nice thing to say") can also substitute antagonism for community, in constituting a face-threatening act, something like the "reproof valiant" in Touchstone's declension of courtly agonistics (Shakespeare 2006, 366). In general, it is necessary for the relations symbolized in the discourse and the relations established by the symbolizing discourse itself to be kept in dynamic balance, with frequent interchanges and neither being allowed to predominate for long periods. A highly marked orientation to the message or a highly marked encoding of politeness may be experienced as icily authoritarian, and as itself an infraction of personal space. Formality, and the increased self-reference it implies, in other words, can be experienced as both retractive and attractive. The flourishing of any discourse community may be measured not by how formal or informal its interactions characteristically are but rather by the complexity and intimate complicity of these exchanges between the said and the saying. Movements between these logical levels are equivalent to different inflections of open and inclusive space.

These movements and corresponding inflections of letting be and letting in are enacted in another primary tension, between saying and unsaying, balancing advance and retreat, assertion and mitigation, in the fluctuating pattern that makes it appropriate to speak, as we sometimes do in legal or academic circumstances, of a declaration as a "submission."

The most important principle of politeness is the mediation of sign and symbol, through the making of symbolic space. We may understand this in two ways. The most obvious way is simply the symbolizing of space, often through allusive or abbreviated gestures, in particular the extended open hand, a hand that literally seems to "give way," indicating a passage into which another may move. This gesture, like many others, uses abbreviation to amplify the sense of the space available, which may literally constitute only the narrow track between where you are currently standing and the only available chair in the room but is made to seem like a broad, daisy-sprinkled meadow across which you are being invited to trip. The fact that gesture so often moves us from the precise to the vague is suggested by the difference between "pointing to" something and "gesturing toward" it. This amplification performs an important function, because it diminishes the space that I occupy, which has clear and visible limits, in relation to the unbounded space that I seem to be withdrawing from or ushering you into. The word *usher* derives from *ustium*, door, because an *usher* or *huisher* would be a doorkeeper. But the function of the usher was in fact to take you from the determined and determining space of the door into the more undetermined space of the interior (in the cinema the space is literally indeterminable, because dark). So the bodily gestures of making way also open up a passage from determined to undetermined space.

This then shows us the second sense in which "symbolic space" may be understood. For the space in common brought about by polite relations can be open precisely because it does not exist or does not exist merely spatially. It is not so much undetermined as determined socially, through the very shared understanding induced by gesture. The symbolizing of space requires the metaphorical space of symbolizing, a space that can be, as it were, laid over or mapped on to actual space—and in order to be effective must be able to be so mapped—but must also be infinitely more elastic than actual space, precisely through being able to be projected or produced at will. It is language and the symbolizing body, with which language always productively cooperates, that constitute this space, with particular parts of the body acting as the gateways between, or transformers of, actual and symbol space: most notably the hand, the most polymorphous producer of and projector of imaginary space, but also the mouth, eyes, and, most neglected but almost as powerful as these, the shoulders. The next chapter explores in more detail these corporeal conjurations of space and the making and giving way they effect.

Politeness often involves maintaining impersonal space by restraining the incursions into it of the personal, most obviously by curbing bodily processes, especially in their more expansive or explosive aspects. By keeping my body in its place and keeping "myself to myself," I also keep open the space in and into which others may move. I may benefit from the use of this common space only if I consent to keeping it in common. But, as a means of sharing space, politeness is in much larger terms the deterrence of pollution, construed by Michel Serres (2011) fundamentally as a form of appropriation. By dirtying something, smearing it with my symbolic waste, I withdraw it from social use, affirming it as my own.

Noise has a special place in the work of social cohibition. An important principle of the regulation of conduct in dense human associations is the need to control accidental, which is to say, nonarticulate bodily noise: snoring, spitting, sneezing, nose blowing, and, most particularly, the noise associated with the digestive process, such as eructations and the incontinent slurping of food. Even in their greatest intimacy, new lovers will work hard to avoid the mortifying interjections of the mucous membrane during sexual relations. A long history associates this kind of unwilled "belly speaking" and other kinds of nonvocal quasi utterance, with ventriloquism, itself often understood as the effect of demonic possession (Connor 2000). To regulate one's speech means to strive to purge the pure act of vocal production from all the suggestions of the bodily, identified in particular with alimentary functions of intake and expulsion, that come from unwilled and accidental noise. Arguably, the process of civilization begins with the transvaluation of the relations of threat and hostility that in most other animals are concentrated in collective eating, into the socially cohering action of the meal, which Martin Jones describes as "the very essence of conviviality that defines humanity" (2007, 2). No greater profaning of the idea of the sacramental body could be imagined than the appreciative smacking of lips and audible gulping while consuming the body of Christ in the Mass. As the transubstantiation into the community of spirit of the act of transforming substance involved in eating, the Eucharist is the apotheosis of table manners.

All noise is related to this idea of demonic effluent. The combination of urbanism and industrialism produced, if not a huge increase in the production of noise—for it is clear that Roman and medieval cities must also have been full of hubbub—then certainly an increase in the intolerability of noise, perhaps because of the very growth of the counterfactual expectation of quietness. Arthur Schopenhauer promoted the contrast between noise-producing life and quiet thought into a principle of cultural politics:

> Kant wrote a treatise on *The Vital Powers*. I should prefer to write a dirge for them. The super-abundant display of vitality, which takes the form of knocking, hammering, and tumbling things about, has proved a daily torment to me all my life long. There are people, it is true—nay, a great many people—who smile at such things, because they are not sensitive to noise; but they are just the very people who are also not sensitive to argument, or thought, or poetry, or art, in a word, to any kind of intellectual influence. The reason of it is that the tissue of their brains is of a very rough and coarse quality. (1913, 127)

Schopenhauer was particularly incensed by the sound of carters' whips, which had for him the effect simultaneously of invasiveness and distraction, in the literal sense of a pulling apart:

> Every time this noise is made, it must disturb a hundred people who are applying their minds to business of some sort, no matter how trivial it may be; while on the thinker its effect is woeful and disastrous, cutting his thoughts asunder, much as the executioner's axe severs the head from the body. (129)

Thought is a withdrawal from space, producing, but also requiring, concentration. Noise has the opposite vector; it not only propagates, but it is propagation itself, the topophagic expansion into space. Schopenhauer's angry contempt for manual work associates the carter's work with the passage of excrement and undifferentiated matter: "I really cannot see why a fellow who is taking away a wagon-load of gravel or dung should thereby obtain the right to kill in the bud the thoughts which may happen to be springing up in ten thousand heads" (129). Schopenhauer allows himself an absurd fantasy of revenge on those who disturb his reflections, in the idea that they might be the source of a similar and matching pain to the careless producers of noise:

> It is obvious, therefore, that here we have to do with an act of pure wantonness; nay, with an impudent defiance offered to those members of the community who work with their heads by those who work with their hands. That such infamy should be tolerated in a town is a piece of barbarity and iniquity, all the more as it could easily be remedied by a police-notice to the effect that every lash shall have a knot at the end of it. There can be no harm in drawing the attention of the mob to the fact that the classes above them work with their heads, for any kind of headwork is mortal anguish to the man in the street. (130–31)

Noise produces not just discomfort and a feeling of helplessness in the one subjected to it but also a kind of outrage hard to match in its intensity at the unjustified invasion and theft of space. Being subjected to noise is like being showered in a spray of spit, or being daubed with excrement, or forced to inhale another's odors—smell being a kind of nose noise, which colonizes the commons with one's colonic stink. The sound of a wild party deliberately invading not just the space of hearing but also the time of repose has as its alibi the memory of celebrations that kept the threatening dark at bay with collective noise, but it is in fact the appropriative menace of collectivity itself, collectivity spitting on communication: "Parasitic noise prevents us from speaking to or hearing our neighbour, thereby monopolizing communication" (Serres 2011, 52). Nobody who aligns with the Beastie Boys in fighting for the right to party—and polite requests to refrain from murdering sleep can produce violent excesses of party rage in revelers—should ever be believed if they say they disapprove of gang rape, that act that turns the bed into the jakes, since this kind of assault is the source of all their transgressive delight. To make a noise is to put the commons in contempt and to foul shared space with the auditory emissions (sperm, spit, piss, shit, all sounding like churnings of the same undifferentiated stuff) that every mammal seeks to put at a distance. There are two ways of establishing this distance: in nomadic creatures, through movement away; or in sedentary creatures, the term *sedentary* recalling the action of appropriation known as squatting, which also, as Serres observes, "describes the crouching posture of defecation and that of females when they piss or give birth" (4), through the work of sewage systems that are the sign and complement of every kind of human civilization we know. Noise is antisocial because it destroys the internal distanciation that is an essential feature of every space held in common.

The space opened up by forms of politeness is both positive and negative. It is positive in that it may in fact be measurable: humans in different groups feel comfortable at different distances away from each other. But it is also negative: not just empty space but emptiness itself, a space to which I temporarily surrender any claim. That is why it can be the virtual space implied by language, which in one sense exists "between" speakers but in another sense has no relationship at all to the space they occupy (they can be speaking by telephone or Skype and so not be "in" the same physical space at all).

Politeness is intimate distance, the distance required for humans to live noncombustibly in close proximity to each other, thereby keeping within measure what Norbert Elias calls "the passionate ferocity of communal feeling" (2001, 6). As human communities become literally and metaphorically more densely entangled with each other, so the need grows for more versatile and delicately maintained forms of internal distancing in order to open up symbolic spaces that can compensate for the constriction of physical space. In order for there to be a symbolic space that can exist (as it were) in the space between social interlocutors and interagents, there must also be an internal space within each interlocutor. No matter how naturalized my habits of politeness are—and unnatural politeness is always impolite—they will always constitute a kind of internal abeyance in myself. The rule seems to be that any compression of physical space must produce an equal and opposite expansion of psychosymbolic space. Manner makes up for the pressing in of matter.

The effects aimed at and achieved (or not) through politeness are usually measured in terms of what they do for the addressee. But there are also complex costs and benefits involved in the act of being polite. The persuasive view articulated by Gudrun Held is that being polite depends on gestures of submission, with submission characterized as "any type of self-withdrawal, self-denigration and personal submission in favour of the interactional partner, which a polite individual is constrained to perform for social-ethical reasons" (1999, 21). Educating individuals to be fluent in the means of symbolically "humbling oneself before *alter*" (22) is decisive for the sustaining of community. This results in a differentiated pattern of "self-denigration and *alter*-elevation oriented towards stabilizing power in the reciprocal valuation and devaluation of social status" (23). It may be generalized into a claim like that of Britta Baumgarten, Dieter Gosewinkel, and Dieter Rucht that civility has "a common core element which, in one condensed formula, might be called the 'recognition of the other'" (2011, 304). Inquirers into traditions of European civility have tended to recoil from what has increasingly been seen as a contradiction between the principles of civility and its association with the dominative history of Western imperialism. But it is impossible to protest against the unjustifiable generalization of European ideas of civility to non-Western societies, as, for example, Jack Goody has influentially done in his view that Norbert Elias's analysis of civilization "is entirely eurocentric and does not even begin to consider that a similar process occurred in other cultural areas" (2006, 166), without at the same time depending on some generalized idea of the necessity of allowing a respectful space of acknowledgment between self and other, an idea that then confirms performatively the very principle of civility, and the necessity of generalizing it, that is being denied in the objection to its overgeneralization.

Almost, it seems, in passing, Gudrun Held observes that "GSs [Gestures of Submission] are omnipresent; they make up almost the whole of social discourse" (1999, 29). This is an amazing claim, with far-reaching implications, not least for a view of communication that depends on the metaphor of "speech acts." For it suggests that much, and even perhaps most, social discourse consists not exactly of positive acts but rather of unactment, the stylized enactment of restrained, suspended, or canceled action. It is no mere metaphor to say that the form of comportment permitted by such spoken unsaying is "self-effacing." Jacques Ellul (1985) wrote of what he called the "humiliation of the word" to refer simultaneously to the incarnation, in which *logos* is both itself cast down and the means of humiliation, and to the degrading of living discourse into image. Can we take seriously Held's suggestion that social discourse not only allows for acts of mitigation or self-abnegation but is essentially constituted of it? Might humiliation be in some sense a necessary part, if not of language then of languaging or discourse? Why should this be?

One way of explaining the motivation for people to be polite is to point to the advantages it can give. Children learn early, or at least we try to teach them, that they have a better chance of getting what they want if they ask nicely. Held puts this in a slightly more elaborate way, in respect to the conventional formulae that often accompany the potentially invasive act of making a request: "The more frequently and the more subtly the speaker submits to alter, thereby rhetorically handing her/him the freedom to decide, the less probable it is that alter will refuse the request without having to carry out a correspondingly elaborate set of formulaic utterances" (1999, 32). So giving your interlocutors the apparent freedom to turn you down ("I know this is an imposition, but do you think it might be possible for me to . . . ?") is a means to increase the pressure on them to accept, lest they appear more boorish than the petitioner.

But we need not see politeness as always driven by strategies as obvious as this. Another way of understanding the stakes of polite self-abnegation is through the phrase "giving way." Members of the British House of Commons employ this phrase in a rather quaintly archaic way to refer to allowing somebody else to speak, which technically requires them not just to stop speaking themselves but also to relinquish their standing position. It is rather a generous expression and implies a willingness on the part of speakers not only to acknowledge the right of others to occupy their position as speaker but also to get out of their way as they do so. To "give way" is a vernacular form of the expression "cede passage" and of course survives in road signs and the British highway code. To give somebody free passage, or to agree not, for the time being at least, to impede is not to give the person everything. Indeed, in the House of Commons, to give way usually means to allow an intervention for the purposes of asking a clarifying question, for example, rather than to relinquish the floor altogether in favor of another speaker.

But it is often treated as though it were a complete relinquishment of one's standing, which may perhaps account in part for the fact that to give way also means to collapse. The idea seems to be that a structure, such as a building or a personality, subsists in its integrity only by a process of straining instress, which bears up against all the forces, both external and, it seems often to be implied, internal, which would otherwise reduce it to ruin. When a building gives way, the understanding is that it gives way entirely and irreparably. Only persons can give way to in the sense of allow, it seems, whereas to give way in the sense of collapsing is characteristic of both persons and things, or, we may think, persons giving way to the condition of being a thing. Such an identification of person with thing is perhaps at work in the military use of "give way," though the earliest uses of the expression suggest retreat, with its possibility of reversal rather than complete rout. Interestingly, in rowing usage, to "give way" meant something like the opposite, that is, to begin, resume, or renew one's efforts, perhaps registering the influence of nautical getting "under way (weigh)."

Giving way in the parliamentary sense, like "giving up" in more ordinary uses, seems close to the word *yield*. Though it is related to common Germanic words, its use as an equivalent for Latin *reddere* and French *rendre* means that it has the distinctive implication in English of requiting or giving what is due (which accounts for its links with guilt). In other Germanic languages, this complex idea of paying back does not seem to be present, and derivatives of Old Germanic *gelðan* like modern German *gelten* tend to mean to be worth, or count as (as in German *Geld*, money). The *OED Online* rules sternly, however, that "the connection commonly assumed [of *guilt*] with the Old Germanic root *\*geld-*, *gald-*, *guld-*, to pay, yield n., is inadmissible phonologically."

This means that there is a double yielding in yielding, equivalent perhaps to the supererogatory rendering enacted in the word *surrender*, in which one not only gives what is due to another, but one also acknowledges the person's claim to or title in it. It is in this respect coupled with demanding, which is an asking that articulates entitlement. But this surcharge also means there is a benefit, or what is also called a "yield," a harvest or the return that one gets back from an investment, for the yielder, who thereby keeps some dignity and power of self-determination, in not having been forced to give anything away but having agreed that it is right to do so.

We might wonder why, if discourse is so governed by the modulating qualification or socializing weakening of speech acts, the act of withdrawing one's words should be so painful and sedulously avoided. What does it mean to be made to "eat one's words" or to "eat humble pie"? Eating does not countermand speech, but it compromises it, through corporealization, as brilliantly demonstrated in James Joyce's rendering of words overheard in a restaurant full of greedy feeders in the Lestrygonians episode of *Ulysses*: "I munched hum un thu Unchster Bunck un Munchday" (2008, 162). The injunction not to eat with your mouth full seems to participate in this same logic. Greeks thought wind instruments undignified because they did not allow for singing to accompany one's music and contorted the face (Connor 2004b). Speaking sublimates the body by transforming substance into spirit. Reversing that process turns speaking back into eating, and spirit into spit, reducing articulation to grunts and slurps. More than this, it debases corporeal ingestion into coprophilic self-consumption. You symbolically eat the symbol degraded to mere substance; even before you have eaten them, your words have been turned into bitter bile.

More evidence of the operations of civic self-humbling may be found in the operations of comedy, in which humiliation plays such a leading role. Here we may draw valuably on the work of Norbert Elias, whose investigation of the "civilizing process" often suggests important connections with the forms of affective self-limitation. Elias began work on an essay on laughter in 1956 and never completed it. Eight thousand words or so of what he did manage to compose were edited by Anca Parvulescu and published in *Critical Inquiry* in 2017 (Elias 2017). What remains of the essay reviews previous theories of laughter, principally those of Thomas Hobbes and Immanuel Kant, and breaks off just at the point at which Elias has made his suggestion that the history of laughter theories has perhaps been asking the wrong kind of question. Elias argues that laughter theory has naïvely focused on the question of what inner states might cause laughter, rather on the laughter itself, as sociophysiological phenomenon:

> We take it for granted . . . that the peculiar configuration of movements in our face, which forms an essential part of smiling and laughter, is merely the outward expression of an inner feeling state and that this inner state is, as it were, the essence, that which we have to explain, while the facial expression, as we call it, is merely regarded as something secondary, a consequence for which this inner state is the pivotal cause. The very term *expression* suggests as much. (287)

Elias spends a great deal of time carefully detailing the physiognomics of laughter, especially as they affect, and in a sense even effect, the face. He also seems to be drawn to more mechanical kinds of explanation, such as the

*Discorso del riso* of Basilio Paravicino, which explained laughter as a necessary relief from the fatiguing work of meditation (289–90). He is impressed by Kant's itself rather risible account of the origin of laughter in a sympathetic oscillation communicated by the intellect to the intestines, approving it as "an attempt to link what we call physical and mental aspects of laughter, one of the earliest I have come across." He also notes Henri Bergson's paradoxical and often overlooked conclusion that "laughter itself is a mechanism" (299).

For Elias, accounting for laughter is part of the much larger question of why human beings should have such uniquely expressive faces, capable of so many and such subtle variations of expression. So the question is not what laughter expresses but why humans should have the facial expressiveness that allows for laughter:

> If the prevailing focus is on the intentions, feelings, traits, characteristics, and properties expressed on a face, the wider question is why man, of all creatures, has developed a face capable of so many different expressions. How did it come that man is an organism in which something can be expressed in the face? Why should it be necessary for what goes on inside, as we say, to be expressed at all? (Elias 2017, 303)

Elias's essay seems to leave the question suspended at this point, though not before he has hinted that the phenomenon "is biological as well as psychological and sociological" (302).

Interestingly, Elias suggests that the mistaken focus on the expressed rather than expressivity belongs to "the implied evaluations of our animistic heritage" (2017, 301). Animism usually refers to the human tendency to attribute soul to nonhuman things, not to the human assumption that other humans have soul. Elias may perhaps mean that the animistic prejudice encourages us to think of things we express as things we mean to express rather than, in Philip Larkin's phrase, "what something hidden from us chose" (1988, 153).

How might Elias have extended and completed his discussion of laughter, having established that the problem of defining laughter is part of the problem of accounting for the extreme and seemingly unique variability of the human face? I think he might well have accounted for it in terms of the face's central role in human society, and in particular its role in making the inner states of individual human beings legible. As such, the face is what we call the interface between the inner and outer, and the means of adjusting them one to another.

The face is also the location of the mouth, and more specifically the teeth. It is not just the meeting place of inner and outer; it is the meeting place of violent appetite and symbolization, considered as the deferral of appetite ("Can I tempt you to another piece of Battenberg, Vicar?"). In other creatures, with more stationary faces, the face is really just a weapon, a mouth with a set of sensory guidance systems. The more enraged we may be, the more fixed and masklike our face may become.

The clue is contained in an undeveloped paragraph in the middle of Elias's essay, in which he emphasizes that "provided the fit is free and hearty enough, we are defenseless. Laughter does not agree with any strenuous exercise. We are not ready for physical combat as long as we laugh" (2017, 283). There is something very striking in the way in which Elias couples freedom and defenselessness: If we give ourselves over to laughter, it is the laughter that is free, not us. We restrain the laugh precisely by retaining our capacity for self-government and, therefore, the capacity to exercise control over others.

Elias devotes some time to the Hobbesian tradition that sees laughter as "sudden glory arising from some sudden conception of some eminency in ourselves; by comparison with the infirmity of others, or with our own formerly" (quoted in Elias 2017, 292), and what has become known as the "superiority theory" that arises from it, that is, the view that laughter is fundamentally a triumphant response to the humiliation of others. This is important for Elias because it allows for the deployment of an argument through what might be called performative denegation:

> This is one of the most characteristic features of laughter: the teeth are shown, though not threateningly; they are kept in check by the tightly drawn upper lip, like a weapon playfully shown in a state in which it cannot be used. . . . Laughter, even though it might be hostile and aggressive, indicates to the beholder that the person who laughs is not in a state ready for physical attack. If you are in danger of being physically assaulted, make the attacker laugh (if you can). For the time being, he will be unfit to go on with his assault. Momentarily, laughter paralyses or inhibits man's faculty to use physical force. (284, 288)

Laughter, it seems, exists in order for us to demonstrate our helpless submission. And insofar as we depend very largely on others to "make us laugh," it is fundamentally a submission to the social itself. It not only shows helplessness; it performs helpless submission to the necessity of showing. It is a salute to sociality, the display not only of the fact that we are for the time being no threat but also of our constitution as social creatures. Where weeping is the display of helplessness as a petition, laughter, which involves some of the same "loss of face" or literal discomposure as weeping, is the display of helplessness as joyous acknowledgment of heteronomy. In laughing, you do not so much "lose face" as lose out *to* your face, showing how little it is really in your keeping.

This principle is complicated by the fact that males and females in different cultures seem to act out different relations to their faces. In many cultures, females are expected to restrain the extravagant facial displays that may be permitted to, or even expected of, males, an expectation that gives extra potency to transgressions of it, as in the obscenely protruded tongue of the Gorgon. Even in European societies, women seem to feel more need to inhibit or disguise the opening of the mouth or display of teeth involved in laughter than men do, hence the association of the giggle with the female rather than the guffaw. The female face seems to be experienced more reflexively than the male face, as a continuous work in progress, to be carefully monitored rather than deployed or surrendered to. Yet the very self-protectiveness of the mouth-shielding gesture, or the covering of the eyes, may function as an equivalent display of helplessness under the eye of the other.

In his "Notes on a Lifetime," Elias connects his later, uncompleted investigations on laughter to earlier apprehensions that he owed to his early medical training that sociology must not neglect biology (and is not in any danger of collapsing into it):

> Later, I worked at one time on problems to do with laughing and smiling. They show in paradigmatic form, it seemed to me, that people are biologically attuned to each other, in a way that should not be overlooked even when one is primarily concerned with attunement acquired by learning, that is social adaptation. . . . I knew of the unique diversity of the musculature of the human face, observed how much more complex this musculature was than that of existing humanoid apes—how much more developed is, for example, the risorius muscle which plays quite an important part in human laughter. From this side too therefore, I was made aware that human beings are by nature attuned to living together with their own kind, to species-specific forms of communication which, partly if not exclusively, may be and must be activated and transformed by the assimilation of learned social patterns. (1994, 86–87)

Facial signals and feelings are not related to each other in the same way as effect and cause. Both are originally aspects of one and the same human reaction. Feeling and expression belong primarily together (87). Elias connects this to his criticism of the "animistic" view of expression:

> It is an example of the *homo clausus* mentality, which inclines us to think that anything directed outwardly, that is, especially towards other people—in this case the signal field of a face—is a kind of accidental accompaniment to the solitude of that person's inner existence. In reality the communicative signalling of feelings to other people is a primary feature of the human constitution.... No doubt all this only became clear to me much later, but then it became one of the main pillars of my theory of civilization and of my sociological thinking in general. (87–88)

Elias demonstrates in his own painfully elaborate attempts to describe the smiling and laughing face what may have been an important strand in his argument that though the signs of laughter are immediately recognizable, indeed "unmistakable," when it comes to describing them "our fount of words, our conceptual schemas are not well developed for such a task. One is often groping for words" (2017, 286). Laughter is not only difficult to capture in words; the uttering of words is also one of the actions it characteristically inhibits. Laughter effaces the face's role as the source of speech and makes it perform as part of a signifying body. Rather than speech orchestrating the body, laughter makes utterance dance to the spasmodic shudders of the body. And more than in any other kind of communication, that body is not singular but collective, the prosody of laughter being rapidly transmitted between bodies. So even as it overcomes articulate speech, the essential, empty articulation of laughter affirms the essential attunement it both allows and relies on.

One might define laughter as a particularly dramatic form of the principle of unactment I earlier identified at work in language, the capacity for language to put itself in abeyance that seems pervasive in and essential to all human discourse. We may perhaps relate this to the principle of "impotentiality" that Giorgio Agamben makes out in the work of Aristotle. Agamben illustrates this capacity for non-being in the visual experience of darkness, pointing not to the capacity to see in the dark but rather to the capacity to see *that* it is dark, to see that there is nothing to be seen, and to see that nothing: "human beings ... can experience darkness: they have the *potential* not to see, the *possibility of privation*" (1999, 181). This is the sense in which "all potentiality is impotentiality" (181). Agamben follows Aristotle in declaring this to be a defining characteristic of human beings: "Other living beings are capable only of their specific potentiality: they can only do this or that. But human beings are the animals who are capable of their own impotentiality. The greatness of human potentiality is measured by the abyss of human impotentiality" (182). This insight, though richly provocative, is somewhat less so for being articulated as a metaphysical principle. If it is really true that, for humans, all potentiality is impotentiality, then this gives us no very interesting way of making out the force of particular kinds of unacting, abstention, or determinate nonrealization of potential, though of course, it may encourage us to that work. It is precisely that force, found in the pressure to reserve or hold back force, that is so pervasive in human communication, that constitutes politeness.

## Magic Words

A name that is commonly given to the force that inhibits force is form. Form is often taken to be the opposite of force but may be better thought of as its reflexive elaboration. The recognition of form is intimately bound up with what Norbert Elias saw as the interchange of involvement and detachment. He made this interchange the subject of an essay published in 1956, which begins with the observation that "as far as one can see, the very existence of ordered group life depends on the interplay in men's thoughts and actions of impulses in both directions, those that involve and those that detach keeping each other in check" (226). In the essay that follows, Elias treats the question of involvement and detachment as primarily a methodological problem of particular application to social scientists. But it is also, as he clearly recognizes, an issue that powerfully structures whatever we understand by social life, which itself produces, and in characteristic ways works to mitigate, this tension between involvement and detachment. Polite behavior, for example, creates forms of solidarity that are dependent on the maintenance of forms of safe distance, following a socialized version of the principle Buckminster Fuller (1961) called "tensegrity." The principal medium of this is language, the function of which is to balance immediacy and delay, excitement and calm, transmitting urgency while at the same time tranquilizing it.

 A bearer of a great deal of this is formality. Human groups, like complex systems in general according to the systems theory of Niklas Luhmann, tend in the direction of greater formal self-reference or, to use a term that suggestively mediates between the mathematical and the social, *self-similarity* (2013, 70–82). If we can say that this is literally a kind of entropy, or turning inward, we can see it as a kind of decay of chaos into coherence. This is the kind of progressive detachment from natural life through forms of styling that increase self-similarity, which allows human groups to recognize, approve, and reciprocally include each other. That is, it is a kind of detachment (from nature) that permits and promotes involvement (with humans). To belong to a group is to agree not to break into these circles of inward and self-referential address.

Formality exists on both sides of the intimacy-distance polarity. Formality can constrain my freedom of movement, in physical, linguistic, and psychic space, by keeping me in my place. But through the creation of enclaves of self-similarity, it can put others and, perhaps more important, "the open" or unstructured space as such, at a distance and thereby offer me a limited but sanctioned sphere of sanctuary in which to exercise my freedom. The university furnishes a good model of such an enclave: by creating a space known as *academic* (a word that originally had reference to an actual space apart from the city), it allows for the creation of the thing it knows as academic freedom. A sports arena offers another. I could just set off running and see where I end up: but humans prefer to run in circles that bring them back to their starting point.

Formality can mean the subjection of free speech or action to rigid codes. But this is in fact very uncommon. Far more common is the use of politeness formulae to create informality, the conjoined sense of freedom and security. This apparent paradox can be resolved by the suggestion made at the beginning of this chapter that politeness enacts the mattering of manner. For one of the ways in which manner can matter in politeness is in making things seem to matter *less* than they otherwise would. Urgency turns speech into an imperative tool or weapon; the soft answer that turns away wrath does so by dispelling urgency, often with a smile or a joke. The fact that human conversation is so threaded with polite jokes and polite laughter, in what Robert Provine calls "*laughspeak*, a form of blended, laughing speech that communicates emotional tone" (2001, 37), may suggest how important the sheer pleasure of communicating the fact of the nonurgency of communication can be. Robin Dunbar's argument (1996) that the evolution of language may have had more to do with the communication of tone and good temper, in the same way as grooming does in chimpanzees (and household cats), than the transmission of information, gives support to this view of the politeness function. To soothe is often to smooth, with soothing words often accompanied by smoothing actions. Perhaps we call the act of transmitting information "communication" in order to communicate the fact that communication is about transmitting the sense of having things in common rather than the transmitted things themselves.

This sense in common is what is called pleasing. It has been mooted that Latin *placo*, I please, shares a root with *plancus*, flat, plain, level (Ernout and Meillet 2001, 513). The three commonest forms of polite transaction are requesting, thanking, and apologizing. Children are told to say "please," as the "magic word." You might well say "please" if you plead, but saying "please" is much more a matter of pleasing than pleading, which is from Anglo-Norman *plaider*, to argue or litigate. *Please* is a contraction of "if you please," a formula preserved in modern French *s'il vous plaît*, which is a reminder that "if you please" might sometimes have been "if it please you" or "an't please you," making the *you* actually an accusative and so the object rather than the subject of the pleasing. The complex history of the relations between the subjects and objects of pleasing in English have been explored by Cynthia L. Allen (1995). Indeed, the use and point of the "if-you-please" formula seems somehow to detach the prospect of pleasing from its object so that it floats agreeably between the parties, allowing for the playful handy-dandy of a lyric like the Beatles' "Please please me like I please you." The indeterminacy of intent in the word *please* goes with its syntactic indeterminacy, leading some to wonder whether it can be regarded "as a syntactic item at all" (Stubbs 1983, 71), along with the variety of positions it can occupy in phrases and sentences. *Please* often has the feel of an adverb and is categorized as such by the OED, since it is usually attached to a requested action, as though "open the door, please" implied "open the door pleasingly," but it does not otherwise behave as an adverb (it cannot be comparative, for example; "more please" can only make sense as "more, please"). Requests require politeness because the one making a request is at a disadvantage and because the simple act of requesting is likely to impose on the requestee a cost, either in fulfilling the request or in being required to find a way to refuse it politely. It is not likely that either will result in any positive pleasure, so that "if you please" really means "if you don't mind" or "if it is not too much trouble." But the act of requesting with the word *please* itself supplies a compensatory pleasure, the very pleasure of being asked politely, or having the question of one's pleasure formally, or with the particular kind of informal formality we know as politeness, taken account of. So a request, which always represents a possible delimitation of my freedom of action, is represented as an expression of concern about the effect of the request on my feelings. Certain male fruit flies honey their advances to females by presenting them with a little drop of sweet liquid before things get under way. A polite formula like *please* functions similarly as a preliminary *amuse-bouche*. A sort of grooming is put in train, a calming, comfort-giving diversion from the anxious main business of asking and agreeing. The pleasure of diffusing the slight danger of the request is itself diffused, adding minimally to it.

The most important point about all this is that, for the most part, it is scarcely marked at all as anything formal. In most cases, the formal act of saying "please" is itself diverted or dissimulated into a sort of routine, of which the most that is required is that it be recognized as having been said or just not having been omitted. The pleasure, if pleasure there is, is the pleasure of participating in the informal, scarcely noticed ceremony of everyday politeness. Formality and informality keep each other in balance. If one says "pretty please," the formula makes a joke of the request, which diffuses some of its force by seeming to accentuate it, precisely because the formula is marked as something silly, an artless bit of prettiness, or petty little ditty, effected for its own sake. Normally, though, as in other politeness formulae, the more marked the act of saying "please" may be, the more it threatens the equilibrium established in the politeness relation. So if a child is being teased or tickled and the pleasure tips over into discomfort, this may be marked by a disassimilation of the word *please* from the phrase in which it features, with the giggling ripple of "no, no, don't, please, don't" modulating to the jaggedly imperative "stop, ple-ease."

In English, the word *pray* had a comparatively brief career as an alternative to *please*, coming into use not much earlier than the early 1600s (though the clipped *prithee* appears in the mid-sixteenth century) and beginning to seem somewhat archaic by the end of the nineteenth century. Nowadays, it is almost always used to impart a kind of mock ceremony, this function tending to be marked by its separation of subject from verb: "What, pray, is the meaning of this?" But the word does indicate the way in which polite formulae may function in the act of prayer. The idea that praying somebody for a favor might do him the favor of representing him, with mild but complimentary impiety, as the kind of divinity to whom one should pray, points to the ways in which prayer itself might enact these performative relations of pleasing petition and propitiation. It is unsurprising that poetry should often involve the act of praying, since praying so often depends on something like poetic performance, the patterned pleasure and pleasure in pattern of the poetic in formal play being part of the enacted transaction. To pray is often to praise, this implying a kind of unconditional gift of grateful admiration, which one seems to assume will be pleasing to the Lord. Though it is hard to imagine why an omnipotent deity should be susceptible to such unsubtle shifts in his creatures, it remains a rather charming notion that God should be thought vulnerable enough to face threat to appreciate its mitigation in polite address. Timothy Kendall's neat epigram makes a pleasing song out of the alternations of pleasing, praising, and praying:

> Be sure not long the worlde will laste,
> *Please*, *Praise*, and *Praie* therefore:
> Praie to the Lorde, hym praise and please,
> and care thou for no more. (1577, 22)

The act of pleasing by praise urged here is in fact performed in the second and third lines, with the permutation of elements they set in play (a toy ghost of the words *please*, *praise*, and *pray*). The final line may be read both as advising the reader to be content with the act of giving pleasure in praising prayer and as a warning that there may be some virtue in having a care for what will come after there is "no more" life or world, for which a life of prayer may in fact prudently prepare.

The links between politeness, pleasure, and variability were observed by Henri Bergson in a lecture he gave on politeness to students at the Lycée Henri-IV in 1892. He characterized politeness as "intellectual flexibility" and invited his audience to consider politeness in terms of a "gracious dance performance." It is not clear whether Bergson means us to compare politeness to the dance itself or to the experience of emptying oneself into the dance while watching it, and he probably means both:

> The feeling of the gracious dance performance enters into our feeling of grace. At the same time as there is a sympathy for the weightlessness of the artist, there is the idea that we are freeing ourselves of our weight and of our materiality. Enveloped in the rhythm of the artist's dance, we adopt the subtlety of the dancer's movement without participating in his effort. And, in this

way, we rediscover the exquisite sensation of those dreams in which our body seems to have freed itself from its own weight, in which existence abandons resistance, and form its matter. Therefore what I'm saying is that we find again all the elements of physical grace in this politeness, which is a grace of the mind. Like grace, politeness awakens the idea of a limitless suppleness. Like grace, politeness makes a current of mobile and light sympathy pass between souls. Like grace, finally, politeness transports us from this world where language is bolted to action, and the action itself to interest, into another, ideal world, in which words and actions overcome their utility and have no other objective than to please. (2016, 5–6)

Bergson's "grace of the mind," carried across into the dancing grace of speech, suggests a kind of gratefulness in pleasing. The complement of "please" in polite speech is of course "thank you" (*gracias*). However, the expression of gratitude differs from the saying of "please" in that gratitude is an emotional attitude as well as a particular verbal performance; you can feel grateful without saying so, whereas it is hard to imagine what it would be like to feel "saying-pleasey" without actually saying "please."

The philosophy of gratitude tends to be pursued in terms of ethical reasoning and so to be concerned with questions of rightness, justification, and duty, typically concerning itself with questions such as what gratitude consists of, when we should feel it, when it is justified or misplaced, when it is genuine, and what its moral value might be. The observations developed here take it as a given that we often do feel grateful, and in various ways express that gratitude, and asks what the meaning and significance of that gratitude may be. So the leading question is not, when is gratitude due but what does gratitude do?

Gratitude is a willing curtailment of independence and acknowledgment of obligation, an acknowledgment made explicit in Italian *obrigato* and the slightly old-fashioned "I'm obliged." It appears that men are less likely to express gratitude and very likely for that reason less likely to feel it, than women, perhaps because men tend to be, or at least think they are supposed to be, warier of dependence than women. At the same time, gratitude, and more particularly the expression of gratitude, considered as a form of admiration or compliment, may be regarded as other-elevating and so self-lowering. The complimentary function of gratitude is brought out by the fact that complimenting itself elicits quite complex impulses to and orderings of gratitude. If somebody compliments me on my suit or sun tan, the most acceptable response is simply to say "thank you" (Herbert 1986). And the most acceptable response to the phrase "thank you" is "you're welcome" or "not at all," in apparent accordance with the rule that one should not accept the gift of admiration involved in being thanked without the minor self-lowering of an answering admiration.

In fact, gratitude is a pseudorestitution, a restitution that does not and cannot give anything back. Georg Simmel suggests that gratitude is a supplement to the various forms of legally enforceable contract and transaction in society and "establishes the bond of interaction, of the reciprocity of service and return service, even when they are not guaranteed by external coercion" (1950, 387). Gratitude therefore "emerges as the motive which, for inner reasons, effects the return of a benefit where there is no external necessity for it" (389). The fact that it is an unnecessary supplement to more formal interactions makes gratitude precisely gratuitous; yet this very fact is what gives it its binding importance: "Although it is a purely personal effect, or (if one will) a lyrical affect, its thousandfold ramifications throughout society make it one of the most powerful means of social cohesion" (389).

Gratitude is therefore restitution in the oblique case, or subjunctive mood. The odd thing about the state of being obliged by being put in a state of gratitude is that one can never in fact be formally obliged to say "thank you." The infirm but implacable Mrs. Williams in *Human Wishes*, Samuel Beckett's dramatic fragment about Dr. Johnson's circle, plays with these two senses of obligation in responding to a piece of consolatory "twaddle" that is being read to her, in which Jeremy Taylor advises that death may enter into us by many means, including "by a horse-hair": "I know if death were content to enter into me by a horse-hair, or by any other manner of hair for that matter, I should be very much obliged to him" (1983, 165). Mrs. Williams's caustic mock courtesy acknowledges by pretending to suspend the awareness that the obligatory nature of death involves much more, or rather less, than good breeding.

Thanking is as syntactically insecure as pleasing. *Grateful* was used not only to mean filled with a sense of thankfulness; it could also, from the sixteenth to the nineteenth centuries, mean welcome, pleasing, or agreeable, as in the complaint made in a pamphlet of 1698 that religious dissent encouraged wicked impulses:

> This gratifies the Spleen and Animosity that some have against their Neighbours, thus to vent their malice in Censures and evil Reflections on their Life and Manners; a Religion that allows and commends these things, must be very grateful to Flesh and Blood, and cannot want many Followers. (A. B. 1698, 55)

The quotation makes it clear that here *grateful* means gratifying, or giving cause for gratitude. A similar subject-object switch happens with the word *thankless*, which, well into the nineteenth century, could mean ungrateful, as in Gaffer Hexam's reproach to his daughter in Dickens's *Our Mutual Friend* (1864) about her attitude toward the river that provides their living: "How can you be so thankless to your best friend, Lizzie?" (1997, 15). But by this point, the usual meaning of *thankless*, found most commonly in the phrase "thankless task," was something for which you got no thanks, or perhaps gave you no cause to be thankful, or even, odd idea though it is, something that would itself give you no thanks for performing it.

Thanks, like praise, which may anyway be a kind of thanks, is often given to God. Why? Perhaps, as the imaginary benefactor, God exists in order to be the beneficiary of human gratitude and to give the gratification of pleasurable self-curbing that offering thanks does. Gratitude may in large part be defensive, an indemnity against the removal of that for which one gives thanks by acknowledging that it has not come by right. Thanking God is turning a state of gratefulness into an action of gratitude or, in philosophical terms, "propositional gratitude" (a is grateful that b) into "prepositional gratitude" (a is grateful to b for c). This way of thinking, which Sean McAleer calls the "agency requirement" (2012, 55), may be a combination of two principles of magical thinking. The first is that every event, good or bad, must have an author, or causative agent, some entity who meant it to happen. The second is the Freudian principle of omnipotence of thoughts, which makes our thoughts the secret authors of all events, good and bad. This logic might suggest that we give our good wishes to the principle of goodness in order sympathetically to secure our wish that the goodness not cease. The fact that the English word *thank* is in fact a modification of *think* may reinforce this sense of the power of thoughts, with the genitive *thankes*, meaning of thought, being used to signify with goodwill or voluntarily: thus *Godes thankes* is the equivalent to the formula *Deo volente* (DV), God willing. To say "I thank you" is to say that you give the gift of good wishes or are thinking well of the person. Just as one propitiates an angry deity lest it inflict suffering, so one praises a benevolent deity perhaps lest the omission of praise turn it into an angry deity.

The clue here may be that we say "thank goodness" as an almost exact equivalent to "thank God." Whether we thank God for his goodness or thank the goodness itself, there seems to be an attempt to keep the circle of arbitrary, unlooked-for, and incoercible goodness going. The apparatus of formal gratitude furnishes the prepositional circuit that prevents magical thinking from recognizing itself in operation, as it gives its good wishes to its wish for goodness. There seems to be only a sound relation rather than an etymological one between goodness and God, but the echo itself, as in the expression "good God" seems to signify this possibility of pure redoubling. The etymology of *God* itself is (appropriately enough, one might think) obscure, but it has been suggested that it is a derivative from one or two Indo-European matrices: *glheu*, meaning a pouring out (with some suggesting a religious intoxication from the product of the pouring), and *g2heu*, meaning to invoke (Bradley 1889). One might readily imagine that the evocation of the process of evocation might have been conceived as a kind of self-pouring, the word containing and magically decanting that to which it ineffably but prolifically refers.

There is some warrant for this in the magical evocation by Melanie Klein in her essay "Envy and Gratitude" of the breast as the primal and ultimate "good object," from which she supposes that all notions of goodness emanate. Patricia White similarly argues for the strong link between ideas of generosity and the parental relation, noting that "the Indo-European root of *generosity*—*gen*—points us toward the mother-baby relationship and family. It means 'give birth, be born, offspring'; it evolves through Latin, Old English, and Middle English to its modern derivations: *kin, kind, gentle, generous*" (2011, 233). Despite her essay's title, Klein finds it hard to say anything analytic about the principle of gratitude that is embodied in the good breast, in contrast to the many forms of envious attack to which the breast is thought to be subject. Klein writes that "the breast in its good aspect is the prototype of maternal goodness, inexhaustible patience and generosity, as well as of creativeness. It is these phantasies and instinctual needs that so enrich the primal object that it remains the foundation for hope, trust, and belief in goodness" (1997, 180). She sees gratitude as a redoubling of the principle of generosity in the breast, with her own explication depending on what seems like a purely magical principle of like producing like, for which no process or preconditions can be offered, for it is simply what happens when things turn out well: "Gratitude is closely bound up with generosity. Inner wealth derives from having assimilated the good object so that the individual becomes able to share its gifts with others. This makes it possible to introject a more friendly outer world, and a feeling of enrichment ensues" (189). A closely allied notion is that the good breast signifies the principle of "creativity," the causeless and ceaselessly self-perpetuating something from nothing of pure outpouring: "The 'good' breast that feeds and initiates the love relation to the mother is the representative of the life instinct and is also felt as the first manifestation of creativeness. In this fundamental relation the infant receives not only the gratification he desires but feels that he is being kept alive" (201).

Ultimately, like so much in Klein's writing, this creativeness swirls inward to encompass the analytic process itself, along with its own explication, and the aggressive reactions of the patient to it, through "envious and hostile feelings directed against the creativeness of the analyst" (1997, 211). One of Klein's patients reported a dream in which she saw a woman in a queue ahead of her taking two or three little petits fours, which she misidentified as "petit fru," which reminded her of "petit frau," hence, apparently, "Frau Klein." Klein writes that "the analyst who went away with the two or three petits fours stood not only for the breast which was withheld, but also for the breast which was going to feed itself" (205). In the (very limited) critical literature on gratitude in psychoanalysis, resentment and ingratitude are sometimes awkwardly focused around the question of payment for the sessions, or whether the analysis represents good value (White 2011, 231). With its peculiar mixture of extreme intimacy and therapeutic distance the psychoanalytic relationship puts the norms of polite behavior under particular pressure, even if it offers some insights into the psychosocial dynamics of politeness.

Sean McAleer proposes that we understand the value of propositional gratitude—the state of feeling grateful that has no possibility of return of a benefit to a benefactor—as the expression of a sense of humility. Humility means "an appreciation of one's finitude" ("I could never have done it without you"), a feeling with which gratitude is essentially linked:

> It is the reaction of the virtuous person when she appreciates her finitude and her neediness: . . . when circumstances remind her of her finitude and dependence, of the role of good fortune in her life, she responds with gratitude—not just gratitude to her benefactors, but gratitude that she has benefactors, gratitude that things worked out well when no deliberate agency was involved. (McAleer 2012, 61)

Indeed, propositional gratitude, which does not require or even logically permit thanks to be "returned" to a putative agent, not even to "goodness," may be regarded not as a local aberration from the rule of gratitude but as its essential condition, precisely because gratitude does not seem to be owed when someone has received a fully-deserved benefit: "The feeling of gratitude involves, among other things, the judgment that the benefit one has received is undeserved, which itself is an expression of humility" (61). This would allow us to see the exchange model of gratitude, in which saying "thank you" is the requiting of a debt incurred by a benefit, as the aberrant case, or a mistaken rewiring of the gratitude relation into the pseudocoherence of transaction. This remains true to the principle articulated by Kant in *The Doctrine of Virtue*, the second part of *The Metaphysics of Morals*:

> Gratitude must be considered, in particular, a sacred duty, that is, a duty the violation of which (as a scandalous example) can destroy the moral incentive to beneficence in its very principle. For, a moral object is sacred if the obligation with regard to it cannot be discharged completely by any act in keeping with it (so that one who is under obligation always remains under obligation). Any other duty is an ordinary duty.—But one cannot, by any repayment of a kindness received, *rid* oneself of the obligation for it, since the recipient can never win away from the benefactor his *priority* of merit, namely having been the first in benevolence. (1996, 203)

There may be a clue to the understanding of this obligation that seems to include or be expressed in the obligation to express the obligation, by saying "thank you." For such an expression is an answer rather than a canceling of a debt, where an answer gives the relation of response as amplifying expression. The earlier relation of swearing one's innocence in response to a charge, which is implied in the Old English *andwyrd*, and German *Antwort*, from *anda-*, and-, against, back + *word*, has enlarged to allow an answer that precisely enlarges and allows that to which it responds.

As Kant notes, there is always a potential hostility in the gratitude response, because gratitude is a willed belittling and an irredeemable posteriority, in relation to the gratuitous and so self-begetting benevolence to which it must always seem to come second: "In gratitude the one put under obligation stands a step lower than his benefactor. . . . We fear that by showing gratitude we take the inferior position of a dependent in relation to his protector, which is contrary to real self-esteem" (1996, 203, 207). The beneficiary often cannot help feeling resentment that the benefactor has gotten the retaliatory kindness in first. Kant twins envy with ingratitude, a vice that, though it shockingly "stands love of humanity on its head," is common in humans because of the inferiority that gratitude demands and "in order to hide this relation of inequality" (207). The fact that there is always the capacity for envy of the one to whom thanks seem due may account for the wish to construe gratitude as the requital of a finite and reversible obligation and accordingly the discharge of a debt. There is therefore within practices and understandings of gratitude a kind of contest between contest and noncontest, between gratitude as acquittal and gratitude as amplifying echo. There is no gratitude, no matter how free and gracious, that is not vulnerable to being taken up into relations of exchange. Gratitude cannot be enforced but equally cannot resist being forcibly transformed into an enforceable requirement. But this debility at the heart of gratitude, its incapacity to resist the operations of force, is just what *does* resist them, since it makes it clear that it is only by force that gratitude can be deformed into enforceability.

This is why merely polite gratitude that scarcely requires one to feel anything like real gratitude is so important. Such politeness delegates gratitude to language, a delegation that might seem to allow for moral indifference, irresponsibility, or dissembling. But in fact, this delegation is the means of ensuring and honoring a kind of artificial intelligence of the impossibility of independence that language requires and performs. It is the very generic nature of language that allows this inbuilt generosity. Politeness points toward what Jürgen Habermas called an "ideal speech situation" (2001, 97), but not because it is wholly transparent and purged of domination or strategy in the way that Habermas specifies but because it is an ideally gratuitous relation of speech, speech that gratefully invokes and answers to speech. Thanking is what good thinking becomes in utterance, and thanking is the good of thinking. We can be human, that is, exist in the condition of relatedness that is essential to being human, only "thanks to" the language that constitutes our relatedness, in the gratuitous articulation of gratitude. The gratefulness of this relation is the very goodness we thank without needing to mean it when we thank goodness.

## 3   Backing Down

I WANT TO continue the discussion of symbolic civility, but with an emphasis on the bodily rather than linguistic forms of that symbolism. This emphasis enlarges the focus beyond intrahuman relations. In the animal world, submission is a matter of corporeal rhetoric, operating within a dynamic field of sociospatial relations. For most animals, space is fundamentally agonistic, that is, territorial. Relations of submission form part of a complex language that balances tolerance and intolerance of the presence of other creatures and correlates the active desire to occupy space with the willingness to share or surrender it. This is not to say that spatial relations are entirely corporeal, as opposed to being symbolic, since one of the earliest ways of coping conservatively with aggression is precisely through bodily symbolism, which substitutes the signs and synecdoches of victory and defeat for the expensively exhausting and injurious real thing. Nor is submission just symbolic. In fact, we might say that the reverse is the case: In that the purpose of submission is to avert dangerous or expensive physical confrontation, all symbolism may be said to perform a submissive function. The aggressor who satisfies itself with a bellowing simulacrum of attack, or is appeased by the adoption of a submissive posture, is itself submitting to a work of gesture that is apotropaic on both sides. We may say that the function of language in dispelling urgency applies equally to the language of gesture and posture. Indeed, this language not only accompanies spoken language; it is deeply embodied within linguistic usage in the form of the conceptual metaphors identified by George Lakoff and

Mark Johnson's *Metaphors We Live By*, especially what they call "orientational metaphors," having to do with relations of "up-down, in-out, front-back, on-off, deep-shallow, central peripheral" (2003, 14), which often depend on the meanings given to and by inhabited space.

There are two principal spatial dimensions in which aggression and submission are enacted: the vertical, top-bottom axis, and the forward-backward axis. Lateral, left-right relations, in the third dimension of space, have their importance too, but these appear to be used for variations on advance and retreat and ascent and descent. Rather than existing a priori as a kind of containing Cartesian frame, these dimensions are called into being and given their social meaning first of all through these dynamic relations, governed by unstable ownership and the adversarial alternatives of advance and retreat, with submission lying between them. Territoriality does not play itself out within the neutral algebraic cube of possibilities provided by geometry; rather, geometry is the precipitate of territoriality, of a dynamic of owning, wanting, advancing, receding, and yielding.

Submission is signaled in many animals either by sinking to the ground or by retreating: either down or away. Lowering has the disadvantage that downward space is finite, for one will quickly meet the ground; retreat allows one to absent oneself from the scene of danger altogether. For this reason, lowering, or the retreat from height, depends more on symbolism, even if presenting the back and hiding the head can offer some degree of physical protection, and so involves the entry into what might be called "symbolic space." Offering the hand for a handshake, or in that abbreviated allusion to the handshake used between car drivers, the raised open palm, is an advance into space that signifies vulnerability by presenting oneself as a target rather than a projectile (the receptive skin of the open hand rather than the quasi-ballistic bone of the pointed finger).

In both cases, one may say movement involves either an expansion, or advance outward into space, or a retreat inward from it. Advance in many animals takes place through a multidimensional expansion to give the impression of occupying an increased volume: this can be effected through inflation of the lungs, as in bullfrogs; or piloerection (bristling), as in cats; or, in some species (humans included), through the production of sound that suggests a larger, more cavernous body shape. The arts of camouflage skillfully advance and retreat at once, by effecting an expansion into space that in fact allows the creature vulnerable to attack to melt into it and become invisible. Alternatively, creatures may display eyespots on their own bodies that may suggest the presence of a much larger creature, thereby activating alarm in the predator. Such displays are sometimes called aposematic, literally "away signaling." This is another form of the interchange between physical and symbolic space.

## Posture

As Sander Gilman has shown in his history of posture, to be upright is not just the way in which things have biologically fallen out for human beings but is regularly taken also to be a "posture of the mind" (2018, 28–62). Seemingly drawing a lesson, as many others have done, from the fact that human beings are not born able to walk but have to learn to walk upright, G. W. F. Hegel declares that "man is not erect by nature originally: he makes himself stand upright by the energy of his will" (2007, 138). Even as he acknowledges that erectness has become habitual, Hegel still believes that it therefore "must always remain pervaded by our will if we are not to collapse instantly" (138), therefore sharing with Andrew Marvell's speaking body, in his "Dialogue of the Soul and Body," a sense of the sickening imminence of fall—the soul complains of the "tyrannic soul, / Which, stretched upright, impales me so / That mine own precipice I go" (2005, 104). One is tempted to declare of this fantasy of the dependence of uprightness on the vigilant exercise of will what Jeremy Bentham did of the doctrine of natural rights, that it is "nonsense on stilts" and as wobbly as the condition it absurdly imputes to human beings (2002, 317–401). Gilman's history itself seems to take this willful imputation of the exercise of will on its own terms, taking the history of posture to be identical with the idealization of uprightness and so representing slouching, limping, or kneeling simply as the feared and despised negative of military uprightness rather than any kind of impotential resource. Yet even the examples that Hegel goes on immediately to supply following his declaration of the identity of will and uprightness suggest irresistibly the expansion of signifying dignity given by willed symbolic lowering:

> It is sometimes not altogether easy to discover the ground of the determinate *symbolic nature* of certain looks and gestures, the connection of their *meaning* with what they are *in themselves*. We do not wish to discuss here all the relevant phenomena but only the commonest of them. *Nodding*, for a start, means an *affirmation*, for by this we indicate a kind of submission. *Bowing* as

a *mark of respect* is in every case done only with the upper part of the body by us Europeans, since in doing it we do not wish to surrender our independence. Orientals, by contrast, express reverence for their master by throwing themselves on the ground before him; they may not look him in the eye, for by doing so they would be asserting their being-for-self, and only the master has the right freely to survey the servant and slave. *Shaking the head* is a *denial*; for by this we indicate making something wobble, knocking it over.... We pull a *long face* when we see ourselves disappointed in our expectation; for in that case we feel, as it were, let down. (2007, 138)

To be sure, to be upright is to have enhanced risks of being humbled but also for this very reason gives us possibilities of humility that are unavailable to nonerect beings ("the bigger they come"). The ambivalence of humility has much to do with human feelings about the ground after which we name ourselves, the *humus*. So-called humble plants are not just unflamboyant; they also grow close to the ground, like the mosses and lichens, "humblest of the green things that live," praised by John Ruskin in *Modern Painters*, that "are not merely close to earth, but themselves a part of it,—fastened down to it by their sides, here and there only a wrinkled edge rising from the granite crystals" (1905, 129). Uprightness is as much a mode of grounding as an aspiration to eminence, and there is always something in humility that strives to stand out from the earth toward which it sinks.

Almost all human societies symbolize social status along a vertical axis, with power and importance being seen as high and humility being conceived or enacted as approach or closeness to the ground. The Fall is engineered by Satan in the form of a serpent that forfeits its own uprightness for its role in bringing humanity low, this condition signaled in the seventeenth-century term *humi-serpent*, meaning crawling on the ground (Latin *serpere*, to crawl), as in the complaint in a 1642 text that "the Apostles were accounted by Pagans, when they lived amongst them, a people unworthy of any esteeme, or thought, both base of birth and breeding, not onely humi-serpent, but like Job his abjects, the sons of villaines and bondmen, more vile than the Earth they crawle upon" (Udall 1642, 39). *Groveling* derives from a Middle English adverb *grovelynge*, signifying simply the prone position, with face to the ground, rather than an action of lowering. Philémon Holland's 1601 translation of Pliny's *Natural History* offers the intriguing pseudofact that "the dead corps of a man floteth on the water with the face upward, but contrariwise women swimme groveling" (Pliny 1601, 165). But groveling had also by this time come to signify a base or degraded condition, as in the words of Criticus in Ben Jonson's *Cynthia's Revels*:

> O how dispisde, and base a thing is Man,
> If he not striue t'erect his groueling thoughts
> Aboue the straine of flesh. But how more cheap
> When, euen his best and vnderstanding part,
> (The crowne, and strength of all his faculties)
> Floates like a dead drown'd body, on the streame
> Of vulgar humor, mixt with commonst dregs? (1601, sig. C4v)

To grovel came to be thought of as an action through a back-formation from *groveling* as a present participle and therefore began to suggest a kind of futile clawing or scraping at the ground, perhaps from the influence of words like *shovel, scuffle, shuffle, scrabble,* and even *hovel* (the last originally an outhouse for animals but acquiring from the mid-seventeenth century the sense of a rude or wretchedly reduced human dwelling). The action of groveling suggests that one may be trying to escape into the earth or inhume oneself. "Bowing and scraping" appears from 1645 to mean dragging the feet backward as one retreats bowing, often in what the *OED* meticulously and exactly characterizes as "contemptuous reference to over-ceremonious politeness or reverence."

Few writers have been as attentive to questions of posture as Samuel Beckett, and one of the commonest postures of his indigent or defeated characters is the bowed head. It is a posture that Beckett himself evoked in a brief, pompously overblown homage to James Joyce he wrote in 1980: "I welcome this occasion to bow once again, before I go, deep down, before his heroic work, heroic being" (Bushrui and Benstock 1982, vii). The posture of abasement and the humility-humiliation it betokens in Beckett is at the center of a rich physiosymbology of inclinations and bodily declensions, which encompasses walking, crawling, kneeling, lying, reaching, and all the other dynamic and expressive "modifications of the upright posture" to which Erwin W. Straus pointed in his 1952 study of uprightness, including especially "the voluptuous gratification of succumbing" (1952, 540, 538). Straus stresses the importance of distance in the upright posture and the consequent homology between inclination and sociality:

> The strict upright posture expresses austerity, inaccessibility, decisiveness, domination, majesty, mercilessness, or unapproachable remoteness, as in catatonic symmetry. Inclination first brings us closer to another. (539)

Humility may be related to the principle of distance that Straus points to as the most important phenomenological consequence of the upright posture. As Straus observes, "Distance is ambivalent. Sometimes we want to preserve it; sometimes we want to eliminate it" (547). In one sense, humility establishes a modest and submissive withdrawal from the other, breaking off the eye-to-eye contact that can signal aggression. But at the same time, the inclination toward the other, along with the approach to the dimension of the ground, in which existence seems less differentiated, suggests amicable intimacy. The handshake performs a similar ambivalence, distancing the hand from the fist or other weapon, while mingling bodily space with one's partner and so distancing oneself, as it were, from the distance necessary to strike a blow, as when boxers defend themselves from attack by swamping their opponents in a clinch. Linguistic "gestures," such as intimate or honorific forms, exist in a symbolic equivalent to the elastic "between space" of bodily gesture, operating always between the alternatives of advance and withdrawal, threat and defense, desire and disgust. In the case of Beckett, this dynamism of posture is instinct with a more fundamental ambivalence regarding existence, as the "standing out" of being—in Latin, *exsistere* often has the suggestion of coming forth from obscurity or from death—not only from the world and from others but from itself. To stand out, for Beckett, is to stand aside from standing out.

To abase oneself is to surrender both sight and the imaginary dominion over unlimited lateral space it promises. The speed and flexibility of lateral movements, embodied in the multidimensional fluidity of the arm and hand, give way to the laborious toil of the crawl, in which the advantage given to the front-facing optical apparatus by erectness is lost, making the quadruped crawler effectively sightless, barring occasional tortoise-like craning of the neck. Just as verticality makes available dynamic lateral space, underpinning the complex cooperative action of dividing and connecting space, in the "manifold of directions" provided by the upright body schema (Straus 1952, 554), so declension away from the vertical or descent to the horizontal shrinks the possible into the actual, canceling the creative distance between eye and world. To descend is to diminish, surrendering shared occupancy of the interactive space of recognitions and becoming an unseeing object of sight for the one who can "look down" on us. If "man in upright posture, his feet on the ground, his head uplifted, does not move in the line of his digestive axis; he moves in the direction of his vision" (558), to relapse to the horizontal is also to advertise the subordination of noetic to alimentary functions. Speech, made possible by the modifications of the mouth in the upright creature, loses its reach and distinctiveness—the creatures crawling through the mud of Samuel Beckett's *How It Is* are scarcely able to utter anything distinguishable as they mutter their muddy words into the circumambient mire. To descend is also to move backward in time, to the helplessness of infancy, or even away from progressive temporality itself: the old sink and shrink from verticality too, on their way away from all wayfaring and back into atemporal terrene churn.

However, the gestures that enact this surrender of vertical space are never absolute, since they are themselves a part of the "manifold of directions" (Straus 1952, 554), which is inhabited, made, and remade by the upright body. The head that bows, the hand that shades the eyes in salute, the knee that bends, can and do also resume their positions, because they are signs of their own signaling function. Gestures that seem to cede social space always in fact intercede in it. The space of communication is solidified by the gestures of humility that seem to introduce distances and differences in it, since, as a result of the upright posture itself, social-communicative space is formed of the play of these distances. Hence the importance of the formality of gestures of abasement, for example, in their abbreviation, the nod as token of the bowed head, the bowed head as substitute for the full bow from the waist, or, by contrast, in their elaboration in the imaginary spreading of the skirts performed as an accompaniment to the curtsey: to crumple in a dead faint of awe at the feet of a tyrant would be the height of disrespect, for humility requires the communication to the other of one's own consciousness (and therefore manifest communication to oneself), of one's lowliness, this entailing a certain degree of precautionary self-possession. Such gestures of abasement will always strike us as in some manner stiffly formalized and watchful over themselves, because movement in the vertical dimension requires more skillful and purposeful exercise of balance and self-control than movement in the lateral plane. This may be part of the reason that the word we use for a well-managed rhythm is a *cadence*, or falling.

This vertical sensitivity can lead to ambivalence. For those who bow inhabit two social spaces at once, retaining in some ghostly way the memory or possibility of uprightness as they temporarily relinquish their upright condition. Like the striptease artists who, according to Roland Barthes, "wrap themselves in the miraculous ease which constantly clothes them" (1972, 86), thus seeming to conceal themselves in the very manner of their seeming display, the ducking retainer or bobbing undermaid inhabits two spaces, the literal and the symbolic, at once. The one to whom visual space is ceded, who is saluted, and for whom the spectacle of servility is served up, is, by contrast and consequence, petrified in the singular space of his ascendancy. Those who submit thereby have more freedom and variability than those to whom they submit. The emperor receiving tribute is more constrained, because more trapped in his mesmerized column of eminence than those who dance out their deference below the line of sight before him. Who has not felt this imposition of the fossil posture transmitted by the bowing maître d' or the commissionaire sweeping open the taxi door?

The constitution of gestures seems to require some relation to the ground, a relation formed almost always in some kind of stylized resistance. Indeed, as I have just suggested, it might be said that declensive gestures, or gestures of delayed or arrested fall, actually display a more careful and purposive intentionality than gestures of reach or aspiration, mostly because to subside with grace or solemnity requires a slowing, and slowing will always suggest a subordinating stylization of the natural body. Gestures that seem meant, in the sense of intended, seem correspondingly charged with meaning, in the sense of standing for something. We should not therefore see in gestures of submission a simple and asymmetric passage of agency, or the assumed power of voluntary action, from the one submitting to the one submitted to. Rather, every such gesture redistributes agency, understood as the assumption of the possibility of action, between them and never only in one direction.

We can measure the effect of this in the little word *lowly*. Its primary meaning is simply an adverbial form of *low*. Where this literal sense survives, as in John Clare's evocation of sinking light, "The silver mist more lowly swims / And each green bosomed valley dims" (1984, I.350), it is still intelligible but odd. But lowness signified wretchedness of condition as well as physical position at least as early as the thirteenth century in English, a usage that survives in the idea of a "low blow" (below the belt and so beyond the pale) and in lordly contempt for the figure of the estate agent's clerk expressed in T. S. Eliot's *The Waste Land*: "One of the low, on whom assurance sits / As a silk hat on a Bradford millionaire" (1969, 68). So lowliness, seeming to chime with holiness even where it is not explicitly rhymed with it, means lowness lifted or enlarged by some countervailing disposition, an acceptance of lowness that elevates one above one's literal condition. This meek, modest, humble kind of lowness is signaled, at least as early as the fourteenth century, in the development of *lowly* from an adverb into an adjective, as exemplified in Felicia Hemans's imagined "Inscription for a Cottage" (cottages are almost the embodiment of lowliness): "Oh! give me, Heaven, whate'er my lot, / Or in the palace, or the cot, / A noble generous mind; / Exalted in a lowly state" (1808, 53). The complex internal inclination of the word *lowly* begins to lay it open to imposture, as in Olivia's rebuff to the elaborate politeness of Viola (as Cesario): "My servant, sir? 'Twas never merry world / Since lowly feigning was called compliment" (Shakespeare 2008, 258), which allows the suggestion that the feigning of lowliness is itself to be seen as a kind of lowness.

Elevation is different from orientation. One can be close to the ground with one's face and eyes lifted. All religions seem to depend on some ritual stylization of the body, but, as we saw in the discussion of signation in Chapter 1, the centrality of the Crucifixion in Christianity puts at its symbolic disposal a potent and paradoxical posture. The Crucifixion combines lowering with elevation. To be fixed to a cross is to suffer a restraint equivalent to that of being pinned or tied down. When one wishes to refer to the incapacity of the limbs to move freely relative to each other, one will say that the victim is tied up; when one wishes to emphasize someone's incapacity to move the body through space, the person will be said to be tied down. Yet the posture of the Crucifixion gives rise to an ascensive gesture of the arms, which at once subjects itself to some higher force and seems to rise to meet it by some inward impulsion. Witnesses to the Crucifixion look up at it. After the main event, the body must be gotten down from the cross, in that ceremony, which is so recurrent a motif in Christian art, of *deposition*, a word that might stand for all actions of corporeal lowering. Salvador Dali's *Christ of Saint John of the Cross* (1951) is one of the very few images of the Crucifixion that forces one to look down from above on the crucified Christ. Yet the bottom half of the painting shows an earthly scene over which Christ may be imagined to be hovering in blessing and protection, which, like Gerard Manley Hopkins's Holy Ghost, "over the bent / World broods with warm breast and with ah! bright wings" (1970, 66), in a perspectival compromise between ascension and abasement. The more rapturous or mystical practices of prayer adopt the arms-spread posture, arms wide and palms turned receptively upward, usually combined with kneeling, to emphasize the paradoxical combination of humility and spiritual uplift. There may also be some visual recall of the Moro reflex, present in human babies from twenty-eight weeks of gestation, in which the baby suddenly deprived of support will fling its arms out wide and then draw them back together. The spreading of the arms suggests simultaneously defenselessness, exposing the face and breast to assault, and a comprehensive gathering together, a duality recalled in Emily Dickinson's evocation of "spreading wide my narrow Hands / To gather Paradise" (1975, 327).

The preeminence of the symbol of crucifixion means that it is itself available for humble modulations or declinings, like that of Saint Andrew, who is said to have petitioned to be crucified on a *crux decussata*, or splayed cross, in a posture that did not profane Christ's Crucifixion by seeming to mimic it. In fact, the X-shaped cross does not seem to appear in images until the tenth century and does not become dominant in representations of Saint Andrew until the seventeenth century—Caravaggio's 1607 painting shows Saint Andrew on a conventional cross (Réau 1958, 3, 79). Tradition has Saint Peter being crucified upside down for the same reason. Being upside down risks joining absurdity to piety. Caroline Walker Bynum points to the account of the Cistercian nun Lukardis of Oberweimar who habitually prayed upside down—during which "the nun's skirts clung, modestly and miraculously, around her ankles" (1987, 210). Although sinners are often depicted toppling or being pitchforked headfirst into Hell on the Day of Judgment, an inverse logic seems to lie coiled in the complete inversion of the body, which can suggest too much of the versatile mastery of the acrobat or dancer rather than saintly abasement. The compound words we use to describe this condition—*headfirst, upside down, topsy-turvy, head over heels*—can be suggestive of this exhilarating comic resilience rather than the willing subjection to gravity. The grandeur or triumph attaching to the action of grounding in rugby, and the substitute bringing to earth in the act of catching, also complicates the iconography of saintly self-lowering. In human gestures, which depend on mnemonic persistence of vision, keeping active the memory of relinquished positions, all dispositions must also be superimpositions.

There is an internal division between bodily and specifically manual gestures that partly reproduces the division between speech and gesture itself. Gestures of hand and fingers seem more closely twinned to the act of speech than gestures performed with other parts of the body. Quintilian remarks that "other parts of the body assist the speaker: the hands, I might almost say, speak for themselves" (*ceterae partes loquentem adiuvant, hae, prope est ut dicam, ipsae locuntur*) (2002, 128–29). Indeed, some bodily gestures, especially the shrugging of the shoulders, seem specifically designed to express the withdrawal from articulation into dumbshow, or the stifled movement into expression. It is as though gesture divides the body into its articulating and merely enactive functions. Some of these gestures (defensively folded arms, looking away) may seem more like embodiments of a general state of mind than statements. Both kinds of gesture are expressive, but the hands and fingers seem particularly active in what Adam Kendon terms the "*utterance uses of visible action*" (2004, 1–2).

If the vertical dimension is of paramount (from *par*, according to + *à mont*, up to the summit) importance in human gestural relations, the space of horizontal variation made available by uprightness is also powerful. The phrase "giving way" indicates an important lateral dynamism in the inhabitation of social space. For the collective intuition of spatial relations depends not just on states of advance, occupation, and retirement but also on complex plottings of approach, convergence, and avoidance. Gerard Manley Hopkins says gloriously of the sand in an hourglass that it is "mined with a motion" (1970, 52). Any place of crowded movement is a similar compound of actual and potential movements, directions, projections and corrections, actions and anticipations, *anticipactions*. A human group in movement, most notably in the place of compacted passage we know as a station concourse—from *con-* + *currere*, a running together, that is not far away from a corporeal *discourse*, or running in all directions—is a ferment of corporeal prepositions, a sociogeometry dominated and given impetus, not so much by lines of parallelism as by the slopes and swerves of diagonals (from Greek, διά-, *dia-*, through or across, and γωνία, *gonia*, angle) through which we avoid collision. The angle at which I sheer away from the person with whom I am about to collide is not only determined by a projection of the person's speed and direction but must also factor in the calculation that that person is also making of my course and avoiding action, all monitored by the action of glancing that applies both to looking and to moving. The diagonal is the integration of the to (*ad-*) and the fro (*ab-*) in the *apo-*, the off-from, in the kind of convergence of divergences that is imaged in Beckett's bad-dream ballet *Quad*. In this geometrical "piece for four players, light and percussion," four cowled figures enter a lit square and pace around its perimeter and diagonally across its center, slewing each time around a central "danger zone" (Beckett 1986, 453). When all four players are in motion together, their concerted deviations form a kind of sinkhole-swirl of avoidance that is the shared hologram of their noncontact.

I wish time remained to me to build a complete anthology of these glancings, tropisms, and turnings aside. When I move into somebody's intimate zone of contact for a social kiss, I am aware that, right at the last moment, I will need to move aside for my lips to graze against either the right cheek or the left. But which first? Most couples performing this maneuver go for the right cheek first, it seems to me, but one must be prepared to respond decorously and in time to a southpaw kiss to the left cheek, as a fighter watches for the feint that disguises a left hook. The penalty for joint miscalculation is an accidental meeting of the lips, which is too close to desire and therefore assault to belong to polite social life. A social kiss between two spectacle wearers carries extra risks, of physical entanglement, and will, in skilled operators, sometimes require a preliminary whisking away of the spectacles by both parties, giving the resultant contact an extra dimension of blinking vulnerability. The miraculous sway of the diagonal is the expression of the fact that proximity requires approximation to accuracy and accurate approximation. Inappropriate behavior is not only that which is improper, that does not belong and so is unclean, but that which does not apprehend the appropriate angle of approximation, which is to say abproximation.

For all movement is projective. It is like a melody in that my position is determined in relation to where I expect myself to be in a few yards' time, a future position that is implicit in my mobile intending present. To in-tend is to bend or stretch toward, in a tending or tension that alludes to a bowstring but is present also in the reaching out of the word tune. The only way to move purposively is to get ahead of myself, to occupy in projection the space that is my aim. When they lose the spring in their step, the old lose the curve of their walking motion and start to stump like toddlers or a jerky antique film. In social space, I must make a medley of my own move-music with the melody of intentions made out in the movements of those people through and amid whom I move. Some people, especially perhaps those skilled in contact sports, are much better at calculating these movements than others; the tendency for so many nowadays to be absorbed in devices while they walk through turbid social space makes them seem inattentive to or tuned out of this dance of approaches and approximations, meaning they warp social time and space around them like a stone in a stream.

In a moving crowd, these approaches and avoidances occur physically, with minimal speech accompaniments, which mostly exist to cover or themselves to deflect near collisions—"sorry," "pardon me," "please," "after you"—but there are also trajectories and deflections in the cat's-cradle sphere of speech. To speak is in itself to make an advance, to approach or encroach into locutionary space. Especially if he is male, the lecturer or the bar haranguer may physically lean forward into the space of his audience in order to "advance" his propositions. But every utterance is a kind of move made in an actual or implied space of engagements.

When I was a new lecturer, I was given an afternoon's instruction in the reading of interlocutory space by an educator of general practitioners whose name I long ago forgot, though I have never forgotten the range of ways of soliciting and directing discussion that he demonstrated to us; indeed, I recall it almost every working day. Chief among them was the system of traffic signals that may be relied on by the leader of a seminar. It is possible to stay the swamping spate of a "high contributor" by using an abbreviated version of the rugby handoff or traffic policeman's cocked-wrist "stop" gesture, which need rise no higher than the level of the midriff. Equally, one can bring on or bring out a thought that one sees forming in the widened eye or mouth of a shy or, as we so kinetically say, unforthcoming member of the seminar; all this requires is to show the back of the hand, accompanied by a little inward wag of the middle two fingers to encourage an advance into the discursive crossroads. The role of the chair in a committee meeting may be to act as this busy node of distribution, allowing the discussion to be conducted fairly and equably in the conductance the chair himself embodies, balancing selective solicitation with inhibition.

Another important and powerful feature of gestural interaction is postural echo, which may be seen as the bodily ground bass to the more rapid exchanges of manual gesture involved in gestural mimicry (Kimbara 2006) or "parallel gesturing" (Graziano, Kendon, and Cristilli 2011). The principle here is that a posture that mirrors that of one's interlocutor functions as reassurance and encouraging amplification, whereas contrary postures act as an impediment. If my interlocutor has hands, arms, or especially in the case of males, legs spread, and I sit with legs crossed and arms folded, my closed posture will seem not only defensive but antagonistically forbidding. It is not that closed postures are inhibitory in themselves, as might perhaps be thought, for a failure to echo folded arms, say, through what might otherwise seem like an open and relaxed gesture like leaning back with hands behind one's head, will also tend to be experienced as an aggressive barrier, because it will form a spatial contradiction or countermove. Similarly, what might otherwise be seen as a submissive gesture, like lowering the eyelids or head, may be experienced as a restriction of space for the speaker marooned in her own high ground of performing without any answering and so expanding echo. Here the logic of acquiescent resemblance or the rebuff of contrast displaces the primary logic of spatial command.

Human beings find it exceedingly hard to discount or overrule these sympathetic postural principles (or bodily postulations, as I wish it were possible to call them, given the unhelpful connotations of "posturing"), though they can be marshaled more or less self-consciously to assist certain outcomes. One of those outcomes is to put one's partner at ease, encouraging more relaxed thinking and confident speech, but another is to increase the quality of our own energy-imparting attentiveness. To adopt a posture that appears in tune with that of one's interlocutor is to submit to a lead, to enact the obedience that is embodied in audition. It is to suggest that our body has eyes only for the interlocutor's body and is concerned not to obstruct its movements, by literally "giving way" to them. To refuse this echoing is like refusing the interlocutor free passage, offering a cold shoulder by removing the shared investment in social space, in a sort of antagonistic retreat that, rather than giving ground, actually constricts the space of operation.

The term *expression* makes it seem as though the flow is always from inward states to outward manifestations, but there can be flow in the opposite direction. A squash coach used to say to me as I panted out my drills on the court, "Why aren't you smiling?" When I gasped, "Because I am dying," he would reply, "That's because you have forgotten to smile." One echoes not just one's interlocutor; one intercepts oneself in this act of autoecholocation.

## Standing

To be upright means to be standing, that action that seems to be both a state and a movement to achieve it—as when we are strangely enjoined in British courts of law to "be upstanding." The idea of standing does a huge amount of the work involved in thinking and communicating about human relations, especially in relation to questions of persistence and change. The importance of standing is neatly indicated by the fact that the word *standing* in fact means importance. Standing is status. To be *in good standing* means more than that one has reputation or eminence: it indicates that one occupies one's place reputably and reliably. Something said to be standing is also permanent, remaining in place through changes of circumstance, as in a *standing committee* (which is why a standing committee can be said to *sit*) or *standing army*. Although standing implies—we can truthfully say stands for—permanence and immobility, it always also has the suggestion of an oxymoronic state of dynamic protrusion, always more or less assertive or aggressive. This need not be in a vertical dimension, for things *stand out* from a background as well as *stand up* to assault. Stands and standing express legal right or authority, as in a *locus standi*, meaning the right to appear before a judicial body, and therefore more generally a state of being. In legal terms, to have standing means to be recognized as a legal entity, having rights and interests and therefore capable of making claims, or having them made on one's behalf, an expression played with wittily in the title of Christopher Stone's (2010) defense of environmental rights, *Should Trees Have Standing?*

The gesture of standing therefore seems essentially to involve two contrasting modes: standing up or out, as oneself; and standing as, or in for, or standing in one's own place, or standing in place of another. This seems to involve the fluctuation between two modes of space, the one literal and existing in present time, the other virtual and involving the memory of past time or the projection of future time; for if I am in somebody else's place, I can avoid breaking the physical law forbidding what is called superposition only through a superimposition of imaginary on physical space. This superimposition is just what language and sometimes other symbolic renderings of space allow. And it does so, intriguingly, by the fact that language itself can be regarded as a symbolic substitution for physical gesture.

It is tempting to range gestures as Adam Kendon does, on a spectrum that runs from the less linguistic to the fully linguistic (sign language). This has its own pseudospatiality, since it seems to put the linguistic at a distance from the corporeal. It is phenomenologically plausible, since it feels as though language can operate at a distance from the body, and it is indeed necessary for language to be abstracted (literally drawn away) from the individual instances of bodily sign making; for something to count as language, you have to be able to quote it. Yet, though seeming to move away from the literal spaces in which the body lives and moves and has its being, language carries those spaces with it in its hand luggage, because language depends on the assumption and conjuration of physiocorporeal space. Language is therefore not aspatial but metaspatial, hyperspatial, cryptoquasispatial. It allows for spaces to be projected and recombined but rarely to be negated altogether.

It is physically difficult for English speakers to say, or even think, yes, while shaking their heads, or no while nodding. It is not even clear what *physically* means in that statement. It feels difficult to perform the physical action, as though one were required to occupy two bodies simultaneously, but there is also a strange sense of strain in the act of articulation, even if it is silent, as though one were being forced to pull against some implicit gesture carried by the very word.

Gesture may in fact be regarded as carrying with it the idea of carriage, given its origin in the highly generative Latin word *gerere*. In contemporary usage, gesture is distinguished from posture as bodily movement is distinguished from pose or disposition, but the earliest uses of *gesture* in English in fifteenth-century English suggest the total bearing or general demeanor of the body. During the seventeenth century, the word could be used to mean not only a form of bodily movement but also a posture, or way of holding or placing the body, often with particular reference to religious actions of prayer or reverence. One might even suggest that the holding of a bodily posture must in fact be thought of as a kind of arrested gesture, or gesture of arrest—the gesture of actively refraining from movement, a keeping still, or bearing of stillness. So in 1577, the English translation of a sermon by Heinrich Bullinger advises:

> Some foolishly imagine ye prayer is made either better or worse, by ye gesture of our bodies. Therfore let them heare *S. August. lib. 2. ad Simplicianum Quaest. 4.* saying, It skilleth not after what sort our bodies be placed, so that the minde beeing presente with God, doe bring her purpose to passe. For we both pray standing, as it is written, The Publicane stoode a farre off: and knéeling, as we reade in the Actes of the Apostles: and sitting, as did Dauid and Helias. And vnlesse we might pray lying, it shuld not haue bin writen in the Psalmes, Euerie night wash I my bedde. For when any man seeketh to pray, he placeth the members of his bodie after such a maner as it shal séeme most meete to him for the time to stirre vp his deuotion. (1577, 928–29)

Devotional writers in the sixteenth century were particularly concerned with the postures and actions of the body at prayer, and kneeling was certainly regarded as a form of bodily gesture. Thomas Becon commented in *A Newe Pathway vnto Praier* on "the externall gesture in prayenge, as knelyng, knockyng on the brest, lyftynge vp of the handes" (1542, sig. M4v). In fact, if gesticulation may be regarded as a kind of intensification of gesture, with a strong expectation that the fingers will be the particular focus of attention, gesture itself has progressively been focused in the hands, leaving us progressively poor in terms for what might be called mobile postures, effected not through the hands but the body's other cardinal points of flexure—neck, elbows, and knees.

Precisely because gesture seems to be increasingly localized in the hands and fingers, it can sometimes rival or interfere with speech. Gesture comes to be regarded as a shadowing or spectral doubling of the word, the hands and fingers performing a sort of diacritic dance in air. The increasing interest in gesture among seventeenth-century writers like John Bulwer, in particular in relation to the practice of sign language among the deaf, focused attention more and more on formalized gestures, signs to which meanings could be securely assigned. Bulwer's two books on the language of gesture identify it as a kind of ventriloquism, or throwing of the voice into the hand:

> The *Hand,* that busie instrument, is most *talkative,* whose *language* is as easily perceived and understood, as if Man had another mouth or fountaine of discourse in his *Hand* . . . and to these signes, God attributes a voice, for He saith, If they will not hearken to the voice of the first signe, they will believe the voice of the latter signe: (and as there is in the supernaturall, so there is a signifying voyce in the naturall signes of the *Hand*). (1644, 1–2)

In that it is visual, the voice of bodily signification is really closer to a kind of writing, or indeed a writing out of what is more remotely suggested by the movements of the body more generally. In fact, however, the work of gesture often forms something more like an affective commentary on what is being said, a doing of the meaning rather than a picture of it. Gesture then provides something equivalent to the marks of accent in language or the indications of tempo and quality that began to accompany musical notations in the nineteenth century. In one sense, gesture fills out meaning with bodily mood, or modality. In so-called motor or beat gestures, the principal function may be to underline the rhythm of what is being said, providing a kind of visual percussion, or conducting of the meaning. Indeed, gesture may often be thought of as a kind of visual sound track, or bodily "mood music," accompanying the principal action of verbal utterance, this an inversion of the modalities at work in cinema, in which the principal action is visual while the background affective commentary is aural. If gesture furnishes the sense of the quality of an utterance, this is often by means not so much of amplifying but precisely of *qualifying* it, focusing it by physically constraining its application or providing some way or other for it to take place. As one might expect, there is considerable overlap between the kinds of visuospatial enactment manifest in gesture and the conceptual metaphors identified by Lakoff and Johnson (Cienki and Müller 2008).

Most writers on gesture emphasize the necessity of limiting it and keeping it subordinated to the voice. Gesture provides what Quintilian calls "décor" (2002, 121), seemliness, fittingness, the word having in Latin an implication similar to that which it has today, of a background that is well accommodated to a foreground. Quintilian evokes a chain of command in which the mind governs the voice, which in turn controls gesture. In fact, though, there is always a risk that gesture will escape this control: gesture, he says "conforms to the voice and joins it in obeying the mind" (*qui et ipse voci consentit et animo cum ea simul paret*) (118–19). Like many other writers, Quintilian recommends the practice of looking in a mirror to regulate gesture visually, as though to guard against the body's tendency to expressive insurgence, pointing to the example of Demosthenes, "who used to plan his performance in front of a big mirror; despite the fact that the bright surface reverses the image, he had complete trust in his own eyes' ability to tell him what effect he was making" (121). Centrifugal wildness of gesture, especially of the head, which should be the headquarters of reason, is to be guarded against: "Nodding the head frequently is also a fault: tossing it about and shaking out the hair [*comas excutientem*] is for fanatics" (122–23). The one who exhibits decorum seems to stand in front of or outside himself, monitoring and constraining the movement to what is necessary and no more.

*Gesticulation*, a word that comes into use in the early seventeenth century onward, seems to be presumptively manual and, even as it lifts gesture to the status of a language, also seems to convey the sense of vulgar exhibition, or lack of control. Would it not be odd to read of somebody vigorously gesticulating with nods of the head, or, even stranger, gesticulating with splayed knees or wagging ankles? Gesticulation is used to indicate a certain kind of excited or excessive gesture, as early definitions make clear: in 1616, John Bullokar's *English Expositor* defined it as "a moouing of the fingers, hands, or other parts, eyther in idle wantonnesse, or to expresse some matter by signes, in daucing, singing, or other such like exercise." Bulwer includes examples of the "apocrypha of action" (1644, 97), or gestural "prevarication" (lit., plowing a crooked track), which arise from "hands too active in discourse" (111), or the agitation of other parts of the body to absurdly excessive gesticulation:

> To shake the armes with a kinde of perpetuall motion, as if they would straightway flie out of the sight of their Auditours, or were about to leave the Earth: is a Praevarication in Rhetorique. Such Oratours have been compared to Ostriches, who goe upon the ground, yet so, that by the agitation of their wings, they seeme to thinke of flight. This happens to some by reason of a certain Plethorique wit and ardor of Nature, which scarce suffers it selfe to be kept down and holden by the body. *Cresollius* once saw such a Divine, whose habituall mobilitie of his *Hands* was such, that the strongest men could scarce emulate, unlesse by an incredible contention of labour. Some, through a puerile institution, or by a contracted custome doe the same; imitating little birds, which being not yet fledged, nor strong enough for flight, yet in their nests move and shake their wings very swiftly. These the Greekes call [μεγυσιζειν, *megusizein*], which they use to object against those who by a foolish gesticulation appear in the posture of little birds. . . . This gesture is most proper to Mimiques, and the Theater; and can scarce stand with the gravitie of the Forum, or the reverence of the Church; unlesse some part of it well moderated, may be permitted in signification of Gladnes of heart. (113–14, 115)

Gesticulation is to gesture, it seems, as ejaculation is to utterance. Hegel prolongs this theme. Though he finds the gesticulations of Italians charming, seeing in them the way in which "their mind spills over without reserve into its bodiliness" (2007, 46), he rules that

> the cultivated man has a less animated play of looks and gestures than the uncultivated. Just as the former bids the inward storm of his passions to be calm, so he also observes outwardly a calm demeanour and imparts to the voluntary embodiment of his sensations a certain measure of moderation; whereas the uncultivated, lacking power over his interior, believes that he can make himself intelligible only by a luxuriance of looks and gestures, but is thereby sometimes seduced into grimacing and in this way acquires a comical air, because in a *grimace* the interior at once completely externalizes itself and one thereby lets each individual sensation pass over into one's entire reality, with the consequence that, almost like an animal, one sinks exclusively into this determinate sensation. (139)

In all this, gesture is secondary to speech. When we say that a particular body of speech or writing is a gesture toward something or, quite often, "merely a gesture," we imply always that the gesture in fact holds back from that on to which it opens. James Joyce writes of Stephen Dedalus, listening in polite discomfort to Mr. Garrett Deasy's speech about the history of unionism, that "he sketched a brief gesture" (2008, 31). We don't know what the gesture is, meaning that Joyce himself merely gestures toward telling us about the gesture. We are told that Stephen's gesture is brief, but this does not tell us whether it is the kind of gesture that is speedily accomplished, like tapping the forefinger, or whether it is a gesture in abbreviated form. So Joyce's account of the gesture succeeds in being something like a gesture in itself, capitalizing on the fact that almost all gestures are in fact sketches of gestures, gestures toward, movements that stand in the place, and ahead, of other, fuller embodiments. But in "gesturing at" or gesturing toward," gestures also for that very reason stand aside from full embodiment. Gestures are therefore gestures at gestures. They are not substitutions for speech but rather modulations of it, that always stand aside from the figures they cut. This justifies the distinction between gesture and gesticulation, for where gesture cedes place to utterance, gesticulation attempts to double or even replace it in exaggerated mimicry.

Where gesticulation asserts itself in rivalry with or mockery of speech, gesture seems to keep the counsel that it conveys. Elizabeth Barrett Browning employs the archaic form *geste* to convey the sense of restrained expression and expressive restraint in her poem "A Vision of Poets," in which a poet is granted a vision of other dead poets in a chapel: "still as a vision, yet exprest / Full as an action—look and geste / Of buried saint in risen rest" (1897, 219). The poets are as silent as the "phantasm of an organ" that "booms" through the space, Homer displaying "the broad suspense / Of thunderous brows, and lips intense / Of garrulous god-innocence" (219). The poem is a spelling out of their collective poetic "geste," which presses upon but never fully into speech, forming a kind of prospective meaning, in the sense of meaning-to mean, that remains prior to the expression of any definite meaning. Or rather, the poem attempts to maintain through all its articulations something of the sense of inarticulate impending that belongs to gesture. Here language attempts to complete itself by reaching forward into the incompleteness, the holding back from language, that characterizes gesture.

Natural though it may be to see gesture as a shadow of speech, this is also in a sense an odd inversion, for we often experience speech contrariwise as a minor, incipient, or residual form of gesture: this is why speech so often seems to need to be filled out or made definitive by gesture. Emphasis is from Greek ἔμ- + φασις, in outward appearance, implying making fully explicit what might otherwise be veiled or hinted. The oral formation of words suggests possibilities of gesture with the space of the mouth, in which the frontal and the posterior, the upper and the lower, the spacious and the constrained, can seem to be spatially enacted, in the phonememic relations of what I have called the dream theater of the mouth (Connor 2014, 12, 15). The word we often use to suggest this internal or subliminal gesturing in language, whether spoken or written, is *suggest* itself, another of the modulations of *gerere*. In Latin, *suggere* could mean literally to carry, bring, put or lay under and, from that, to furnish or supply; in English, the word seems to retreat from explicitness, to imply that which is implicit, or conveyed indirectly or immaterially. A suggestion is a subgest, an undergesture, or underbringing, as though through some movement of the body that occurs beneath what is declared. This is perhaps what Giorgio Agamben proposes when he writes, explicating the use of the Latin word *gerere* in contrast to *facere*, to make and *agere*, to act, that "what characterizes gesture is that in it there is neither production nor enactment, but undertaking and supporting" (1993, 140). Gestures are "carried out" and are themselves "carryings out."

In this sense, it is as though speech were the shrunken vestige of more fully enacted movements, with writing being a withdrawal even further from the living body-in-motion, as the vestige of that vestige. If the gestures of sign language have sometimes been despised as witless mockeries of the word, the defense of gesture has often suggested that it is the living word made flesh of which speech and writing are the eviscerated residues. For, as Vilém Flusser maintains, a gesture is to be distinguished from a simple movement because it is intentional: "A gesture is one because it represents something, because it is concerned with a meaning" (2014, 4). The fact that one never seems to be able to go far into the history of any word without finding embedded in it some kind of physical gesture, or gesture toward the physical, has encouraged the theory among some linguists that gesture may in fact be the origin of spoken language. But this is a merely theoretical history, a history that is a back-formation from the fact of gestural speech. Human beings are not alone in using gestures, but the blending of gesture with speech means that they are always joined in reciprocal intimation and implication, in which each stands substitute for the other, standing in for, or behind, or to the side of the other.

The idea of bearing or carriage is a complex of action and passivity. To bear means to support the weight of something, so that one's own bearing has the suggestion of carrying the weight of one's own body, or more generally one's social self. But bearing also has the sense of conveying, in the sense in which something may have a bearing on some matter, the idea of meaning here being suggested through the idea of bringing some force to bear. In one's bearing or carriage, one wields oneself, subjected to the burden of self of which one is the subject. Authority resides in those who are able to carry their own bodies, but through and in their own bodies.

The idea that the posterior region of the body is to be thought of as the "bottom" or "fundament" seems to testify to a memory of the horizontal alignment in which the two polarities of the body are mouth and anus. This means that the head, the most elevated portion of the body, actually has two antipodes, the feet and the anus. This may be part of the reason that sitting is associated both with docility (schoolchildren and well-trained dogs must be taught to sit still) and with authority: on the Day of Judgment, the Almighty will be seated, not striding back and forth between the ranks of the damned and the blessed like a baseball coach. When one is seated, one has seceded authoritatively from the space of literal antagonism or defense, as a sign not of defenselessness but of being beyond the need to resort to self-defense. When seated, one's person is lowered, but one remains on one's feet (hence the childish wantonness of feet that do not reach the ground, but dangle or swing uncontrollably or irresponsibly, and the unimaginability of a potentate giving orders seated on a swing). Throne, from Greek θρόνος, seat, chair of state, reign, has the same Indo-European base as Sanskrit *dhṛ-*, to hold, keep, carry, as found also in Sanskrit *dharma*, law. The one enthroned is often the one who is carried, "in state," as we say, just as the corpse of a monarch or important person will be said to "lie in state," even though state implies *statuere*, to set upright like a statue, allowing the person thereby to lie down standing up, like the "risen rest" of Browning's resurrected poets (1897, 219). But the one enthroned is also the one who holds or carries, hence perhaps the importance of objects borne, whether orb, mace, or sword. The gliding ceremonial movements of the magnificent imply the carrying of a weight of a crown even when one is not there, and holding one's head up implies, not so much altitude as a willing assumption of this imaginary weight that bears down on one. Borne, one's bearing has, and is itself, a bearing.

Many gestures tend in this way toward the *reflexive*, a word that in itself implies a bending or declension away from the vertical, bowing the head or flexing the knees. The language of human gesture depends on the fact that we are not only an upright but also a jointed creature and capable of deploying ourselves by the rotation of neck, elbows, wrists, waist, knees, and ankles.

The comportment of bearing can never be separated from the future-directed act of bearing a child. To bear a child is not just to carry it; it is to be given a temporal bearing toward a future event, one that will involve the action of "bearing down," the event that, appropriately enough, does not have an obvious agent. The homophones *borne* and *born* are past participles of the two senses of the verb to bear, to carry, and to give birth to. One can bear and one can be born, but one can never birth, or "born" oneself, as a willed action, in the way one is said to be able actively to die. This possibility of bearing is exclusive to females, for the time being at least; but the nonexperience of having to have been born is universal, making bearing the gesture that most essentially holds itself apart from being an action. Such a view seems to be in accord with the proposals made by Adriana Cavarero for a different "geometric imaginary," centered on, or tilted through, "maternal inclination" (2016, 130) to replace the philosophical mirage of the solitary, self-sustaining *Homo erectus*:

> In light of the verticality that dominates the history of ontology, the task is to change our register or reposition our gaze, trying to imagine ontology as a geometry of variable postures inside of which inclination may assume a "modular" role. . . . Adam, who was created as "a perfect man," probably did assume an erect posture right away. Those born from women, by contrast, evoke a kind of subjectivity already caught up in folds, dependencies, exposures, dramas, knots, and bonds. (128, 130)

Where we might go even further than Cavarero (though in her own direction) is by allowing for the necessary inclusion of what she calls the "dream," "mirage," "anomaly," "pretense," or "pathetic blunder" of sovereign verticality (129, 130, 219) in the geometry of inclinations she tries to set apart from it. If she is right to say that uprightness is a mistake, she must compound that mistake in making uprightness a kind of unique exception from inclination, in something of the way she writes that it must strain to maintain its own phantasmal exceptionality. The fabric-in-the-making of gesture-space does not allow for such absolute shearings. Her own argument makes unavoidable an inclination to the view that all human posture, and acts of postulation through it, are part of a general topology, a morphological dreamwork of corporeal-symbolic space, in which noon is just another position ticked off around the dial.

Behaving is caught up in a similar field as bearing, since *behaving* is *be-* + *have*, so the way in which one actively has, owns, or holds oneself. Behaving in English therefore implies the reflexive relation of "behaving oneself." The inconspicuous and hugely adaptable prefix *be-* implies a minor but telling modification of the mode of self-having, to imply the way in which one has oneself in relation to some other need, implying the kind of habit, deriving from the same Latin root *habere*, to have, that is at work in the *-hibitive* zero degree of words like *inhibition*, *prohibition*, and *exhibition*.

The odd history of the word *demean* illustrates this reflexive self-reference of forms of physical behavior. Up until the early seventeenth century, *demeaning* was still close to the word *demeanor*. It could be used in a transitive sense to mean manage or control, as in the description of reckless Phaethon in Geoffrey Chaucer's *House of Fame*: "Loo, ys it not a gret myschaunce / To lete a fool han governaunce / Of thing that he can not demeyne?" (1988, 359). The route to the words *demesne* and *domain* is from Latin *dominicus*, a lord or master, but the suggestion of control in the two words must sometimes have caused them to chime one in another. The uses of the word *demean* in Shakespeare seem to hint of a word in transition: In *Henry VI Part 2*, the Earl of Salisbury complains

> Oft have I seen the haughty cardinal,
> More like a soldier than a man o' the church,
> As stout and proud as he were lord of all,
> Swear like a ruffian and demean himself
> Unlike the ruler of a commonweal. (1999, 161)

Here it seems clear that *demean* simply means behave or conduct, since the only way in which it would make sense to demean yourself *un*like the ruler of a commonwealth would be to swear like a ruffian. In *Comedy of Errors*, the Courtesan complains, "Now, out of doubt Antipholus is mad, / Else would he never so demean himself" (Shakespeare 2017, 254), but the account of his unaccountable behavior that follows emphasizes craziness rather than behavior that would be regarded as lowering his dignity.

But by the middle of the seventeenth century, the word *demean* began to be used to mean to lower, or debase, often, though not invariably, used reflexively, as in debasing oneself or, as we somewhat coyly say nowadays, "letting oneself down." *Demeaning* begins to be understood not as deriving from Latin *minare*, to drive or conduct, but as a making mean, or of little account, the adjective *mean* itself having declined from the idea of being of average or middling quality to being inferior. Eighteenth-century commentators complained about the lowering of status of the word *demean*, seeing its usage as a self-exemplifying sort of linguistic vulgarity:

> When the illiterate are desirous of "talking fine" they use *demean himself*, instead of their accustomed Phrase *"let himself down."* The French—*demener*—means to conduct or behave. It relates to *Deportment*, and never indicates *Disgrace* or *Dishonor*. The Vulgar use also *bemean*—"He bemeans himself by such Conduct." (Withers 1789, 208)

The OED contributor Fitzedward Hall wrote a detailed defense of the legitimacy of this new use of *demean* as debase, arguing, against the OED entry, that demean-debase was just a different word rather than a debasement of demean-behave, the relation between the two being analogous to the two kinds of deferring, transitive and intransitive, signaled in the nouns *deferral* (in time) and *deference* (to rank or standing) (1891, 379). Whether one sees *demean* as the result of a complex history or simply a homonym, it does seem as though the ways in which simple acting becomes behaving tend to become more complex and more reflexive rather than less. Though there may be a somewhat courtly cast to the idea of demeaning oneself, as there is to a word like *demeanor* itself, and the sense of corporeal quotation marks in behavior that might be described as demeanor, they nevertheless widen the range of dimensions in which physical action operates.

Theorists of gesture from Quintilian through to Adam Kendon emphasize the difference between incidental or unwilled bodily movements and postures and deliberate or intended movements. Kendon found that gestures were understood as movements that seem to stand out in certain ways from the normal background actions of the body: "Deliberately expressive movement was found to be movement that had a sharp boundary of onset and offset and that was an *excursion*, rather than resulting in any sustained change of position" (2004, 12). Such movements are *"features of manifest deliberate expressiveness"* (13–14) and are then understood to move the body from being to meaning. This emphasis on standing out may seem to pull against the argument made in this chapter about the essentially recessive nature of gesture. In fact, however, the work of making one's body mean is an assertion of the body's subordinate condition. The very fact that gesture should be so universal among human beings and yet should have taken so long to come under critical scrutiny may imply that there is something in gesture that hangs below the threshold of conscious action. One should perhaps distinguish between deliberate and conscious gestures. It may be possible for somebody to be making vigorous gestures to accompany excited speech, gestures that it will seem to an audience are just as intended as the speech they accompany and accentuate; and yet such gestures will be largely unobserved by the person making them, and he or she will find it hard to recall them even immediately afterward (Morris et al. 1981, xvii). The fact that people born without limbs have the sensation and neurological traces of gesturing (Ramachandran and Blakeslee 1998, 41), and that people blind from birth who have never seen gestures nevertheless gesture even when speaking to other people they know are also blind, seems to be a strong indication that gesture is a powerful and inseparable complement to speech rather than a deliberate and therefore separable supplement to it (McNeill 2012, 13). Susan Goldin-Meadow sums the matter up well when she writes: "We don't need to think about gesturing in order to do it. All we need to do is think about talking and gesturing comes for free" (2003, 242).

Of course, there are many gestures that are intended to be understood as assertive rather than concessive. But we might recall the ambivalence of the action of Latin *asserere* from which *assertion* derives. Its primary meaning is to join together a person or thing to one's self, but this could take two contrary forms: the action of *asserere* meant the laying on of hands to declare someone either *in servitutem* or *in libertatem*, either taken as a slave or given liberty. When one asserts, the object of one's assertion is given its being. Even in the most assertive gesture, there may be an act of allowance.

It should be recognized that, although gestures are usually actions that can be seen as defined and complete, with clear beginnings and endings, they are also, in relation to what they may seem to be representing, almost always curtailed or attenuated. This can involve selecting only one aspect of an action, typically that part of it that implicates the hand or arm, or in showing only a representative section of the action without following it through to completion—the beginning rather than the full arc and follow-through of a blow, for example. Strikingly, this abbreviation is a feature even of gestures that might be thought of as exaggerated or violently "over the top." Desmond Morris identifies a large class of "intention movements" that consist of incipient or preparatory movements (1977, 173–8). In some cases, like the clenched fist or the curtsey, which may be seen as an initiation then aborting of a movement of kneeling (144), the curtailed version of the movement has become autonomous. Many of the gestures of auto-intimacy—stroking or twisting the hair, touching the lips, bringing fingertips together—provide minor forms of the comfort that the infant derives from being hugged or supported by a protective adult; they are among the many gestures that seem to demonstrate a retraction from more obviously assertive or self-advancing behaviors (102–5).

This may explain why the use of gesture has been found to aid learning. Miriam A. Novack and Susan Goldin-Meadow conclude that "although gesture may be an effective learning tool, at least in part, because it is a type of action, it is the fact that gesture is abstracted action, or representational action, that likely gives rise to its far-reaching learning outcomes" (2017, 660). An abstract or otherwise attenuated gesture may act as an invitation to the receiver, an invitation that the co-constitution of human cognitive systems makes it very hard to resist, to "complete" the gesture. Gesture thus enacts a kind of giving way even where it may seem most forcibly to be pointing the way. A gesture that accompanied forceful talk of laying down the law would also be asking for consent to and assistance in the process, no matter how domineering the gesture might seem. Simulation is here stimulation, in a collusive work of allusion.

One might see this kind of simulation as circular and reciprocal. For gestural simulation not only stimulates answering and prolonging mental simulations in a communicative partner; it may also be a simulation of a mental motor simulation. This would be to follow the Gesture as Simulated Action framework proposed by Autumn B. Hostetter and Martha W. Alibali, which assumes that "gestures emerge from the perceptual and motor simulations that underlie embodied language and mental imagery" (2008, 502). The essence of gesture is then simulation, defined as "partial motor activation without completion" (Novack and Goldin-Meadow 2017, 653).

This argument finds some support in David McNeill's analysis of what are often called "beat" gestures, meaning gestures the function of which is to give prosodic emphasis. McNeill's suggestion is that the function of beat gestures—chopping the air, wagging a finger, patting a table in time with stressed words and syllables—"is like that of yellow highlighter—the beat emphasizes that something else, speech or gestures other than the beat itself, is important in some larger context" (2012, 15). In this sense, the beat is an indication of giving way or giving on to some other thing than gesture.

Gesture may therefore resemble a kind of conducting as well as an indispensable form of sociolinguistic conduct. The conductor of an orchestra provides a dynamic image in gesture of the music, a sort of composite of what is being heard and what the conductor would like to hear. This forms and is formed from a conductive flow from the orchestra to the conductor and back again, each soliciting and filling out the other. Gesture in conversation similarly institutes a flow of representations, in which leading and letting be continuously replace and call each other forth. This is in tune with the view suggested by Susan Goldin-Meadow that gesture may form a kind of undertalk, or back channel between partners in a conversation:

> An underground conversation can potentially be taking place every time we talk. Speakers are not always aware of the ideas they express in gesture. Listeners pick up on these ideas, but may themselves not be aware of having done so. An entire exchange can take place without either speaker or listener being consciously aware of the information passed between them. (2003, 245)

The view of gesture I have been developing here, as having to do with some essential relation of giving way, is in contradiction to many of the more positive readings of the power of gesture. There is no shortage of claims for the special power of gesture to enhance thought, utterance, or experience. Carrie Ann Noland and Sally Ann Ness propose that "gesturing may very well remain a resource for resistance to homogenization, a way to place pressure on the routines demanded by technical and technological standardization" (2008, x). They go on to suggest that "gesture can indeed transmit a predetermined, codified meaning, but it can also—and simultaneously—convey an energetic charge or "vitality effect" that overflows the meaning transmitted" (xiv). The contributors to the book they are introducing provide repeated reinforcement of the view that gesture exceeds or transcends mere meaning: "We should not attempt to decipher the meaning of the gesture but rather look to the intensity of the gestural formation" (Stern 2008, 201). In arguments developed over some decades, as summarized in his book *Why We Gesture*, David McNeill represents gesture as the orchestration or animating energy of utterance:

> Gesture is not a representation, or is not only such: It is a form of Being. From a first-person perspective, the gesture is part of the immediate existence of the speaker. Gestures (and words, etc. as well) are thinking in one of its many forms—not only expressions of thought, *but thought, that is, cognitive Being, itself*. . . . To the speaker, gesture and speech are not only "messages" or communications, but are a way of cognitively existing, of cognitively Being, at the moment of speaking. (2016, 14)

It is indeed hard to avoid the strong sense of the positivity of gesture in this claim or the unashamed phonocentrism on which it seems to depend, which suggests that language without gesture, that is, writing, is somehow deficient in this quality of present being and only alive at all in the spectral traces of gesture or "intrinsic imagery" (McNeill 2016, 4) that remain in all language. But there is no need to rely on any kind of Derridean reproof to keep the hypothesis alive that gesture is a kind of withdrawal. The help it needs is supplied by the explicitly Heideggerian account of Being, signaled by the capitalization of the word, on which McNeill draws. In this account, one does not produce language as much as inhabit it. You cannot inhabit something you have yourself produced, or rather you can do so only once it is allowed its autonomy from you. The kind of inhabitation of language produced by gesture is well characterized by the statement by Maurice Merleau-Ponty quoted by McNeill, that language "presents or rather it is the subject's taking up of a position in the world of his meanings" (Merleau-Ponty 2007, 193, quoted in McNeill 2016, 14). In fact, thought here could be nothing we could think of as a world in which a subject had meanings that were exclusively that subject's own. The role of gesture is to put the speaker in the world of communication, a world that can never be the speaker's property and that can be inhabited only as a latecomer or guest, however active and extensive the home improvements they effect. There is no gesture one can make, however assertive or even frankly aggressive, that does not acquiesce or make accommodation to this condition of being accommodated in language.

For McNeill, this worlding of the gestural word is achieved by means of what he calls Mead's Loop, named for G. H. Mead, who wrote that "gestures become significant symbols when they implicitly arouse in an individual making them the same response which they explicitly arouse in other individuals" (1974, 47). Mead's suggestion is given physiological substance by the discovery in apes of mirror neurons and the postulation of their existence in human brains as well. And if they do not exist, then some other mechanism for the matching of mental simulation to the sight of movements performed by others would need to, given how widespread the experience of such sensations is. Gesture is bound to language because gesture is precisely what binds us into motive community, a community that makes it possible for there to be the kind of linguistic communication that has evolved in humans and, indeed, in McNeill's view, argues "the unlikelihood of language evolving in any species that lacks hands" (2012, xii).

Gesturing creates a shared space, which it substitutes for the actual physical space inhabited by interlocutors, in an act that might be called copropriation. What is held in common is not the specific spaces and simulated traversal of them constituted by individual gestures but the clean sheet or Freudian "mystic writing-pad" (1953–74, 19.225–32) that gesturing together both avails itself of and by doing so makes available to others. In fact, gesture copropriates a joint fund of imaginary space stuff, characterized not just by extension but also by weight, texture, and resistance, allowing it not just to be navigated but also itself manipulated, in postulated cutting, pouring, stretching, sifting, stirring, compressing, and so on. This copropriation is to be distinguished from that of Heidegger, the word being used by French translators to translate *Ereignis*. Heidegger evokes with this word a reciprocal belonging or *Zusammengehörigkeit* of humanity and being in general, while, following him, Michel Henry evokes a similarly general reciprocal inherence of Body and Earth (2012, 45). But the copropriation of gesture is always privative, an appropriation of the plenum of space as such for the purposes of a particular encounter, which makes space its own. This colonization is necessary for the act of reciprocal yielding or giving over of space by gestural speech. Bodily gestures both depend on the assumed availability of a neutral plenum of space to furnish a stage for communication and corporealize that space by charging it with meaning. The space of gestural communication thus gives us a way to give ourselves away in it.

## 4  Refraining

I REMEMBER BEING given as a child tantalizing glimpses into the rather exotic rituals of what I thought of enviously as normal families. Later, I would realize that many children were like me in believing their own family circumstances to be weird and pathological and in their longing to be part of the normal families that they read about in books or saw on television. One of the things that normal families did that we never did was to have people round for dinner (they also had "dinner"). Neither happened in our house. We had aunties who sat with their coats on holding cups of tea on their knees, thin-lipped and looking anxious to go. I once heard from one of my friends from one of these putatively well-adjusted families about a behavior that would be expected if there were a particularly large group of dinner guests, or perhaps an unexpectedly small casserole to feed them. "FHB," mother would beam across the table to her children, or big sister hiss in younger brother's ear: "Family Hold Back."

Holding back has developed a very bad reputation. We tell ourselves that we must learn to avoid or attempt to outwit everything that might hold us back and should be especially on our guard against all the ways in which we might turn out to be holding ourselves back. Just as one might expect, where the expression "holding back" occurs in titles of recent books, it almost always indicates some undesirable impediment that is to be overcome. An unsorted selection from Amazon: *No Holding Back: The Autobiography*; *What's Holding You Back?*; *Stop Stopping: How to Finally Break Free of What's Holding*

*You Back*; *How to Stop Feeling like Sh\*t: 14 Habits That Are Holding You Back from Happiness*; *Conquer Negative Thinking for Teens: A Workbook to Break the Thought Habits That Are Holding You Back*; *Don't Bullsh\*t Yourself!: Crush the Excuses That Are Holding You Back*; *How Women Rise: Break the 12 Habits Holding You Back*; *No Holding Back: My Story*; *The One Thing Holding You Back: Unleashing the Power of Emotional Connection*; *Myths of Work: The Stereotypes and Assumptions Holding Your Organization Back*; *Moving Past Perfect: How Perfectionism May Be Holding Back Your Kids (and You!) and What You Can Do About It*; *Unfrozen: Stop Holding Back and Release the Real You*; *Rebel Entrepreneur: How to Win the Game of Business and Break Free from What's Holding You Back*; and (obviously my favorite, given the preceding list) *Invention: Think Different; Break Free from the Culture Hell-Bent on Holding You Back*.

In *You Must Change Your Life* (2013), Peter Sloterdijk reports in detail on the many rituals and routines that constitute the programs of self-formation, or "anthropotechnics," to which in his view all religions amount. Nearly all those forms of apprenticeship or discipleship involve the exercise of Agamben's "impotentiality" (1999, 182), not doing things or, more precisely, the action of inaction, or refraining from doing things. We are used to thinking of doing things together as a signal feature of human affiliation—eating, talking, playing, working. But human beings are also very drawn to not doing things together and drawn together through them.

I am going to call this holding together in holding back *cohibition*. There are only a few English verbs that deploy the Latin *-hibere* stem: the most familiar are *exhibit*, *inhibit*, and *prohibit*; to *perhibit*, meaning to esteem, repute, or attribute, flared up briefly in the early 1600s, while to *adhibit*, meaning to apply, allow, assign, or append, had a longer career but is now a fussy exotic. As so often, one wonders about other possible prepositional prefixes, such as *transhibit*, *dehibit*, *dishibit*, *obhibit*, *subhibit*, or *enhibit*, for which no sensible uses seem to have been found; the passing over of *prehibition* seems like a particularly lost opportunity. Latin *-hibere* is a modification of *habere*, to have, and the meanings of this family of words alternate between ideas of owning or holding (to exhibit is to display or hold out) and disowning, or holding back. Perhaps the most interesting exhibit from this family of words is *cohibere*, which conjoins the meanings of holding together and keeping in, on the one hand, and restraining, restricting, curbing, or warding off, on the other. Most notably, it is the word used by Lucretius in what would for later generations, and perhaps for many still today, be the most scandalous proposition of the *De rerum natura*, that the mortal soul must diffuse into the air once the containing force of the body is dissolved:

> In fact if the body, which is in a way its vessel, cannot contain it, when once broken up by any cause and rarefied by the withdrawal of blood from the veins, how could you believe that it could be contained by any air [*aere qui credas posse hanc cohiberier ullo*] which is a more porous container than our body? (1975, 3.440–44, 222–23)

The work of the word *cohibition*, which was used to signify both restraint of impulses and as a medical term for staunching or suppression of bodily flows, appears nowadays to be done by *inhibition* or *prohibition*. The latest printed citation supplied by the *OED* is from an 1882 lexicon of science and medicine, which gives German *Beschränkung* and *Verzähmung* as equivalents to *cohibition* and offers the following definition of a "cohibiting medium": "A substance which prevents the passage of electricity from one body to another when placed between them; the term has the same meaning as isolating medium, with the addition of an idea of activity" (Power and Sedgwick 1882, n.p.). Cohibition is then the inhibition of dissolution in inhabitation. In the seventeenth century, *cohibit* was in fact sometimes used for, or perhaps confused with, *cohabit*, for example, in the allegation made in a text of 1661 that, among Persians, "men might contract matrimony and cohibit with their Daughters, Sisters, or Mother" (Pererius 1661, 47). Though *cohibition* has itself almost entirely evaporated from English, I revive it here to suggest the cohibition that is necessary for cohabitation, where the habit (from *habere*, to have), of inhibiting, abstaining, or relinquishing, is what you have, and hold, and thereby what holds you together in and with your habitat. Family Hold Back.

The styling of human actions almost always involves reduction of complexity—to remove all the differentiations of gait involved in ordinary walking for the purposes of marching or processive walking, for example, or to bring the ordinarily mobile and mutable body to a state of repose in prayer. Indeed, action abstention may be, more than merely one feature of human affiliation among others, the most important way in which human beings withdraw themselves from nature or distinguish themselves from other humans. To be sure, human beings assert themselves through aggression and conquest; but it is remarkable how often they also assert themselves through inhibition. Judaism, for example, strongly identifies sanctity with withdrawal and renunciation. Holiness is strongly associated in the Pentateuch with *qedûšâ*, or the exercise of spiritual withdrawal, associated in particular with commandments to withdraw from forbidden foods, ritual impurity, forbidden relations, and the practices of Gentiles (Diamond 2004, 76). Most of the Ten Commandments concern prohibitions rather than prescriptions, with even the positive exhortation to "remember the sabbath day, to keep it holy" (Exodus 20:8) involving a refraining, since to keep the sabbath holy means keeping it apart from other days by various kinds of ritualized abstention, that is, maintaining its integrity through subtraction.

Human beings are perhaps governed by the resolve articulated in W. B. Yeats's "Sailing to Byzantium": "Once out of nature I shall never take / My bodily form from any natural thing" (1956, 192). If human beings for the last few centuries have more and more frequently felt the pressure to do the thing known as fulfilling themselves, that fulfillment will always have to depend on some primary abstention, or *holding away* from creaturely, merely Calibanic existence, eft-nibbled, idly appetitive. Abstention is the means of achieving willed rather than merely willy-nilly existence. Even cults of naturalness will usually be driven by the human mania for purification, the cleaving away of the inessential in favor of the essential. The most unfulfillable instruction you will ever hear is to "act naturally," because no natural creature is capable of performing anything approaching an *act*, that word that always doubles simple or spontaneous doing with the self-conscious performance of that doing, just as the idea of "nature" is by definition part of the method and apparatus of hoisting oneself out of the in-itself condition of nature.

Human beings are governed by the injunction not to be and by the often violent recoil from certain primary forms of what we seemingly cannot not be. So, a human being will always be a kind of object in the world; but to be accorded human dignity is not to be, or be taken to be, an object. Human beings are a kind of animal; but to be human is to be more or other than an animal, to be, in fact, in its own view, the only nonanimal animal. Human beings refrain and abstain and can maintain their understanding of themselves as human only in those refrainings and abstentions.

However, holding oneself back is twinned with going beyond, and unmaking with remaking. The Greek ἀσκεῖν, which gives us *ascetic*, meant to work, fashion or elaborate; though it came to be applied to athletic training or practice, therefore implying the self-denying severity of striving, it could also be used to mean to deck, adorn, or ornament. This can lead to seeming paradoxes. Shaving of the hair is often a form, and a style, of self-privation. Yet many sects also forbid the cutting of hair, as a way of abstaining from the vanity of self-adornment with which the styling of hair is associated. That sects should need the work of scissors should not surprise. The mode of abstaining followed by a Nazirite in Judaism forbade cutting of the hair: "All the days of the vow of his separation there shall no razor come upon his head: until the days be fulfilled, in the which he separateth himself unto the Lord, he shall be holy, and shall let the locks of the hair of his head grow" (Numbers 6:5). Rastafarians observe the same prohibition. Although letting the hair grow belongs to the class of abstentions from social convention that return humans to nature rather than lift them out of it, this is complicated by evolutionary explanations of why humans uniquely have continuously growing head hair, even though they have lost the fur on their bodies. As Alison Jolly suggests,

> Truly untended hair implies that the wearer is desperate or insane and, furthermore, has no friends. Pseudo-untended hair signals ritual mourning in some cultures or, more often, cultural revolt (hippy ponytails, dreadlocks). To convey social status or sexual attractiveness it doesn't matter whether you curl, uncurl, braid, blow-dry, or use powder or mud: The signal is that somebody has clearly done something to the bits round the back. (2005, 5)

So when it comes to head hair, untended and intended are in fact equivalent conditions, since the "natural" function of head hair is to be able to be unruly and therefore available for styling: "Coiffure and coiffure-demanding genes could be at least as old as *Homo sapiens*" (5). Abstention from style is therefore as much a hairstyle, as much a way, as we oddly but tellingly say, of "doing your hair," as the most elaborate plait or piling. In this respect, at least, "culture" is part of "nature" as far as humans are concerned.

It seems as though in the case of the Nazirites, hair may participate in the preservation-destruction ambivalence that characterizes the sacred. Building on the suggestion that they may on occasion have been called on to shave their hair in order to make ritual sacrifice of it, Elizier Diamond offers the following explanation:

> The essence of the Nazirite vow is that by means of consecrating one's hair for a certain period and then offering it on the altar, one symbolically offers oneself to God, and in doing so one is both offering and officiant. Once one has

dedicated one's hair to the altar, it follows as a matter of course that it may not be shorn, for this would constitute the misappropriation of sancta. (2004, 108)

Edmund Leach offers another suggestion, which hinges on the separability of the hair from the body:

> The social anthropologist is concerned with the publicly acknowledged status of social persons and he notices that ritual acts in which part of the individual's body is cut off are prominent in *rites de passage*, that is to say "rites of separation" in which the individual publicly moves from one social position to another. (1958, 162)

On this reading, one might suggest (though it is not a suggestion Leach himself makes) that the hair is not preserved or renounced because of what it might specifically stand for (life, soul, the penis, etc.) but because it embodies separability itself, and thus the condition of being able to live with and in privation. In social life one is a part of a system of apartness. The symbolism both of giving way and giving away allows one to keep what one loses and lose what one keeps. It is what imparts sweetness to the sorrow of parting.

Rituals of separation do not merely follow the partitive logic of *pars pro toto*, as Leach describes it (1958, 150); they are also in some sense about the acts of parting, in which all partition rituals participate. Shaving is often associated with mourning, and also with transition from one state to another, thus leaving an earlier condition behind, even as shaving can seem to turn the clock back to a purer, more uniform time. It seems apt that the two primary operations on which humans perform variations with the hair are twisting and parting. Leach alludes to the Sīmantōnnayanam ceremony practiced in South India, in which a husband parts the hair of a woman in her fourth, sixth, or eighth month of pregnancy:

> The husband stands facing his wife, and holding in his right hand a quill of porcupine with branch of Udumbara *Ficus racemosa* (Atthi leaves) and parts her hair, beginning from the middle of her forehead leading backwards; this he repeats thrice chanting, "May Rākā (Full Moon) listen to my prayers; may she help me to carry out this ceremony without any defect or omission, and bless me with a male child endowed with praiseworthy qualities, with valour and generosity." (Nanjundayya and Iyer 1928, 372)

Leach insists on the overtness of the symbolism: "parting the hair = parting the genitals in parturition" (1958, 155). At the same time, the act of symbolic parting is itself a conjoining, of the orders of act and symbol, flesh and meaning.

The ambivalence of hair is that, as the barber says in the sad, sinister haircutting scene in the Coen Brothers' *The Man Who Wasn't There* (2001), like time itself, "it just keeps coming." You cannot go back in time, because time itself keeps on coming back, to keep coming apart from itself. Time is what divides us from ourselves and from each other, just as, on a much larger scale, the grand narrative of human history is made up through and through of the tragic agony of partings, divergences, and desertions, recapitulating the primal departure into being in the event of birth and anticipating the let-up of being in death. Rituals of passage seem to hold us together in those partings, making it possible for departing into and departing from to be experienced as continuous being-in-departure.

There is a growing curiosity in a number of different fields about the nature of refraining and, in particular, the question of whether it should be viewed as an action or a simple omission of action—a nonaction, or inaction, as might be said. Philosophers regularly return to problems in the definition of refraining as part of the philosophy of action; though there is little mystery or disagreement about what we mean by refraining, finding a logical description of what it entails proves to be a complex matter (Brand 1971; Moore 1979). It looks as though pigeons find performing an action more absorbing than refraining from that action, so much so that time seems to pass more quickly for them when they are doing something than when they are not doing it, even when they have been trained to perform both actions, such that the not-doing may be regarded as instrumental (Zentall and Singer 2008).

Is the abstaining in abstinence the same as the abstaining in abstention? Yes, in one sense, since one may he said to abstain in both circumstances. But the sense of abstain is in fact different in each. In the case of abstinence, I must have a wish to do something I nevertheless refrain from. In the case of abstention, I may have such a wish but need not; I can, for example, abstain from voting on a particular question precisely because I do not have any feelings one way or the other about it. It would be very odd to call this abstinence. In the case of abstinence, by contrast, there is work to be done, in overcoming or deciding against the fulfillment of a desire. In the formulation offered by Brandon Johns, "there is a distinction between not-doing and refraining:

refraining is a special case of not-doing that requires work on the agent's behalf" (2009, 214). In the case of abstention, such work may indeed be done (I may be strongly drawn to an action that, because I also believe it to be wrong, I nevertheless do not endorse) but need not necessarily be done. In the case of abstention, I can abstain indifferently or, indeed, precisely out of indifference; this is not possible in the case of abstinence. The external conditions seem relevant. Abstinence relates to any kind of action to which we might be drawn. Abstention relates to the specific action of indicating a preference or performing an action that amounts to the indication of a preference. Actually, abstention is usually in fact the indication of a preference for not committing oneself to a preference. Abstinence is an action; abstention is a predication. In the case of a political strike, discussed later in the chapter, the word *abstention* seems more appropriate to the withholding of labor than *abstinence*, since abstention seems closer to the act of refusing something to another than the practice of refusing something to oneself.

The difference between the two modes, or even moods, of abstaining is significant for the purpose and method of this book. Abstaining in the sense of positively refraining from an action (drinking, smoking, eating meat, taking revenge) is usually a more determined action than abstaining from making a choice. It is not that the second kind of abstaining is not itself definite, even definitive, for it certainly is, and in some ways can seem even more positive than refraining in the sense of self-denial (for one thing it may take place in public and may involve resisting quite a lot of pressure from one's peers, in the case where only one more vote is needed to carry or defeat a motion, for example). But abstinence is more positive than abstention in the sense that it is more intensely polarized. The abstinence-abstainer refuses what the abstention-abstainer merely declines. There is more tension in abstinence than in abstention, as you pull away from what you feel pulled toward. Abstinence acts on a choice, where abstention is the act of declining to make one. There can thus be abstinence in abstention, for it may be a way of austerely denying an impulse not to make a particular kind of choice, but this is not a necessary condition of it. Abstinence is therefore concentrating and conservative, where abstention is diffusive. Abstinence usually presents itself as a program of action, maintained through time; abstention can be a solitary act. The higher levels of cohering stress requisite to abstinence make it more apt for the socially formative work of cohibition: it would be hard to imagine a society built around abstention. (This distinction is heuristic rather than literal, since abstention is often used to refer to the kind of willed abstinence I have distinguished from it.)

The ending of Kafka's "A Hunger-Artist" might dramatize the difference. As usually understood, the self-starver would be an abstinence-abstainer, who would deny himself something he wanted. But Kafka's hunger-artist can be indifferent to food, because he has never found any he liked.

> "I always wanted you to admire my fasting," said the hunger-artist. "We do admire it," said the overseer placatingly. "But you're not to admire it," said the hunger-artist. "All right, then we don't admire it," said the overseer, "but why should we not admire it?" "Because I have to starve, I can't do anything else," said the hunger-artist. "Well, take a look at that," said the overseer, "and why can't you do anything else?" "Because," said the hunger-artist, and he raised his little head fractionally, and with his lips puckered as if in a kiss, he spoke directly into the overseer's ear, so that none of his words was lost, "because I couldn't find any food I liked. If I had found any, believe me, I wouldn't have made any fuss, and I would have eaten to my heart's content, just like you or anyone else." Those were his last words, but even in his broken eyes, there was the firm, if no longer proud conviction that he would go on starving. (2007, 262)

Kafka's hunger-artist is forced to abstain from eating as an act of, as it were, proudly impassioned indifference: in other words, as a principled abstention rather than an abstinence. He does not fast through wanting not to eat, like a mystic, anorexic, or a performer determined to show powers of endurance, but rather simply through not wanting to eat anything that might be available to him.

This distinction is not new in the modern world. Caroline Walker Bynum points to the similar distinction made in the medieval world between inability to eat and asceticism, as indicated by the fact that holy abstainers from food such as John the Good of Mantua and Columba of Rieti sometimes exhibited their capacity to eat before audiences: that is "the very fact that ... they *could* eat—i.e., that their abstinence was voluntary—suggests that medieval interpreters drew a clear distinction between inability to eat and asceticism" (1987, 196). In Kafka's German, the hunger-artist tells the supervisor "ich hungern muß, ich kann nicht anders." The German verb *hungern* preserves an ambiguity that is tidied up in English by separating into different words the action of fasting from the condition of being hungry. It is not that the hunger-artist is not hungry, only that he is not hungry for anything that might ever satisfy him. English does, however, have the phrase "go hungry," which might seem adapted to the case of Kafka's abstainer in its evocation of the peculiar kind of progress embodied in a holding back.

Kafka's hunger-artist is not like a hunger striker, because his fasting is not tied to any cause, not even that of demonstrating his fortitude or earning his living (in fact he earns his dying). Though abstinent individuals mark themselves off from their communities, abstinence is also often practiced in common. Taboos and prohibitions define communities: "We of the kangaroo clan voluntarily but irrevocably refrain in perpetuity from kangaroo bothering. Thus we make ourselves who we are." Selective eating prohibitions are much subtler and more powerful than sexual prohibitions, precisely because refraining from eating altogether invariably leads to the cessation of existence, but it is possible to make a prohibitive cut within the field of eating itself by denying oneself certain kinds of sinful, unclean, or enfeebling food. The result is to turn appetite into a willed action, tendency into intention. Dietary codes seem rarely to be based on a theory of what it might be positively good to eat; human beings are much more strongly motivated by aversive theories of what they should avoid or deny themselves. It is other peoples who are defined by what they messily and unchoosily put into their mouths (Frogs, Krauts): "we" are defined by what we take care not to eat. For all their admiration of the wolfish predator, many senior Nazis followed Hitler in being vegetarian, thereby, according to Boria Sax, affirming their elite status: "Throughout most of history only elites could eat meat on a regular basis, but only elites could readily afford to refuse it" (2000, 35). The contemporary problem of anorexia nervosa may be seen as an intensification of a systematic assertion of power through selective self-denial that humans have almost universally sought to give themselves. Peter Sloterdijk gives fasting altogether a special place in his arguments for the importance of what he calls "ascetology" in human projects of self-formation:

> It [fasting] is not an artistic discipline like any other; it is the metaphysical discipline *par excellence*. From time immemorial it has been the exercise by which, if it succeeds, the ordinary human who is subject to hunger learns—or observes in others—how one can beat nature at its own game. The fasting of ascetics is the skilled form of the lack that is otherwise always experienced passively and involuntarily. This triumph over need is only accessible to those who are assisted by a great need: when the old master ascetics say that hunger

for God or enlightenment must overrule every other desire if it is to be sated, they are presupposing a hierarchy of privations. (2013, 70–71)

"Ye shall not make any cuttings in your flesh," Jews are enjoined (Leviticus 19:28). I have always thought this particular injunction belonged among the class of spontaneously self-prohibiting behaviors, along with "Ye shall not plunge thy hand into boiling water" and "Ye shall not precipitate thyself from the top of a block of flats." It is a little like the Eddie Izzard routine that imagines the Anglican Church offering its believers a choice of Cake or Death, leaving the grand inquisitor puzzled about why death should have so few takers ("we're going to run out of cake at this rate"). Still, as Freud wisely assumes of the incest taboo, there is no point in prohibiting something unless somebody somewhere wants to do it (1953–74, 13.17). After all, one of the almost-irresistible temptations held out by the Evil One to Christ in the wilderness was precisely to make the jump. Many human societies are still bound together by a solemn covenant, often reinforced ludicrously by law, to resist the temptation to the voluntary ending of their own existences.

Like many collective relations, the relation between abstinence and collectivity is reversible. Abstaining from things is demanding (that of course being a large part of the point), and being part of a community of abstainers, whether nuns, teetotalers, vegans, or kosher Jews, can help spread the cognitive and emotional load. But for this reason, a shared project of self-denial can in itself create and sustain what may be called an abstinent collectivity. The function of the abstaining then becomes to create and sustain the group rather than membership of the group helping its members stick at their abstinence. Indeed, one might say that the capacity for abstinent control of impulses and appetites would be likely to be selected for among members of a group in which setting aside ego claims in favor of cooperation is at a premium. "Refusal is social and affiliative," as Carole McGranahan has observed (2016, 322).

In its active mode, abstinence takes the form of sacrifice. What abstinence gives up, sacrifice gives away; sacrifice is to abstinence as voiding is to avoidance. In Roman life, the person or object who was *sacer* could be both holy and accursed, the logic being that such a person was set aside for the gods, either to consume or to punish. In a similar way, when Cain is driven out and condemned to be "a fugitive and a vagabond" for the murder of his brother and complains to God that "it shall come to pass, that every one that findeth me shall slay me" (Genesis 4:14), God responds in a sort of good news–bad news way by marking him out as set aside for his personal retribution alone: "And the Lord said unto him, Therefore whosoever slayeth Cain, vengeance shall be taken on him sevenfold. And the Lord set a mark upon Cain, lest any finding him should kill him" (Genesis 4:15). The category of the sacred is the reserved, that which is held back from ordinary kinds of transaction and exchange, including that of being thought about, pushing it in a sense toward the condition of being a noncategory. To keep something sacred is to abstain not just from handling it but even from reflecting on it, in particular in the form of handling constituted by language. Thus, one is enjoined in certain religions not to profane with utterance the name of God, or, as used commonly to be the case, someone would be said to have (voice dropping to a whisper and mouth stretching to form a large mime) "*Cancer.*" But the reservation of the sacred is always liable to be compromised in the form of the secret, which must be told, or at least tellable, in order to be kept. Samuel Beckett's *Come and Go* acts out a ceremonial ring-a-roses of secrets imparted and constrained between three women, each of whom in turn whispers to another the sorrow of the third, unknown to that third. The final image of the play is of an auld-lang-syne interlocking of hands, in an image of how formative of old acquaintance epistemic abstinence can be (Beckett 1986, 354–55).

J. Hillis Miller puts the principle of what he calls refraining, which seems to hover somewhere between abstinence and abstention, at the center of the work of Jacques Derrida. The particular thing that Derrida refrains from is joining or belonging, whether to clan, family, or institution. I want to have indicated in this chapter that refraining is in fact, and necessarily, the most powerfully cohesive force in any kind of human group. If we are monads, it is because we catch the infection of singularity from our belonging, a belonging that can henceforth only ever be a community of those who must hold back from being or having everything in common, and yet whose community is formed from the aggregation of these abstinences. Miller recognizes that this impossibility of genuine intimacy is general, so that Derrida's is just the "singular form, *his* form, of the general human situation of not having to be one of the family, of having an urgent obligation not to be one of the family. My obligation to respond without mediation to the wholly other" (2007, 292). But he does not seem to recognize the ethical bond that this aggregated abstinence constitutes.

We may be able to understand the collectivizing force of shared abstinence through reflection on a quality like "continence" (literally "holding together" rather than "holding away"), which suggests a view of society as constituted on the model of an individual human body. Human beings seem powerfully drawn to a conception of the health of individual bodies in terms of an economy, on the one hand, of containment (of strength, energy, vital force, heat, pneuma, etc.) and, on the other, of purgation, the channeling away of invasive or vitiating matter (excrement, mucus, pus, and so on.). It is this economy that suggests the way in which the giving out of impurity can contribute to the sense of the collectivity as held together by an energy of self-containment, making giving up a means of holding in.

A collective abstinence is to be distinguished from an abstinent collectivity. The former may be unreflective and unselfconscious, a simple pattern of behavior rather than a symbolic affirmation of identity—for example, in a simple preference for certain foods over other ignored foods, or the belief that it is natural for all humans to avoid certain objects or practices, to distinguish themselves from plants or other animals. An abstinent collectivity, by contrast, differentiates itself not primarily from the idea of a natural existence but also from other groups of humans. It consequently has an agonistic purpose, which is amplified if it forms part of a regime of physical training in preparation for attack or defense.

Abstinence can be homeostatic or dynamic. It is homeostatic if it is in accordance with a theory that human beings must in the course of things observe certain limits or prohibitions in order to keep danger at bay or keep themselves in being. It is dynamic if it forms part of a narrative of reparative or projective self-transformation to undo, for example, some damage or deficit in the human condition or some weakness into which other humans may have fallen. Arguments in favor of vegetarianism often deploy this idea of a fall into savagery and the necessity for human beings ethically to remake themselves through an undoing or reengineering of their corrupting appetite for meat. The idea of civilization, conceived as an aim rather than a condition, and which is to be achieved through the "civilizing process" and the work of self-culture at an individual and collective level, both of which depend on ever more complex networks of growth through prohibition, involves just this kind of projective structure.

This suggests that abstinence may have a role in the formation of a temporal economy, in which past, present, and future are bound together by a rhythm of privation in the expectation of recompense. This is especially the case with dietary abstinence, which may be regarded as an engineering of a natural rhythm of appetitive depletion and abstinent repletion, often keyed into the rhythms of wakefulness and sleep. In many religions, fasting is required before a ritual or festival, marking the suspension of *chronos* or customary time. Abstaining from sex before marriage structures the individual life course in a similar way, while also coordinating it with the reproductive demands of a society. An apparent aberration like the popularity of "spiritual marriage," the sexual abstinence in wedlock known in the medieval world, is a perverse confirmation of the relation between indulgence and prohibition that exists in, and possibly as, the institution of marriage (Elliott 1993, 17). Abstention in this temporal perspective becomes a means not just of affirming the longevity of a collectivity—we have never eaten purple fruits and never will—but also of controlling the future through acts of self-discipline. The regimes of self-famishing whereby prophets and shamans may encourage or enable the access of visionary knowledge provide one example of this subordinating of futurity through magical self-mastery in the present. It is even more clearly indicated in the acts of collective ordeal, inhibition, and self-humiliation that are practiced by some religions.

Actions of abstinence may be permanent, but they are much more potent when tied to time and thus used to give tension to temporal extension. Given specific measures in time, abstainings themselves become measures of time. Thus, one is enjoined to fast for certain designated periods, the beginnings and endings of which are carefully specified (sunset and sunrise, forty days and nights), in order to allow for synchronization. A hunger strike always has a temporal end point, even if it is death.

The action of collective fasting remains a feature of Judaism and Islam, and what may be seen as ambivalent festivals of fasting were a feature of Christian observance across Europe up to the Reformation. Rather than abandon fasting, Protestantism attempted to harness and intensify its cohering force by making it episodic rather than calendrical, thereby tying it to the intensity of crisis. The function of public fast days was "to instil in the populace a due sense of 'humiliation,'" understood as "the acquiring of an awareness of the insignificance and unworthiness of mankind when compared to God, and a recognition that misfortune was the entirely deserved product of human sinfulness" (Durston 1972, 134). National days of fasting and humiliation were called for in England during plague epidemics in 1563 and 1593, as well as in 1588 during the Armada emergency (129). But releasing rituals of abstaining and humiliation for the calendar also made for fissile outbreaks of potentially uncontrollable piety, as well as the opportunity to assign the blame for reverses on the actions of the authorities. Charles I attempted both to regulate the timing and conduct of days of fasting and to use them to focus national loyalty at the beginning of rebellion in 1641 (131–32).

We are often informed nowadays about the kinds of "national humiliation" that may flow from military defeat, loss of territory and power, economic decline, the antics of an idiotic leader, or other reverses. It has become a standard assumption that the humiliation of defeated Germany by the victorious powers after the First World War created the conditions for the rise of Nazism. The potency of the shared history or prospect of humiliation has often been exploited by regimes wishing to legitimize themselves. Shane Strate describes the "National Humiliation" discourse that arose in Thailand following the revolution of 1932, which ended the rule of the absolute monarchy and the establishment of a series of military governments. Despite the proud claim that Thailand was never colonized, unlike most of its neighbors, the discourse inflected the history of relations between Thailand and the West as "a series of emasculating encounters" (Strate 2015, 6), which needed to be redeemed by a more assertive attitude toward the West. The painful "memory" of humiliation (hardly anybody ever has anything that could count as what is called "memory" in historical matters; otherwise it would not be history but people remembering things) has been used as a justification and motivation for the thrusting off of colonial domination in many former colonies. But force comes just as much from harboring the memory of humiliation as striving to have done with it. Humiliation has been used as a means of gathering energy and commitment in decolonizing struggles, for example, in the National Humiliation Day that Gandhi declared in 1919 to encourage demonstrations against British colonialism (Callahan 2004, 203).

China continues to keep alive the idea of the Century of Humiliation it suffered from defeat by Britain in the Opium Wars of 1842 and 1860 through to the Japanese invasion in the Second World War. The Century of Humiliation has been repeatedly declared to have come to an end, by Chiang Kai-shek and Mao Zedong following the Second World War through to the current regime, even as each new declaration of its ending extends the humiliation beyond the 1839–1949 century. W. A. Callahan writes that "the master narrative of modern Chinese history is the discourse of the century of national humiliation" (2004, 204). The four characters 勿忘國恥 *Wuwang guochi* (Never Forget National Humiliation) reappear constantly in images and ceremonies of remembrance

(Wang 2012). As Callahan writes, "Humiliation is something that you suffer, rather than promote. But in China . . . humiliation is not just about passive 'victimization.' National humiliation discourse involves a very active notion of history and recovery" (2004, 202–3).

National days of fasting, prayer, and humiliation continued to be declared in the United States and Britain through the nineteenth century and beyond. Such days were either to encourage thanksgiving or to mark a time of calamity or threat. The logic seems to be that an act of self-humbling might purchase some remission of misfortune. By 1901, when William Maclagan, the Archbishop of York, called for a National Day of Humiliation to improve Britain's fortunes in the South African War, it had come to seem a somewhat superstitious practice. G. K. Chesterton responded with a column in which he protested against the absurdity of this "access of unreal humility" (1901, 67). He was stung in particular by the sordidness of the temporizing that deployed self-abnegation as a way of currying favor with the Almighty:

> If they do not think their views just, they have been following with every kind of moral bravado and insolence an unjust course. If they do think it just, they are calmly proposing publicly to humiliate justice because it does not prosper. In either case they are guilty of that darkest and oldest form of snobbishness, a cosmic snobbishness. (67)

The work of prohibition is so ingrained in human beings, and in being human, that the very act of prohibition may retroactively create the desire to transgress it, thereby sustaining and even intensifying the prohibition's own necessity. And this is surely because man's first disobedience consists not in breaking a rule but in the very act of self-prohibition or imagining himself prohibited from having a spontaneous unregulated existence. To prohibit is to disobey, or make oneself an arbitrary exception to a norm of nonprohibition. For human beings, mere being is no kind of life at all. In order to be human, it is necessary to create a superego who will perform on our behalf the necessary work of prohibiting (do not eat). The human is himself, like Goethe's Mephistopheles, "der Geist, der stets verneint" (1956, 39). Creaturely existence is existence as merely, vulgarly given. One comes to awareness of oneself just in time to realize it is too late, when one has been in a state of unwilled and unreflective existence for a long time. Every effort to grasp and live out the conditions of one's real existence involves a refusal of that will-less state of being. To be is not to be.

This kind of purification can even extend to the idea of the divine, in that most mystical form of abstinence known as apophatic theology, which promises that, since divinity must be far beyond all powers of human comprehension such that it is not possible to predicate anything truly of God, the only sure way to approach the divine is through willing abstinence from all the ways of thinking that might most naturally occur to one in respect of it. It is an ongoing taking away of the thought that you first thought of. It will also enjoin the cultivation of a mode of speech that will deprecate everything that the very act of articulation seems to assume and require, following the principle announced in the word *apophasis*, unspeaking or speaking away, rather than speaking out, abloquy in place of eloquence. This is, of course, the tallest of tall orders, but that is only appropriate for an intellectual exercise that may be seen not so much as an approach to the divine through denial as a deification of the passion for denial that humans hold so dear, or the apotheosis of abstaining itself.

One of the ways in which groups of modern human beings have tried to assert collective will and the possibility of new forms of political being is through the collective withdrawal from productive labor in the strike. The essence of the strike is contained in the phrase "industrial action," leading to the venerable but seemingly unwearying appearance of gags about it being more like industrial *in*action haha. In fact, a strike often involves a sudden access of activity, marking a change in an existing arrangement or a new beginning—as in "striking up" a tune or "striking out" in a particular direction. A political or industrial strike, used in this sense since the late eighteenth century, draws also from the range of meanings in which to strike means to unfix, close down, or take apart, as in striking camp, or striking a theatrical set, or what was known as "striking work" at the end of the day. Earlier uses were often transitive, so discontented employees would be said from the 1890s to strike their employer: the separation of the action from its object in the condition of "being on strike" or the elaborated periphrasis "taking strike action against" may be a way of registering the somewhat odd mixture of action and inaction, purpose and refraining, involved in industrial striking.

In an ever more tightly integrated world of shared and interlocking responsibilities and expectations, the traditional means for effecting shifts of power, armed uprising, is far too readily absorbed into the scheme of things. Human beings have been practicing armed violence for so long that being a professional killer (soldier) has been for centuries a perfectly respectable, not to say admired, way for someone to make a living. A strike, by contrast, seems to promise transformation precisely through its systematic refusal to participate in any kind of inherited or customary arrangement. This principle is articulated with a kind of cranky brilliance in Georges Sorel's "myth of the general strike" in his *Reflections on Violence* (1999, 126). Sorel realized that, by the beginning of the twentieth century, before any socialist revolutions had been successfully effected, the idea of socialism had already become a kind of second nature, embedded in grimly plausible programs of social improvement. What was needed was a purified and purifying idea of political action that could be negatively distinguished from every kind of practical program. In a melding of Marxism with Bergsonian mysticism, based on intuition rather than reason, Sorel insisted that only a general strike, that is, a refusal of everything that might form part of accepted orderings and understandings of social life, could leave this piecemeal logic properly in pieces.

So it is important for Sorel that one does not waste time weighing the methods and likely political outcome of the strike: "Myths must be judged as a means of acting on the present; all discussion of the method of applying them as future history is devoid of sense. *It is the myth in its entirety which is alone important*" (1999, 116–17). In admirably strict conformity with these principles, Sorel abstains from telling us anything at all about what a general strike might consist of or how it would perform its work. He does, however, devote quite a lot of time to arguing what it is not—why it does not encourage the petty jealousies and desires for vengeance characteristic of ordinary political life, for example (158–59). The action of abstaining from all action and defection from all definition is powerful, according to Sorel, because it is spiritual rather than practical and "awakens in the depth of the soul a sentiment of the sublime proportionate to the conditions of a gigantic struggle" (159). The Sorelian flame is kept crackling in the work of Slavoj Žižek, who similarly urges that revolutionaries should refrain apophatically from ever entering into the vulgar game of trying to spell out the likely gains of political action. The dangerous attraction of this kind of radicalism, of cutting everything back to the roots and thereby rooting oneself in the severity of pure abscission, is apparent in the ways in which it can be appropriated from the left by the right, as in the fervor of those maintaining, not so much in the absence of reasons as in an austerity of reasoning, that Britain must forgo the advantages of belonging to the European Union, a fervor that pragmatic arguments based on self-interest can only fatten.

Sorel's brilliance is in realizing how powerfully cohering systematic abstention has always been for human beings. Strikes, even among academics, turn out to be even harder work than working, not least because you are not getting paid (unless you are in a profession like university teaching where it can be so hard to tell where and when you are actually at work that strikers need to declare themselves to be on strike as a point of honor, a discipline less than universally observed). There are picket lines to be manned, for much longer than regular working hours, pamphlets and manifestoes to be promulgated, marches and demonstrations to be coordinated, confrontations with the authorities to be engineered, in order for strikers to be arrested and impassioned campaigns for their release set in train and, increasingly nowadays in our epistemocratic era, pop-up open-air academies of political theory organized. Nothing can give human beings a more festival sense of common purpose than collective abstinence. Indeed, Sorel is on to this too and points to the prodigious productive power of mobilization possessed by the idea of a general strike:

> The idea of the general strike, constantly rejuvenated by the sentiments provoked by proletarian violence, produces an entirely epic state of mind and, at the same time, bends all the energies of the mind towards the conditions that allow the realization of a freely functioning and prodigiously progressive workshop; we have thus recognized that there is a strong relationship between the sentiments aroused by the general strike and those which are necessary to bring about a continued progress in production. We have then the right to maintain that the modern world possesses the essential motivating power which *can* ensure the existence of the morality of the producers. (1999, 250)

Striking borrows from the drive to sanctify or set apart found in festivals, holidays, or the elaborate provisions for the sabbath found in Judaism and Christianity. Giorgio Agamben finds in such regulated suspensions of time—that both govern time and yet are held outside it—a principle that he calls "inoperativity," which is "not mere inertia or abstention; it is, rather, a sanctification, that is to say, a particular modality of acting and living" (2011, 104).

Many things are subject to inhibition, even inhibition itself. If aggression is met with inhibition, inhibition can itself become a form of aggression—the aggressive production, for the purposes of policing it, of the male gaze in pedagogically politicized forms of female self-exhibition like the SlutWalk (Mendes 2015) or, alternatively, in the apotropaic exhibition of inhibition (keep your filthy eyes off me), through veiling for example. Or, according to one version of the repressive hypothesis, it can produce aggression indirectly by damming up legitimate desires, which are bound to overflow in explosive forms. Under these circumstances, inhibition must itself be inhibited, sometimes allegedly leading to the paradoxical outcome described by Herbert Marcuse as "repressive desublimation" (2002, 75–76).

So substantial are the payoffs of inhibition, amounting, once one includes the effects of the accumulation of capital through the inhibition of expenditure, almost to the entire material fabric of human civilization, that it would be surprising if the practice of inhibition did not often lead to magical fantasies of omnipotence. The inhibition of libido in the celibate and the anorexic can lead to addictive forms of the libido of inhibition, in the intoxication of the apparently limitless sense of self-overcoming power suggested by the capacity to overrule appetite. In such cases the libidinal gratifications provided through the denial of libido become autonomous, displacing the forms of long-term spiritual or social gain that self-denial is traditionally supposed to deliver. The psychosocial work both of sexuality and of revenge depends on this economy of intensifying self-limitation.

It may be that in staking so much on the power of self-limitation or inhibition, human beings are recognizing the evolutionary importance of the principle of self-control in making it possible for intelligent, but ferociously aggressive, creatures like primates to live in large social groups. There seems good reason for believing that, as Patrick McNamara suggests, "if individuals can derive real benefits (e.g., a larger 'return' later) by learning to inhibit current appetitive or consummatory impulses, then natural selection would favour those individuals with the ability to delay gratification of impulses" (1999, 66). McNamara also connects the ability to inhibit distracting impulses to the capacity to concentrate on analytic and deliberative behavior, as well as to deceive, since "deception of others and of self might . . . have been one of the evolutionary sources of the exceptional inhibitory powers associated with modern humans" (68). We are accustomed to the thought that high intelligence and the demands of living among other highly intelligent conspecifics require the capacity to make complex connections between ideas and impulses; but it also requires remarkable inhibitory powers. Not only is the capacity for inhibition of violent or aggressive behavior necessary for life in complex groups; it is also necessary within individuals so that "inhibitory abilities became powerful enough to make complicated cognitive processing possible by protecting against even high-level mental interference effects such as irrelevant memories, images, fantasies, and emotions" (69).

One of the most important forms of structuring inhibition in human life is the incest taboo, which in general terms is almost universal among humans, if highly variable in the specific forms it may take. Robin Fox has connected the incest taboo to what might be called the inhibitive drive in human societies. The unexpectedness of the idea of a drive to, or instinct of, inhibition is part of Fox's argumentative point; we do not expect such a thing as a drive to hold back drives, since its benefits seem so obvious, and we tend to look for causes of things we do not like, such as divorce or dementia, but remain oddly incurious about the causes of things we do like, such as marriage or memory or kindness to animals (1994, 76). Fox is unconvinced by the explanation that the inhibition of sexuality or aggression is a matter of something called "culture" intervening in the state of nature, since what is called culture is so obviously natural, or in no intelligible sense unnatural. The *explanans* here is in fact the *explanandum*, for what the hypothesis of culture leaves entirely unexplained is why the all-explaining thing called culture should have evolved at all.

For Fox, the capacity to inhibit aggressive and other impulses should itself be seen as instinctive. As Freud among others suggested, inhibition rarely acts simply to squash aggressive impulses. Instead, it works obliquely by diverting or reassigning such impulses, in particular through processes of ritualization—for which the analogy among primates and other animals would be actions like display and exhibition. "Behind this propensity to ritualize, especially in *Homo sapiens*, lies the innate ability to inhibit our basic limbic emotional drives," Fox proposes, far-reachingly (1994, 79). *Homo sapiens* is to be understood as

> an animal whose evolving brain was as concerned with the *inhibition* as with the *facilitation* of aggression, and perhaps even more so. It was not that "animal aggression" was absent; it was still very much in evidence. It was that in man the aggression was constantly being monitored by consideration of delayed gratification: *aggression postponed was dominance gained*. The aggression still had to be there and easily "turned on" for the dominance struggle to be effective. But it had to be just as easily "turned off" so that the animal did not make foolish moves and spoil its chances (as is the case with the hyperaggressive animals who end up wounded, dead, or exiled). (79)

The biosocial or, as it has later tended to be called, sociobiological explanation for the capacity to inhibit impulses is that it makes possible the cooperative behavior among complex groups that is necessary for human survival and success:

> The real "causal" question here then is not why so many young males act so violently. This is digestion: it just happens as long as the appropriate stimuli (the analogs of food) are fed in (females, other males, resources). The real causal question is how so many cultures manage through initiation, intimidation, sublimation, bribery, education, work, and superstition to stop them and divert their energy elsewhere. (92)

In a certain sense, we might suggest that this provides a general account of the function of culture, as embodied principally in the capacity to symbolize: culture is just the name for the ensemble of symbolic actions, actions that are not quite actions, or somehow more than the mere actions they seem to be, that humans use to inhibit violence. Apart from anything else, this makes sense of the otherwise anomalous-seeming fact that the primatologist (and painter) Desmond Morris, author of *The Naked Ape*, was for a short time director of London's Institute of Contemporary Arts.

Abstinence and inhibition are effected through symbolic means, most particularly through the richest symbolic means available to humans, language. If this is true, it makes it unsurprising that language itself should be the vehicle and subject of inhibition. Gilbert Herdt remarks that, not only are all human societies concerned with the regulation of sexuality; they are also concerned with the regulation of how sexuality is represented: "All of them, past and present, exert cultural, political, economic and even psychological controls over how people talk about sex: when, where, with whom and why—not why they are motivated, but why they must be stopped from sexual discourse" (2011, 259).

Not only are secret societies common in many times and places; many societies seem to depend on the keeping of certain kinds of secrets—the sacred, for example, being understood in many cultures as that which should not be inquired into or spoken about (Connor 2019, 145–49). Most academic writing about silence, in common with writing about refraining, restraint, and holding back of all kinds, tends to assume that the imposing of silence is an impediment or violation, meaning that silence should ideally in all circumstances be broken. Peter H. Stephenson has suggested, by contrast, that the ability to keep silence may literally have often been a matter of life and death for early humans. As Stephenson observes, "The most essential feature of human control over limbic vocal responses is the ability to not vocalize at all under conditions which elicit involuntary response on the part of other Primates" (1980, 49)—that is, when a jaguar or SS officer is a few feet away. The development of systems of inhibition that could override the impulses promoted by the limbic system may have allowed for the silencing of the spontaneous cries that would announce one's presence to a predator. For similar reasons, it is also the case that the ability to keep silent is also a great advantage in hunting. Noisy animals usually have few predators—and domesticated animals tend to vocalize more (our cat Leila lived wild before inveigling herself into our household and was almost silent for a long time before we succeeded in teaching her how to meow in something like an acceptably feline fashion). The relation between keeping quiet and staying alive leads Stephenson to the speculation that

> sound generated by species may then be grossly understood as inversely proportional to the amount of pressure exerted upon that species by predators. Under great pressure by predators, the inhibition of not only random vocalization, but of an entire emotion laden involuntary call system may have been highly adaptive. Given current data on the predation by leopards on *Australopithecus robustus* I would suggest that such conditions obtained in the past for antecedent human chronospecies. Furthermore I would suggest that rather than rendering the evolution of language impossible, the increased demand in terms of natural selection for individuals who could remain silent may have been precisely that which allowed for the evolution of language ultimately to take place. The development of a prefrontal lobe which is generally associated with inhibition and the consequent increase in cortical-cortical pathways coupled with the relative reduction in cortical-limbic pathways may stem from conditions where individuals who were able to keep silent were selected for, while those who could not became evolutionary casualties. (49–50)

As Stephenson observes, one of the most important things about speech is the fact that it incorporates silence: "The sonic and aphonic are poles existing in one overall medium of communication for neither can exist without the other as the source of its own definition. Speech involves the controlled use of silence and silence can only exist as an absence of what is recognized as sound" (52). One might go even further than Stephenson and suggest that, where the emotional-laden calls of the limbic-vocal system must either be fully on or fully off, speech can be on and off at the same time, because speech includes, exploits, and even depends on "intraphonic" silence. Indeed, many forms of speech can themselves be forms of call inhibition, or *unsayings*: "whatever you say, say nothing," as the Seamus Heaney poem has it, referring to Northern Ireland during the Troubles as the "land of password, handgrip, wink and nod" (1990, 79). Learning to speak does not mean replacing muteness with expressive sound. It means modifying the cry, learning all the ways in which the impulsive demands given being by the howl or scream may be engineered by and into the work of communication. On solemn occasions, often to mark a death respectfully, collectivities commonly practice formal abstinence from speech in the form of the Minute's Silence.

Of course, abstinence and renunciation can be instrumental—a wager placed on the chance of an enhanced return. But there may be a more primary kind of abstinence, one that seems to make its demand on its own behalf or even bring its own immediate reward. One form of this is obsessive avoidance rituals, the performers of which build their life around the shunning of sources of temptation or impurity or sedulously avoid all kinds of danger, whether in the form of unlucky omens or numbers or dangerous bacteria. One might still view such a regime as instrumental, in that it is motivated by the dread of whatever consequences are feared, with the payoff being the preservation of health and good fortune. However, in many cases of compulsive avoidance, or actions designed to neutralize or undo other actions, of which the washing of hands may be paradigmatic, a self-fulfilling delight can develop in the very exercise of this apotropaic power of annulling or heading off. Maud Ellmann's study of the poetics and politics of self-starvation begins with the story of a female hunger striker in Armagh during the protests in 1981, who was released from detention but died a year later of anorexia nervosa: Ellmann writes that "she took her hunger with her when she left the prison as if she had become addicted to the nothingness that she had learned to substitute for food, clinging to it even at the cost of her life" (1993, 1). Ellmann's study concerns itself with a kind of willed hunger that consumes itself in its dark desire for itself, under circumstances in which "one no longer fasts for justice but for jouissance" (13).

The contemporary associations between fasting, slimming, and body image suggest that eating and its disciplines may be strongly entrained by sexual questions. Michel Foucault argues that this is actually a reversal of priorities that obtained in the ancient world, which took a long time to accomplish:

> It is a trait manifested by all Greek and Roman medicine to accord much more space to the dietetics of alimentation than to that of sex. For this medicine, the thing that matters is eating and drinking. A whole development—evident in Christian monasticism—will be necessary before the preoccupation with sex will begin to match the preoccupation with food. But alimentary abstentions and fasts will long remain fundamental. And it will be an important moment for the history of ethics in European societies when apprehensions about sex and its regimen will significantly outweigh the rigor of alimentary prescriptions. (1986, 141)

This kind of fasting may be dissensive rather than collective, in that it may assert a power of self-denial that defies social norms and expectations. As Caroline Walker Bynum suggests, these norms and expectations are often centered on food, as they were for women in the late medieval period. Bynum argues that medieval fasting, among other kinds of privation and self-mortification among women, was not an internalization of patriarchal prejudices that saw the female body as the source of wickedness and sensual temptation, as corporeality itself in contrast with the soul. Rather it was a kind of ontological poverty grab, which capitalized on the powerful idea of the femininity of Christ, where femininity meant a mixture of suffering and bountifulness, for suffering was the gift that could be relied on to keep giving, becoming more affluent the poorer it got. This was surely by no means the last time that the ontological advantage in disadvantage has been exercised by or on behalf of women against men whose phantasmal power (the power that they and others dream they have) deprives them of the much more potently immediate experience of being as being powerless, provoking at times the passionate intensity of male impotence envy.

Women thus asserted control in the area in which they were anyway enjoined to exercise it, in that women were then as now largely responsible for the preparation and serving of food. As Bynum shrewdly observes, "Human beings can renounce, or deny themselves, only that which they control" (1987, 191)—this remaining true even, perhaps, where control is what needs to be renounced. Piously self-starving women, as it were, served in every sense (*serve* being from Latin *servare*, whose primary meaning is to save, deliver, or keep unharmed)—conserving themselves in serving themselves up, as Christ did in the Eucharist: "Women found it very easy to identify with a deity whose flesh, like theirs, was food. In mystical ecstasy, in communion, in ascetic *imitatio*, women ate and became a God who was food and flesh" (287, 275). This was a kind of weakness that powerful men could approach only indirectly, or through paradox, since they "needed to become weak and human, yet spiritual 'women' in order to proceed towards God . . . the man had to see his basic religious commitment as flight from power and glory—for Jesus himself had fled power, no matter how much kings and prelates might wield it in his name" (287, 288). Bynum suggests that the very fact that females were to be thought of as more fleshly than males

> led both sexes to see themselves as in some sense female-human. . . . Religious women in the later Middle Ages saw in their own female bodies not only a symbol of the humanness of both genders but also a symbol of—and a means of approach to—the humanity of God. (296)

Men needed to renounce power and authority to approach God; women could junket on the voluptuous fantasy that lived the flesh as renunciation itself: "Fasting, feeding, and feasting were thus not so much opposite as synonyms. Fasting was flight not *from*, but *into* physicality" (250).

Giorgio Agamben claims, apparently on the somewhat spindly say-so of a passage in Plutarch's *Convivial Questions*, that all festivals may be understood in terms of a ceremony described as "expulsion of bulimia," in which a slave is driven away from the house with blows from a stick. Agamben sees this as a replacement of animal appetite with social and civilized eating:

> What is chased away is not hunger and famine but rather the "hunger of an ox": the beast's continuous and insatiable eating (symbolized by the ox, with its slow and uninterrupted rumination). Chasing away the "bulimic" slave means, then, expelling a certain form of eating (devouring or engorging like wild beasts in order to satiate a hunger that is by definition insatiable), and thus clearing a space for another modality of eating, one that is human and festive, one that can begin only once the "hunger of an ox" has been expelled, once the bulimia has been rendered inoperative and sanctified. Eating, in this respect, is not a *melachah*, an activity directed toward an aim, but in inoperativity and *menuchah*, a Sabbath of nourishment. (2011, 107)

In a sense this is a familiar explication of the workings of Elias's civilizing process, in which animal appetite, understood as an uncontrolled aggression or the loss of self in selfish gratification, is controlled and moderated. Pulsing through Agamben's argument here, however, is a political allegory, which sees the appetite of an ox in terms of the uncontrolled demands of consumer capitalism, and the festival as its sanctified suspension, through strike or other kinds of symbolic resistance. There are some odd wrinkles in Agamben's account—the ox does indeed need to eat constantly, as do many other animals who subsist on a vegetarian diet that does not allow for rest (no gorilla could afford to set time aside from the daily grind of food gathering for a sabbath), but this patient, if relentless nibbling seems just the opposite of "devouring or engorging like wild beasts," oxen being just as emblematic of the pastoral as sheep. One might say that human beings had leisure for festivals only once they had supplied themselves with the forms of nutritive surplus offered by a carnivorous diet (gorging on ox, for example, rather than eating like it), which may itself have led to and depended on the technological discovery of cooking. In this account, the suspension of production and appetite would in fact absolutely depend on the work of production, indeed be nothing but a secondary production of it.

Bulimia nervosa, which has been seen as a particular form of the hunger strike against normal eating, is able simultaneously to indulge and abstain, and on both sides, on the side of eating and on the side of abstinence (the bulimic binges on deprivation as much as on food.) And both anorexia and bulimia can be characterized by a perversely immoderate form of immoderation. The hunger striker prolongs the spectacle of the fast with sips of water, just as the epic abstinences of mystics and saints can often be explained by the midnight nibblings in which they have on occasion been detected. The bulimic reverses this through his or her privy disposals of the engorgement of eating, whether through vomiting or seemingly virtuous whirling hours on the exercise bike.

This power of non- or undoing in abstinence from the food that is necessary to life may be equivalent to and perhaps exemplified by the death drive, or whatever else might lie beside or beyond the pleasure principle. Indeed, the acquiescence to death, grudging or willing as it may be, is the most literal kind of abstention, in that it abstains or holds oneself in abeyance, not from any particular form of existence but from continued personal existence altogether. But, as we see in Chapter 6, perhaps even this form of absolute abstention is condemned to take some positive form or to be inflected in some way by the human horror of unstyled existence, a horror that only collectively sanctioned, and sanctified, practices of privative self-styling can assuage.

## 5   Apologizing

APOLOGY REPRESENTS A voluntary withdrawal or giving away of status. The question of how absolute this withdrawal must be is always alive in apology. Can one apologize unreservedly? Probably not, though the expression opens the show for us in a telling way. You cannot apologize unreservedly, any more than you can surrender unconditionally, because both ideas are self-refuting and in the same way. Unconditional surrender is a particular way of surrendering, that is, a condition of surrender, the condition of imposing no conditions. You can be defeated in many different ways, but you can surrender only discursively, that is, on condition that you acknowledge your defeat and agree to fall in with approved ways of comporting yourself as a defeated party. From this point on, there are conditions all the way, and nothing but conditions. You can surrender unconditionally only if it is specified and articulated in some formal and explicit way as a condition of your surrender, as a promise or guarantee you make in surrendering, usually in some kind of written treaty or public performance, or both. Apology without let or hindrance can similarly be assured only through an articulation that must constitute a reservation, even in its promise to impose none; otherwise you would just apologize fully or, as we say when we suspect that fully doesn't sound full enough so try to fill the word out a bit, "fulsomely," without making any such specification about just how full it is. To say "I apologize unreservedly" is really like heading a notice that you would like to be taken to be polite with the words "Polite Notice." But to give notice not just that you mean to be polite but that you think you have already succeeded is actually rather impolitely presumptuous. When one reads a reference letter that builds to the crescendo "I support her application for this post enthusiastically and without any kind of reservation," it is almost impossible not to start wondering what kind of reservations are in fact being disavowed.

So it might be better if you could leave it to somebody else to make the judgment about whether or not you were keeping anything in reserve with your apology. Yet you can apologize unreservedly, it turns out (or your audience can only be sure you have), only if you yourself offer the assurance that you are doing so. But to specify that your apology is without reservation, therefore without any kind of tacit qualification or fingers-crossed exception, and without any kind of calculation of its consequences, is itself to specify a condition for your apology, albeit the negative condition of having no conditions. Not only that, and probably most important, such an affirmation will always offer a rescuing or preservation of your dignity *de profundis* in an articulation of your right to make an estimate of that condition of making no conditions and whether or not you have met it. To apologize unreservedly is therefore, in however minimal a way, to stand appraisingly outside the act of apology, so reserving some measure of immunity to its evacuating or devastating effects and keeping open the possibility of exaltation in humility we have met with a number of times in this book.

Apology is caught up in the economy of human dealings, in which we do not merely act but assess and exchange behaviors, to preserve and secure various kinds of worth. This is why it seems intelligible to say, not just that I feel I should apologize to you but that "I owe you an apology," and why we may find ourselves saying, surely without the least idea what in most cases it could possibly mean, that we do or do not "accept" an apology. It is a strange kind of debt to enter into, where one's creditor may have the choice of declining one's repayment, forcing one to remain in debt, not just because the interest accrued means the price has gone up (why have you taken so long to apologize?) or because, though one does not have the money to pay, there is no recognized currency in which to pay it. (In a world in which getting into debt has become more of a duty than staying clear of it, and as anyone trying to pay off a mortgage early will discover, such arrangements are becoming as common in financial as in moral affairs.)

## Sovereign Apology

On the other side, there is nowadays the incessant demand from all quarters for apology. This is sometimes represented as an epidemic of apology itself, as though it were spontaneously self-occasioning. Apology occurs more and more in response, not to an expectation but to a demand. We must know explicitly that and when people are demanding apology, because it cannot merely be inferred from one's actions; like declaring war or taking offense, demanding is constituted and not merely evidenced by the performative speech act, known as "demanding," which nearly always amounts to uttering the words "I demand an apology" or some variant of the words that can be taken as identical to it. A swarm of problems buzzes around this act. There is first of all the question of *demanding* itself, a word that is the subject of one of the *OED*'s crisp little masterpieces of historical definition. Latin *demandare* means to entrust, commit, give in charge, or commend. Typically, one would use this word for the act of giving someone or something into the care of another. The transition to the act of intensified request probably occurred, says the *OED*, "through the notion of *entrusting* or *committing* to any one a duty to be performed, of *charging* a servant, or officer, with the performance of something, whence of *requiring* its performance of him, or *authoritatively requesting* him to do it." The movement is equivalent to that between *commend* and *recommend*, on the one hand, and *command*, on the other. Some time between the eleventh and thirteenth centuries, the simple act of asking turned into a sort of "*asking* in a way that commands obedience or compliance," as the *OED* puts it, a request made with legal right or mandate. So you demand something you think you ought already to have, or have no need to request, meaning that your demand actually constitutes a claim to prior ownership.

It seems possible that English *demand* might have weakened into the simple condition of asking that *demander* has today in French—at least one sixteenth-century usage records that somebody "gently demaunded" to be released from a debt, where it does not seem that any entitlement can have been assumed (Hall 1548, f.ccxxxvi). In fact, though, the passage from legal to vernacular use seems to have increased the intensity of the demand in the act of demanding, precisely because the entitlement came to be established not by the fact that it is assumed by an authority that is recognized as able to make demands but by the act of making the demand itself, which had correspondingly to become more demanding. My demand demands first of all the recognition of my right to make my demand—and in the process, if I am lucky, constitutes it.

All this implies that demanding an apology always allows the question, precisely by seeking to rule it out or countermand it in advance, of whether the demand is in fact justified. Can anyone who resorts to demanding an apology ever fully deserve one? Could the demand for an apology ever be mischievous or injurious enough itself to require apology? Demanding an apology may not necessarily turn you into a mercilessly avenging angel, but it cannot help giving you an agreeable inkling of what it would feel like to be one.

Nowadays, the demand for apology is caught up no longer with external relations of force (the power of the king, landlord, local authority) that are represented or referred to in language but relations of force that are enacted internally within language performance itself: so not relations but actions, shows of force that force it into being. Governments or official agencies who inherit in a bureaucratic form the more mystical sovereignty of kings, bishops, and barons still demand the payment of rates or fulfillment of duties by reason of their authority: they are people authorized in advance by other people, including their demandees, to make demands such as this on occasion. But in demanding an apology, I entitle myself, or give myself the right, to be entitled to, or have the right to, an apology.

Where does the right come from in the case of ordinary citizens or groups of such citizens? It appears that in such cases the demand for an apology on the grounds that one has been wronged derives its authority from the wrong itself, so that the wrong that I claim has been done to me, and therefore claim in a certain sense as my own, gives me the right to demand an apology for it. In the case of demands for apology to a group, it may literally be the case that the group derives its identity from the wrong done to it, since your membership of the group may be determined wholly and solely by whether you are held to have suffered the wrong in question, a wrong that gives you your right to apology. Certain groups are constituted and sustained in being by their shared conviction of *victimage*, a word that appeared in English only in the mid-1950s but has already shifted its meaning from the action of scapegoating, or choosing another as an expiatory victim, to affirming one's own condition as a victim of wrong. The prestige attaching to being a victim may be anticipated in the fact that the word *victim* is from Latin *victima*, a beast prepared for sacrifice, possibly deriving from *vigere*, to be lively or thrive, or to be in honor, esteem, or repute.

In demanding an apology, I ask for something for which there should be no need to ask, since in a sense my demand insists that by rights I would already have it. To demand something, as opposed to requesting it, is to ask for something that must be regarded as already mine, because it is mine by right, in the recompense that has been both, as we say, "due to me" and therefore laid up for me ever since, and immediately by, the downpayment of the originating offense. This circle of self-reference ought to make demands for apology socially and logically much flimsier than they in fact are. However, there appears to be an enhanced sociological force in the drama of the demand and compliance with it—where *sociological* means containing and pertaining to the logic of sociality itself—that gives it a kind of power beyond rational inspection, a power that previously resided simply in the external fact of power (the power to beat you up or lock you away). The performing of wrongs confers on the wronged the right to demand from the wronger special duties of symbolic restitution.

Demanding apologies also interferes seriously with the credibility of any apology that may be elicited. Quoting Marion Owen's observation that "apologizing is one of a class of acts that are expected to be performed without prompting" (1983, 139), M. Catherine Gruber argues in her study of courtroom "allocutions," or apologies delivered by the convicted to the court, that the very circumstances of being invited to make an apology just before they are sentenced actually rules out the possibility of meeting this important condition, meaning that "at the same time that a judge invites a defendant to allocute, the judge deprives the defendant of the opportunity to make an unprompted apology" (2014, 22). In fact, these special conditions are partly replicated whenever an apology is demanded, for the demand countermands any possibility of the spontaneity required for a sincere apology. The demand for apology thereby runs the risk of prohibiting its own fulfillment.

To demand an apology feels like squeezing one's antagonist into a corner or effecting a deserved humiliation . But it is always in fact also to offer to one's antagonist a precious ontological opportunity, which is scarcely to be had in any other way. For apologizing offers to one in the wrong the same immunity as being killed for revenge. In both cases, the victim of a wrong can take sadistic pleasure from the thought of the continuing agony of remorse of the one effecting the wrong, while the victim contrives to remain in ignorance that the perpetrator has actually been left off the hook. It is only through supreme self-deceit, or by the mediation of certain kinds of religious doctrine, that you can imagine somebody you have killed in revenge still skewered somehow, somewhere, by the pangs of remorse. And despite appearances, wringing out an apology from someone also puts the apologizer beyond your reach, liquidating rather than legitimating your demand, for forgiveness is acquittal. One of the many reasons that it might be thought we should be willing to apologize is that it is a skillful means of deflecting the aggression that always animates the demand for apology—and many have felt that deflection of aggression is the best, most skillful, and most important thing that humans know how to do. "But surely I have a right to be aggressive, considering what has been done to me or to someone in whose name I speak." No. Some people may have a duty of aggression, to protect others from other kinds of aggression, but nobody has the right to aggression, especially since the purpose of aggression is often to give itself its own otherwise unearned rightness rather than the inverse.

By subjecting somebody to your demand for apology, you grant that person an enlarged and sovereign subjecthood, a subjecthood that only your desire to make the person wholly and abjectly subject to your will can give. For sovereign subjecthood comes not from being able to subdue others to your will but being able and willing to subdue yourself, unnecessarily. Rather than merely laying down the law, the victim of a wrong who demands an apology gives to the one from whom apology is to be exacted an opportunity to demonstrate the power and willingness of self-donation of the law. This is all the more so because in many cases, though perhaps not invariably, the apology will be expected to take the form of a call for forgiveness and reconciliation. So what the one who demands an apology demands is that the apologizer issue an appeal, something like a demand without expectation or against all odds, to the apologee.

The effect is to reverse the direction and object of petition. As Nicholas Tavuchis puts it, "By assuming such a vulnerable stance, and only by so doing, we now unobtrusively shift the burdens of belief and acceptance to the injured party" (1991, 18). The thought of the moral advantage that one offers to the one apologizing can be almost intolerable. When all goes well, however, it can effect a very powerful decathecting or draining away of aggression and hurt from the whole sorry situation. To see somebody surrendering authority in this absolute yet oddly authoritative way can suddenly make the moral high ground seem very low-lying indeed and can even induce in the apologee a desire to join in the jubilee of surrendered authority. The penalty of not doing so is to be stuck in a posture of refusal that cannot avoid seeming stubborn, self-gratifying, and suddenly petty compared with the grandeur to which the apologizer has access. It is very hard, for example, to answer a formal speech act involving the words "I apologize" with an equivalently formal "I forgive you" without actually sounding priggish or preening.

Most of those who reflect on apology assume with Nicholas Tavuchis that it is "essentially a speech act that seeks forgiveness, that is, recertification of bona fide membership and unquestioned inclusion within a moral order" (1991, 27). I do not think that this need necessarily be so. It is in fact perfectly possible for an apologizer to feel, and say, that there is no prospect of the offense being forgivable, and no desire for forgiveness, without the declaration ceasing in the least to be an apology. This is another aspect of the sovereignty in abjectness that apology can grant to itself, the counterpart at the supply end of things, perhaps, to the customary expectation that an apology should not require an invitation or request but should arise of itself. Just as it is possible for an apology not to be accepted, it is conceivable under certain circumstances for somebody giving an apology to decline to accept the forgiveness it can elicit, in what might seem a kind of self-prostrating pomp.

The necessary reflexivity of apology means that it is a phenomenon of shame rather than guilt. "You should be ashamed of yourself," we say, not "you should regard yourself as guilty." Somebody else can pronounce you guilty; in fact, this is probably the only way in which you can be, as we say, "found" guilty, but nobody can pronounce you ashamed. Rather, people are forced to say that "you should be ashamed," in the slightly unwilling acknowledgment of the fact that only you can acknowledge your shame. The self-pronouncement of shame is perhaps what we mean by apology, and sometimes what we articulate in it: "I am ashamed of myself." Apology is the apotheosis of shame, a state lifted, sometimes relievingly, into an action of acknowledgment. Perhaps this is why there is something uncomfortable and even a little disgusting in watching a public apology; apology is the public exposure of what is, or should be, a rather muggy private drama.

This is an enlargement rather than a diminishment in that it gives the apologizer the opportunity for ontic expansion into the space of self-relation, allowing the apologizer to enter the for-itself after previously being coffined in the space of the in-itself. Taking on diminishment gives you the augmentation of self-relation. And this is in turn why apology can offer protection for the very immolation of self that it seems to threaten, for there is a saving distance in the act of apology from the act itself. The Latin formula *mea culpa* is in the ablative case, and so means not my fault but by my fault. I can acknowledge my fault because, by dint of the fact of my apology, I am no longer fault or faultiness itself, and by acknowledging that something is *by* my fault, I ensure that I am no longer fully *at* fault. Apology, the turning away of the word (of accusation), or the word that turns away, is always ablative in this sense.

The earliest meaning in English of *apology* is a defense, whether of oneself or another. In the course of time, its meaning has apparently inverted to mean the abandonment of defense or self-belief, in self-abasement. Earlier than that, however, Latin *apologus*, after Greek ἀπόλογος, both of them preserved in English *apologue*, also meant a fable, usually of an Aesopian kind involving an animal. Apology is therefore to be thought of as apotropaic, a turning away or aside of some imputation, in which it is not clear whether it is the word of accusation that is turned aside or the word of vindication that turns it aside. Marina Warner wonders how it is that this emphatically assertive act turns historically into its opposite:

> How did the concept—and the practice—shift from this righteous reasoning in self-defence to the abject, self-abasing petition of apologizing, as we understand it today? From the Promethean stand of heroic defiance, to the adoption of the Ionic suppliant? (2003, 469)

Nicholas Tavuchis sharpens the distinction between defense or justification and an apology, writing that "now an apology begins where these former rhetorical and essentially self-serving forms leave off. . . . To apologize is to declare voluntarily that one has *no* excuse, defense, justification, or explanation for an action" (1991, 17). Yosef Z. Liebersohn, Yair Neuman, and Zvi Bekerman observe that the Greek *apologia* was not a term for a social but a legal action, specifically the response or "counter-speech" delivered by a defendant in a trial, and suggest that the fact that such a response speech, in cases where it was clear that the offense had been committed, would often have taken the form of a request for forgiveness or mercy may have anticipated the later shift in the meaning of the word (2004, 923). But there may nevertheless be a continuity between the two apparently contrasting modes, of positive defense and negative petition; for apology remains a defense, in a modulated form that finds vindication in culpability, or rather the capacity to assert and embrace it, and so to be the abasement that one enacts upon oneself. The feelings that may niggle at the righteous apology demander who feels somehow ethically outplayed, seen off by being paid off, and in a coin that is not available for spending, except through inglorious crowing that puts the demander further in the wrong, because the demand has been extinguished by being met: all these hint that this kind of defense is much more decisive than the more aggressive kind that leaves the way clear for answering attack. The only way to allow a demand for an apology, in the sense of allowing it to exist, *allowing*, from *alouer*, being close both to applauding and to giving a lease or allocation, is to refuse to meet it, and thereby to outdo and annihilate.

And this comes about precisely because of the necessarily performative nature of apology, which cannot be other than what we call "public." It does not require anything as grandly or glamorously world historical as an inaugural declaration for this self-relation to be established, because it will be in force whenever the force of performance is substituted for the performance of force. As soon as the king has been killed, in an indubitable and irrevocable act of force that puts an end to the crude externality of armed force as the source of kingly authority, the king's authority will henceforth derive not from anything external but from the willingness of the people to accept it. Of course, that force will be real—and substantially displayed, in busbies, bayonets, beefeaters, and so on—but it will also be a pantomime, because its dependence on being displayed will itself need to be put permanently on display.

One might say that this is really an apology for sovereignty. And this head that capitalizes on its own decapitation turns out to be in play with regard to the question that has recently arisen so insistently in relation to the act of apology, that has indeed come to colonize it entirely: Can states, and their equivalents, apologize, and, if so, when should they?

A demand for an apology resembles the demanded apology in being a declaration. It is as hard definitively to declare something without using the words "I declare that" as it is to demand something without using the self-declaring words "I demand that." It is similarly impossible to apologize by simply being sorry; one must say "sorry," meaning that one must perform some kind of declaration of one's remorse. Such declarations partake in the self-doubling nature of all declaration, but perhaps especially political declarations such as the American Declaration of Independence, which, in Jacques Derrida's acrobatic analysis, establishes in and through the fact of its own declaration the right of "the people," on whose behalf the signatories sign, to make it. For the people do *not* exist as an entity, the entity does *not* exist *before* this declaration, not as such. If it gives birth to itself, as free and independent subject, as possible signer, this can hold only in the act of the signature. The signature invents the signer. (2002, 49)

The constitution of a state requires a statement that allows a state to come into being by presuming in the very making of the statement that it already has (53).

There is a curious kind of delirium that can overtake anyone writing about such matters, given that, once one begins to evoke circles of reflexive self-constitution, they seem to develop their own rhetorical momentum so that it is hard to stop making up new ways in which to demonstrate how institutions have to make themselves up as they go along. The particular blend of sly frivolity and slow-moving solemnity that characterizes Derrida's writing on such matters is at once rather addictive, once you've got the hang of it, and intensely annoying for those with less patience for rhetorical self-indulgence. I make this point, not, I'm afraid, as any mea culpa, or promise to do better in future, but in order to put into play the question of seriousness itself in relation to apology. I wish to propose that the serious question that is usually asked of public and political apology—Is it right? (in all of its imaginable aspects and dimensions, is it legitimate, is it necessary, does it do any good or any harm?)—is inseparable from another question: Is it ridiculous?

I will postpone, possibly, you may be relieved to hear, in perpetuity, the question of whether public apology is serious or ridiculous is *itself* serious or ridiculous. But we can be sure at least that the public and ceremonial nature of state apologies makes the question of the degree of their solemnity morally salient. Indeed, *solemnity*, a word of uncertain origin, is itself performative, a solemn ceremony being defined as one performed with due seriousness. A failure of seriousness in matters where solemnity is required (the making of vows, or attestations) is a serious matter, which is why courts reserve the right to punish people who are found to be in contempt of court. J. L. Austin famously observes that felicity in performative statements depends on them being serious and not part of a joke, pantomime, or tragic drama (1962, 121). Strangely, utterances can be properly performative only if they are not mere performances (showing off, simulating, imitating). The point of wondering whether it is ridiculous for nations and corporate bodies to give apologies is to essay and assay the McEnrovian protest: You Cannot be Serious.

## Being Serious

What might be ridiculous about apologies on behalf of nation-states and similar collectivities? It is not that the persons impersonating the nation risk seeming ridiculous, for this is a risk that is in any case built in to apology and constitutes a great deal of its force. Many of the ceremonies of abasement that accompany acts of public recantation are a deliberate and designed exposure of the person concerned to possible derision. So it is not that apologizing makes the apologizer seem ridiculous that matters in collective apology; it is that such acts *render the act of apology itself absurd*, reducing it to a meretricious stunt. Those who are in favor of public apologies on behalf of collective bodies think that they can borrow the power of apology to do good on an economically large scale. Those, like me, who are opposed to it, are so because they wish to protect the huge good that apology can do from being made ludicrous.

Much has been made of the moment on December 7, 1970, when German chancellor Willy Brandt, who was laying a wreath at the Warsaw monument to the victims of the Warsaw Ghetto Uprising, suddenly and seemingly spontaneously fell to his knees. The gesture has become known as the, and sometimes a, *Warschauer Kniefall*. Such gestures and postures (you may recall my having regretted in an earlier chapter the absence of a verb for the gesture of adopting a posture) used to be de rigueur in earlier periods and certainly, as in the case of Henry IV's public self-humiliation, by waiting barefoot and in a hair shirt for admission at the pope's gate in Canossa Castle, had a kind of charismatic force. But it is very difficult to effect such physical gestures with the requisite degree of dignity, especially if you are unpracticed: as a previous master of a college who had officiated at many graduation ceremonies once remarked to me, getting from an upright posture to your knees in front of a large audience is "high-wire stuff." We should perhaps be grateful that Tony Blair chose to give the letter in which he expressed his pain at the memory of the Irish Famine to actor Gabriel Byrne to read rather than perform it himself, say, genuflecting in a shift (Cunningham 2004, 82). My point is that the avoidance of absurdity in apology is a very serious matter.

There are many actions that a state may perform for, to, and on behalf of its citizens, partly because this is exactly what states are for—their prime function being to act as instruments for determining and executing forms of collective action. As such, there is nothing to stand in the way of states performing a range of ceremonial or discursive actions, like declaring war or independence; issuing protests, threats, requests, and ultimatums; and also framing various kinds of intention, just as though they were persons capable of making decisions and performing actions, naturally including the action of giving articulation to these decisions and intentions. States not only have the necessary apparatus for performing this kind of substitution—plebiscites, committees, parliaments, spokespersons, official media of communication, and the like—they themselves *are* the necessary apparatus. Thus, states, like other collective entities such as colleges, companies, and city councils, can certainly also issue apologies.

But what they cannot do is mean them in the way in which people can, and must, mean them. A collective entity may without absurdity say it is sorry, but it may not without absurdity be believed to feel sorry, which is an essential condition for apologizing persons, because states and equivalent collectivities are just not the kinds of things, embodied beings, that can feel anything at all. States can make statements, but they cannot possess states of feeling, except as an animistic projection. They have certain kinds of agency, but only as agents: that is, proxies, dummies, zombies, simulacra, personae.

But given that the apologizers and apologees both seem satisfied with the process, couldn't we just go along with it, in the same way we go along with other kinds of morally efficacious let's-pretends? Yes, of course we could, and of course, dear me, we abundantly do, but only at the cost of making apology itself ridiculous by delegating it to a nonexistent entity. I am not making a hypernominalist point, that the Roman Catholic Church or the United Kingdom does not exist in any straightforward way, because it is plain that they do have existence, and existence that allows them to perform some of the actions of corporeally existent human beings. But they do not exist in all the ways in which embodied beings do, that being a large part of their point and privilege (to point to the most obvious difference, states aim or assume themselves not to be mortal in the ways, or at least on the time scales, that embodied beings are).

It is not just that delegating apology to a symbolic body, or, paradoxically, to an actual person who is required to embody that body, is like the purchase of indulgence or arranging for somebody to go to confession for you, in the way you might send somebody in to a math exam in your stead. An action of this kind is certainly sneaky and distasteful, but need not in itself be ridiculous. What is ridiculous is the solemn pretense that the delegated entity could ever be capable of actually performing the delegated action. Issuing a public apology on behalf of a collective is like sending a cardboard cutout into the confessional or exam hall and *expecting nobody to notice*.

Can statues apologize? No they cannot, any more than they can be apologized to (not that this has stopped human beings having a go at the latter). As their names should sufficiently intimate, states are in fact statues, that is, substitutes, stand-ins. There are clearly identified protocols for making decisions to act collectively in certain ways, not all of them democratic by any means, but most of them understood and accepted. But there are no protocols for deciding how states can or should feel on our behalf, nor ever could be, because, I repeat, states and equivalent collectives are not things that can feel anything at all. The pretense of embodying a nation's fictitious feelings as an address to the feelings of another fictitious entity is as disgusting as, say, the German nation offering to tell survivors of Nazism a joke, or do a dance, to cheer them up.

What makes the whole rigmarole not just pleasantly ridiculous but poisonously absurd is not the doubtless genuine feeling that when an apology has been made, some ritual has been performed that has symbolic meaning. There is nothing wrong in itself with symbolic meaning. But the objection would have to be, not that collective apology is merely symbolic but that it is nowhere near symbolic enough. Imagine a fully symbolic arrangement whereby apologies could be applied for, assessed, and, if appropriate, supplied by automated systems, like online requests for repeat prescriptions. In such an arrangement, only symbols would be involved, from start to finish, though the living parties to the symbolic apologetic transaction could no doubt be informed of the action once it had been approved and had, if only electronically, occurred. It would be perfectly easy to generate an animation if required of some avatar abashedly mumbling the words of apology with bowed head and appropriately stirring music. One can imagine a thriving futures market in apologies quickly arising, a little like the market in orphans hilariously evoked by Dickens in *Our Mutual Friend*, when the newly monied Boffins announce that they are looking for a child to adopt (2008, 195–96). Perhaps apologies would come to be demanded, offered, supplied, and accepted at the blistering speed in which shares are algorithmically bought and sold. Perhaps in a sense such a market is already coming into being. If symbolism were all that were needed, there would be nothing to object to in such an arrangement, and, given the growing volume of apology business, an arrangement for automatically requesting and dispensing them might even come to seem rather useful.

In fact, however, such an arrangement sounds absurd and even (this being the point), the more serious the matter being apologized for, nauseating. Why? Because we need to feel that there is some kind of entity that motivates the action of apology and whose body can embody the subject who articulates it. Although an automatic form of words generated and broadcast by the National Bureau of Remorse and Recantation could take exactly the same form and have precisely the same meaning in terms of what was said as the form of words solemnly intoned by a prelate or head of state, it would be completely different in the form of its performative saying, because nobody would actually have said it. This is the same double ventriloquism as that observed by Derrida in the case of the Declaration of Independence and in fact recapitulated in the case of every such representative speech act—whereby a body of persons first authorizes the state to speak in their names, and then the state appoints some person to clothe the state in flesh in order to speak in its name.

But this is only philosophically absurd in the case of collective speech acts; it is insultingly ridiculous in the case of a collective apology. Apology is always a performance, but it has to be the kind of performance, by a body entitled to speak by dint of its culpable implication in the offense, of which one can always, as a condition of the apology, legitimately wonder about its sincerity. A collective apology is absurd because this is simply not possible or, since it plainly is possible and, sadly, happens all the time, not possible without absurdity.

I imagine that my insistence on the absurdity of pretending that a state has the kind of mortal body that can laugh, weep, shudder, and chuckle as well as the kind of collective body that can invade other countries will be seen as in itself an absurd overliteralism. But that is precisely my argument: ceremonies of apology make literal an action that can only ever be, and only ever should be, symbolic. One could imagine somebody objecting to my high-minded distaste for such performances that it is no different from the kind of performance involved in, say, the Eucharist. There is a logic in such an objection, which helpfully makes explicit the theological dimensions of this kind of moral-political vicariance. It allows me to specify that what is absurd about collective apology and, worse than absurd, impious, is the way in which it assumes that there can be a Real Presence of a suffering-capable body in such matters. Even if the most that rituals of collective apology can usually manage is to be sanctimonious, their intent is to be sacramental.

Among the many undesirable things encouraged by the raree show of official apologies are ridiculous or literally fantastic expectations of them, from serious and well-informed commentators from whom one might expect sobriety. Melissa Nobles, for example, observes that "government apologies most often have been highly-scripted affairs" (2008, 6). As opposed to what? In what conceivable way could a government apologize both spontaneously and legitimately? Spontaneous government can certainly exist, but it is better known as insane dictatorship. Sighing over a scripted apology from a government assumes first that spontaneity is a guarantee of sincerity and second that it is possible to reason about the sincerity of a government, as opposed to the particular officials who may spring forward or be fingered to speak in its name. Both are entirely fishy propositions. It is quite possible for a government to mean what it says when it makes a statement or voices an intention ("This Means War"). But it is quite impossible for a government to mean what it says when it says it feels remorse in the case of the simulated speech act that an apology must be, because it is not possible, despite the casual and unthought-out convictions we permit ourselves, for a government to mean a feeling of or about anything at all. When we are discussing individual acts of public contrition, such as those encouraged by the Truth and Reconciliation Commission in South Africa, the concern, as Rhoda E. Howard-Hassmann and Mark Gibney put it in their introduction to the book *The Age of Apology*, "whether individual apologies offered by perpetrators were genuine, or merely a blatant calculation of interest, a chance for perpetrators to get off by feigning sorrow" may be painfully and consequentially salient. But the move that the authors immediately make, in remarking that "this is a factor that ought to be noted in all studies of political apologies: they may merely be a new form of *realpolitik*" (Gibney et al. 2008, 5), while undoubtedly true, does not have the relation to the question of individual sincerity that they believe it does. Sincere individual apologies can be multiplied, but they cannot be scaled up into sincere apologies by collective entities.

The real issue behind this question of sincerity is therefore not whether states should apologize but whether it is possible for states to apologize at all. It is certainly possible for states to express remorse, that is, to pretend to apologize, by pretending to be able to, but it is not possible for them to do so sincerely, since it is not possible for states to feel remorse, any more than street lamps, statues, or even in fact printed statements of remorse can. The impossibility becomes clear as soon as you ask any of the questions about states of feeling that would also have to seem perfectly reasonable in relation to entities capable of feeling remorse. Does the state feel remorse *as opposed to*, say, wry amusement? Does the state ever get bored? Can states feel happy, skittish, mischievous, languorous, affectionate, vaguely uneasy, as well as penitent? These questions are of course insolently frivolous, but they are so in the same way as the suggestion that states might sometimes be ashamed of themselves. I have suggested elsewhere, in the course of a discussion of the theory of collective feelings, that we should take warning from the fact that collective subjects tend to be believed only to be able to feel "meta-emotions," that is, ascribed or prescribed emotions, things that we feel they should feel (if they existed), rather than the things that an entity capable of feeling would be capable of. I do not yet feel inclined to apologize for what I wrote in that essay:

> The fact that collective institutions only seem capable of having, or laying claim to, emblematic kinds of emotion is evidence of a substantial difference between the emotions we think that individual subjects are capable of feeling and the emotions that may plausibly be attributed to collective subjects. In truth, I think it is a potent hint that we don't really believe collective subjects can have emotions at all. (Connor 2013, 5)

It might also be noted that, while collective entities can establish and maintain various kinds of memorial practice, they are quite incapable, qua collective entities, of "remembering" anything. Indeed, remembrance need have nothing to do with remembering, except in specifically supplying its absence. The willingness to accept without a whimper the strange fiction that the actions of recording and reminding constitute a kind of "memory," as though writing out a speech were the same as learning it by heart, parallels and partners the belief in the possibility of apology by collective entities. The animistic attribution of human cognitive functions to what is oxymoronically known as "historical memory," thereby eliding the essential purpose of history, lends undeserved plausibility to the idea that collective entities can feel regret for actions they somehow remember themselves performing.

I have said that an apology gives power to the ones apologizing because it gives them the opportunity to make their souls. You can apologize only for something you have done or for actions for which you are willing or able to take responsibility. Apology requires a mixture of acceptance and repudiation: it means the affirmation simultaneously of your continuity and discontinuity with your actions. This may account for the feelings both of humbling and enlargement, since I must acknowledge and articulate the judgment I make on myself. The painfulness of apology comes from the difficult balance between the self-lowering that apology must involve and the self-enlargement that it must enable. It is therefore a prime example of the positive action of giving way or yielding ground whose forms I have been exploring in this book. And this can take place only under conditions in which I accept, indeed insist on, my intrinsic self-division, asserting and inhabiting, at least for the time being of the apology, the fact that I must be what I am not, yet cannot be other than the otherness that I currently, excruciatingly, am. Only a subject can perform or undergo this—perform this undergoing, undergo this performing, enact this being acted on—even as being a subject depends on this capacity for standing paradoxically aside from, or being able to be more or less than itself. Substitute subjects cannot perform this nonaction, cannot have this impotentiality, even if we, or they, can pretend they can.

This is why the question of continuity matters so much in collective apology and also why it tends not to be inspected too closely. A government must be able to stand as an allowable substitute for the guilty party (itself) for whose actions it apologizes. It seems plausible, even necessary, for governments to inherit and honor liabilities from previous generations, since this is one of the principal legal functions of governments (Levy 2000, 241). At the same time, the kinds of thing for which governments apologize are often the kinds of thing that under ordinary circumstances would be the subject of prosecution rather than mere reprimand. So governments are likely to apologize not just for rudeness, forgetfulness, inefficiency, or other venial offenses but, being governments and doing the sorts of thing that governments do, for offenses for which they should immediately place themselves under arrest, or at least turn themselves in for questioning by themselves. The fact that they do not is made possible by a kind of self-quarantining, whereby "the government" can apologize for the actions of "the government" that it still is sufficiently to be able to appear to apologize and yet skin-savingly is no longer sufficiently to be held legally responsible. But this is the kind of self-quarantining that serious apology specifically rules out, however it may seem to be hedged ("I don't know what came over me, but I cannot deny I did it").

Again, governments can cut this caper precisely because they are not subjects capable of apologizing but pseudosubjects who are really apologizing for the actions of other people entirely, and often people whom they politically opposed and despised (Willy Brandt was an opponent of Nazism from the

1930s onward, his very name being adopted in 1933 as a pseudonym to escape the notice of Nazi agents when in exile in Norway). They are not saying, like Prospero, "this thing of darkness I acknowledge mine" (Shakespeare 2011, 303), accepting the otherness that they themselves are and cannot be separated from. Thus, as Jacob T. Levy observes, though the present government of South Africa is legally continuous with the governments who enforced the policy of apartheid, and thus might well be thought to inherit their liabilities and culpabilities, "it would be very strange for the current South African government to apologize to black South Africans for the wrongs of apartheid" (2000, 242). It would be more than strange; it would be clownish and grotesque, but my point is that it is clownish and grotesque in all such attempts to impersonate apologies.

The worst part of the cruel farce is the real person who has to perform the put-up job and allow us fleetingly to imagine that the state, government, corporation, or committee in question might have the same kind of feeling body. This is a particular risk given that many apologies are for ethnic injustice and cruelty that has been focused through the mad fantasies of one group about aspects of the bodily appearance of another. It is only by a casually assimilative ethnic bundling or racial rounding up that it seems more believable for somebody taken to be white to appear to apologize for the actions of a group of other, deceased, absconded, or otherwise unapparent people also taken to be white at the expense of other people taken to be black. Obviously, we do sometimes pretend to apologize for the actions of other people ("I am so sorry that my aunt disgraced herself again at your wedding"), but the nature of apology is such that it cannot really be done. On investigation, apologizing for others will turn out to be really either a disguised reproof to them or the voicing of a merely subordinate regret on your part (for your remissness, say, in not hiding the gin bottle as soon as Auntie Lola rang the doorbell). In reality you cannot apologize for the actions of another any more than you can experience another's death on that other's behalf—and, in fact, this is for very similar reasons; for there is no apology without the confrontation, allied with the faint, fluttering hope of surviving it, with the *petit mort* of the soul that apology is.

I allow far too much license, I know, to the tips and intimations winked by word origins, but the etymology of the word *serious* can do some very serious work of getting our thinking in a line about the matter of apology. To be serious in fact means to form a series, a row, line, or continuous sequence, from Latin *serere*, to join together, which shares an Indo-European base with Greek εἴρειν, to join together, and Sanskrit *sarat*, a thread. Collective apologies are nonserious because they pretend to the continuity that they cannot have. No one can doubt the hunger to be serious of people who think that collective apologies should be pursued and considered, but the moral and historical questions that animate the desire for collective apology are of far too much moment to be dishonored by the infantile silliness of actually performing them.

Apology is not, of course, an admission of legal responsibility, and much of the strategic shuffling around apologies depends on the attempts of the apologizer to restrict the practical implications of apology and the attempts of the aggrieved party to insist that apology does indeed imply and promise practical responsibilities. In fact, states are in an extremely good position to determine questions of legal responsibility and cases where compensation is in order: that is the stock-in-trade of states, and something else that they are there for and sometimes good at. Where a wrong has been committed and a harm persists, there are often very powerful arguments for such forms of compensation. But that is no kind of argument for apology—indeed, it is a very powerful argument for avoiding the charade of apologies that can seem to stand in for such entitlements and responsibilities.

Understandably, some historians accept the link between apology and material reparation that is often the de facto assumption. According to Melissa Nobles, "Apologies potentially 'open the books,' whereas reparations close them. . . . A reparations settlement says, we've settled our debt, whereas an apology says, now that you've apologized, what are you going to do next to rectify the matter?" (2008, 139, 141). The assumption of writers like Roy L. Brooks (1999) is that apology should be seen as part of a continuum of actions that constitute reparation and redress of collective wrongs. The nervousness about the financial implications of apology among politicians and leaders of corporate bodies, not to mention physicians, teachers, and others who are increasingly liable to face lawsuits, suggests that this view is widely shared. But the answer to the question "is sorry enough?" must always in fact be no, though not because apology is to be regarded as a minor or merely preliminary form of redress. "Sorry" could never be enough, not ever, because it works to make equation and adequacy beside the point. It is an egregious misunderstanding of apology to think that it is a matter of weights and measures. Nicholas Tavuchis has observed astutely that apology offers a kind of pseudoexchange of the apology for the offense:

> In the case of apology ... the meanings of "consideration" and "self-interest" are radically transformed.... What, may we ask, is offered in exchange? Curiously, *nothing*, except a self-abnegating speech expressing regret. So contrary to the logic of the economic marketplace or conceptions of social exchange based upon exclusively rational calculation, the apology itself—without any other objective consideration—constitutes both the medium of exchange and the symbolic quid pro quo for, as it were, "compensation." The helpless offender, *in consideration for nothing more than a speech*, asks for nothing less than the conversion of righteous indignation and betrayal into unconditional forgiveness and reunion. (1991, 33, 35)

The very point of the apology is to offer a kind of exchange that could never be commensurate, in fact, an absurd parody of an exchange, that offers a peculiarly potent kind of nothing, or nothing but its conspicuous cost to the apologizer.

Apologies are often treated as open-ended promises, not simply to reform but to do whatever anyone may judge to be in one's power to make reparation for the wrong. Nobody has the right to make or exact such promises. If redress is what is required, and it almost always is, then apology is absolutely not the right way to go about getting it. The formalization of apology in the Catholic rite of penance, which Marina Warner seems to suggest might be a satisfactory framework for understanding apology (as opposed to a way of containing it), requires three stages: contrition, which must be sincere; absolution, given on condition that the contrition is sincere; and then only provisionally (so absolution is only relatively absolute), on the satisfactory performance of penance (2003, 462). Warner is quite clear that this is a kind of magic spell, telling us archly that penance is required for the absolution to "take, like finishing the course of antibiotics even after you're better" (462).

Warner thinks that, because apology means taking on a certain position of petition and the relinquishment of power, and because the people known as women are customarily forced into, or identified with, this condition of powerlessness, apology is in a sense characteristically female. I am inclined to agree that there is a gender dissymmetry in apology, but I wonder whether the probabilities may not pull in precisely the opposite direction. Women may well, as some studies indicate (Lazare 2004, 29), apologize more frequently than men. But if this is so, it may well mean that apology is in fact more strongly gendered than may appear, such that apology may have come to mean something different for women than for men. There may, in other words, be both less cost and less possibility of gain for women precisely because of the grandeur and opportunity to display spiritual self-command through the survival of loss of dignity that apology offers. Warner quotes the observation of a schoolteacher friend that the boys in his class whom he forces to apologize find it much more painful than the girls, because apology is "a girly thing" (2003, 464). I think I know what he, and she, means, but this does not make complete sense to me. Apology is an active self-humbling, and because self-humbling can only be from a position of, or because there are no real "positions," a supposition of power, patriarchy ensures, and in fact actually means, that it is much less likely to be a girly thing or only for those trying to be boys. Apology exacts the subjective cost it does because it is a kind of grandeur grab, achieved precisely through the public jeopardizing of the self. There can be no apology from below, because apology is meant to be lowering. Women and men both wear trousers, but it's only supposed to be funny when men's trousers fall down. If women apologize more than men, one may surmise that it is either because they are under more external pressure to apologize, so there is less at stake, or, more likely in my view, because women are at least sometimes able thereby to access a measure of the sovereign power popularly supposed to be possessed by men. There are, of course, many modes of apology that do not claim this dignifying force—the flustered or panicky "what-kind-of-fool-am-I" abandonment of all pretense at dignity or the surly, mechanical, numbly dutiful mumble—but these do not seem to involve the same extreme tension between assertion and the dissipation of dignity, precisely because they can actually protect against exposure. Apologizing and meaning it necessarily offer the chance of an enhancement of honor through shame. The difficulty for humans of backing down or giving way is a mark of how active and demanding a task it really is, compared with the slavish submission to the imperative of agency.

    Warner's reflections ping-pong between a conviction that the magic ritual of apology can indeed be powerfully healing and a vague but insistent distaste at the fact that "public apologies made by leaders of world affairs cast them in priestly roles" (2003, 461), allowing powerful figures like the pope and Tony Blair to pilfer the charisma of apology. But stealing is precisely what magic, as mechanism, must allow for. Magic works only if it can be abused, just as money works only if it can be stolen. Warner would like to harness the white magic of apology for moral purpose and effect, but what if morality were always itself magical?

This recapitulates what used to be the principle of making people confess their crimes before you executed them, since you were thereby literally saving their souls and in the process avoiding condemnation for allowing them to die unshriven. I think there is something in this. When Saddam Hussein was found sheltering in a sewer and summarily strung up, everybody involved in the savage, sorry affair lost the opportunity of the universal gain there would have been from setting him to work for the rest of his life rebuilding houses in Baghdad. Not only would there have been the minor benefit of getting some houses built for nothing, as well as some opportunities for jeering among the righteous and aggrieved, but he might very well have been enabled to become a much better person, bricklaying being the kind of absorbing and ennobling occupation it is.

All of this is evidence of a confusion, or perhaps simply a convergence, between an ethics of honor and an ethics of economy. We might illustrate the difference with the story of a man who has borrowed money from a friend and, finding himself unable to pay the debt at the date when it has become due, begs for more time, pleading a downturn in his business, leaking roof, ailing wife, and so on. "Do not trouble yourself," says his friend. "Let us cancel our formal agreement and call it a debt of honor." At which his friend groans: "Ah, how can you, my oldest friend, of all people, do this to me? Now I will have to pay you straight away." Honor has the force it does because it is not enforceable. As Nicholas Tavuchis proposes, "Apology stands in relation to what is considered just and equitable by reminding us that if we had resort only to accounts or legal sanctions in our dealings with others, civilized life would be greatly diminished or rendered impossible" (1991, 35).

Warner conducts her analysis of apology through a series of literary examples that she rightly calls "scenes" (2003, 460). It may well be that literary writers have thought harder than most about the action of apology, or, even if they have not thought about it particularly hard, their work fortuitously provides particularly rich opportunities for us to think about it under apparently controlled conditions. But the appropriateness of this approach to the topic may lie in the fact that apology is almost all literature, in the specific idiom of enactment we know as theater, whatever we think that is exactly, not exactly knowing being part of what theater is. Obviously, a literary or theatrical staging of apology is always a sort of experiment conducted under controlled conditions rather than occurring, as it were, in the wild. But it must be obvious that apology always takes place under controlled conditions, partly because it is itself a way of controlling condition, and a condition of control. Literary apology is useful for thinking about apology more broadly because apology turns out never to be broad enough not to remain in some sense literary. And the literariness of apology, in the particular modes of control that it attempts or affects to exercise, is also what puts such difficulties in the way of knowing what apology is, or what exactly is happening when it is said to have happened.

The theatricality of apology helps us to understand an important principle of it—that it must be performed. This means, not only that it must be a public action, and be recognized for what it is, but also that it must meet standards of performance. We might once have spoken of a "handsome apology" because apologies have not only to be performed but also to be performed, like Barbara Hardy's indiscernible adverbiality, *well*. We sometimes say we think it important for an apology to be sincere, but what we mean is that it should be convincing. Recently, we have read reports that Australian cricketer David Warner has had to apologize for his tearful public apology after an investigation identified him as the instigator of a plan to roughen up the ball with sandpaper during a match against South Africa (Najem 2018). The meta-apology was induced because the original apology was both too much (no matter how much we think we want to see school bullies reduced to grizzling toddlers, it is always toe-curlingly intolerable when it happens) and too little, because the apology failed to include enough detail about who else was involved, when and how the plan was first conceived, who paid for the sandpaper, how sin first entered the world, and various other matters about which Warner seemed unwilling or unable to make full disclosure.

Most of the writing concerned with political or public apology occupies, and evidently contents, itself with documenting the historical and political conditions that apologies appear to address and the conditions under which the things supposed to be apologies are sought and supplied. Examples here might include the work of Jacob T. Levy (2000), Girma Negash (2006) and Melissa Nobles (2008). While Jennifer Lind assembles reasons for doubting "that international reconciliation requires apologies and other contrite gestures" (2008, 3) and shows the ways in which national contrition can create conservative backlashes from those who oppose them, she has no doubt that states both can and do apologize in pursuit of reconciliation. Such accounts will also often attempt to assess the motivations for seeking and supplying apologies, the disagreements and debates accompanying these processes, and their presumed effects for good or ill. Their tendency is not to inquire into the question of whether apologies of this kind are even possible, or what difference it might make if all such apologies were in fact impostures, or came to be seen as such. If the relevant agents are not kept awake by this question, there is no reason for the historian to be either. It would matter only if doubts on this score were part of the historical texture of the actions and events under discussion. If the record is not raveled by such doubts, it is obviously wholly reasonable to assume that many people think what they are seeking or supplying in such cases are in fact apologies, even if they cannot possibly be right. This phenomenological allowance is intrinsic to many forms of historical and sociological investigation. It is not incumbent on a constitutional historian to sort through and settle all the philosophical conundrums about the reality status of constitutions before they can set about their business. Though the arguments developed here are in part historical, they do not aim either to be or to add much to this kind of history. Nor are they to be taken as any kind of reproach to such historians, except in cases where it may seem that phenomenology has been promoted to ontology and the actuality of apology assumed and/or approved, though it may explain why it has not seemed very necessary for detailed account to be taken of their work.

## Oops

The fascination with apology in recent years has been focused on acts of public or symbolic apology, or "apology by proxy" as Girma Negash (2006) describes them. One can understand the fascination with these events, but we should not expect show-trial apologies of this kind to be much help in understanding the work that apology does in human affairs, any more than High Mass in Saint Peter's should be taken as a guide to serving Sunday lunch. However, looking at apology from the other end of the telescope, that is, the ordinary, everyday instances of apology, allows us to make sense of how apology works, not as occasional performances of ritual magic but as an orienting horizon of human interchanges. Apology is an essential lubricant of polite sociability. The exceptional, ceremonial instances of apology, apology as the performance of existential crisis, lift apology away from its everyday work of marginal self-lowering.

We are amused at how often we say "sorry" in ordinary life. Marina Warner (2002) begins her reflections on apology by telling us that she has been known to say "sorry" when her own foot has just been trodden on. Brendan O'Neill (2007) reported for the online BBC News magazine a survey by Esure Car Insurance that concluded that British people say "sorry" 1.9 million times in their lives (O'Neill 2007)—two or three times per waking hour over a course of an eighty-year lifetime, which actually sounds on the low side to me. British people have a reputation for saying "sorry" even more than other people: it is certainly true that when I am preparing to travel to a country of which I do not know the language, I try to make sure that I know how to say "excuse me" before anything else. But this is not because I anticipate behaving any worse than I would at home. It is because I am aware that the willingness to apologize is an essential part of the pragmatic emulsion that at once holds a society together and gives it fluidity. I may regret looking a fool, but there is really nothing to apologize for in fumbling my change, nor do I have any genuine apologetic feelings when I say sorry for holding everybody up. It would be exceedingly strange if I did. Apology here is an activation of a submission response. It belongs to the phatic dimension of language, and so has a set toward the channel rather than toward the message or its meaning. It is a gesture, part of the suggestive "carrying on" or "carrying out" of language.

This does not make it a cheating imposture, because I can and usually do have a genuine willingness to ease social relationships, asserting my wish neither to impose myself nor to exclude my interlocutor. A public apology, especially when it is performed on behalf of one set of persons and addressed to another set of persons, has no relation to this kind of apology, precisely because it is meant as a literal apology. A state cannot mean an apology because it cannot "not mean" it, or "half-mean" it, in the way that persons can and do and must. Saying "sorry" in English commonly allows for inflections that actually point away from sincerity and toward formula. One of these is the simple use of the word *sorry* on its own, without any specification of what one is apologizing for. If I nudge somebody's elbow in a coffee shop and say "I am sorry to have nudged your elbow just then: I see I have caused you to spill your coffee, which was most thoughtless of me," I am going at least to diffuse the effect of the apology and at worst to seem weirdly and discomfortingly creepy. Very often the word *sorry* will also be abbreviated and deliberately "demarked"—coming out possibly just as a slurred syllabic stub like *sor* or *so'y*. The fact that this usually occurs in cases of physical avoidance or retraction may suggest that the effect here is to increase indexicality in order to gesture away from language to action, as though language itself were being recruited to the action of giving way.

But something else can occur, which actually emphasizes the utterance of the word. This is much more likely to occur at moments of coordinated apology, when two people both reach for the salt at the same time, or when both take avoiding action in the same direction, making for an awkward redoubling of the avoidance. At such moments, one or both may adopt a particular singsong inflection in saying "sorry," characterized by a steep pitch jump from high to low in the enunciation of the syllables, often in the interval of a fifth, or five semitones (not far from the police siren or the classical donkey's "eeyore"). Another typical occasion on which this can occur is when a teenage son in a hurry may jog a parent's elbow on his way out the door. He replies to the parent's irritated "careful!" or reproving "Sam!" with the same two-tone doorbell inflection, as though to supply the word *sorry* with the imaginary caption "here's our old friend the 'sorry' word again." The singsong enacts at once a recognition of the need for an apology and an acknowledgment of its formality, along with a supplementary apology perhaps for the fact that it has again become necessary. It conveys something like: "Oops, I was a bit clumsy there, I realize. We both know it was not very serious at all, and it would be strange for either of us to make a big thing of it, but I do seem to keep doing it, and I realize it's irritating, and it would also be rude of me to say nothing at all to mark the fact; so I am going to do what we both know is the usual thing and deploy the 'sorry' word, which I will both make sure you notice, and also turn into a sort of gift, by taking the trouble to set it to a little tune." Most important of all, the inflection conveys the amicable fact that there is no need at all to say any of this. The increased lyrical emphasis actually deemphasizes the utterance by indicating its conventionality.

This kind of conventional apology is just the opposite of the formal public apology, but not really because it is less formal. The formality of the showtrial apology is intended to mark it out as something of special solemnity and significance; the formality of the everyday sorry-saying is intended to acknowledge and salute the everyday formality—the informal formality, as it were—that is so strong, recurrent, and precious a feature of ordinary social life, that constantly affirms "I hereby acknowledge that I live alongside you." It has sometimes seemed to literalists that we should reserve the act of apology for serious occasions, and therefore say "sorry" only when we mean it. But we do mean it when we say "sorry" to somebody whose space we have momentarily invaded, or whose freedom of action we have constrained. What we mean to signal is that we submit to and are willing to play our part in maintaining the symbolic space of social relations that we are collectively pledged to maintain as the second nature of conflict avoidance. If we say that the act of apologizing not for infractions, but as the deterrence of the possibility that some action might be regarded as an infraction, is a mere gesture rather than a self-conscious action, we are saying something very important indeed about it. For, as I have suggested earlier, it is the fact that gestures belong to the unconscious saying of speech, rather than its said, that helps them form the richly sustaining and vigilantly careful texture of social living. These subliminal actions are much more solemn and powerfully protective than impostures of collective apology. Perhaps they represent, not a diminished form of apology at all but a return of the strong sense of apology as an active defense or vindication—an *apologia pro vita nostra*, or affirmation of a shared commitment to the continuing and indefinitely renewable abeyance of aggression and offense on which all social living depends.

# 6   Losing Well

"BEING A GOOD or bad loser," a phrase that seems to have begun to be used in English only toward the end of the nineteenth century, arises from the new centrality in human life of formalized competition, in the form of sport in particular, but by extension to any kind of trial or competition in which one has the chance of winning as well as losing. The losing in question is therefore the opposite of winning rather than of keeping. Somebody who bore the loss of a favorite watch in the Thames with dignity and composure would not be called a good loser. Losing well cannot be thought of as an entirely new virtue, and there have certainly been modes of losing well, and of winning graciously, in combat or competitive elections, for example, in many cultures and circumstances. But the new prominence of competitive sport made losing well a virtue and moral demand with which many more people than previously became familiar. Losing well is accordingly one of the most recent and widespread of formalized modes of actively giving way.

## Playing the Game

Losing well implies respect for one's opponent. Football managers are much less skilled exponents of this aspect of losing well than one might hope, in that they frequently offer a pseudo-acquiescence to defeat by admitting the deficiencies of their own team that have led to it. But this is a little like the apology that explains that the actions for which you are apologizing are wholly uncharacteristic and you can't understand what came over you. It is much harder to admit that one has played one's best, but it has still not been enough. One loses well when one does not pretend that one had no investment in winning or had no chance of ever winning in the first place (too many players unavailable through injury to make winning a realistic option), that is, when one does not attempt to stand aside from the fact of having lost despite having wanted very much to have won. At the same time, one does not attempt to maintain that one has been deprived of a rightful victory by some aberration or injustice, for that detracts from the performance of one's opponent, as well as seeming to imply somehow that one has not really lost. To lose well, therefore, means not to do anything that would conceal or deny or minimize the fact of one's loss. At the same time, losing well also means not lamenting one's loss extravagantly or storming off the court in self-loathing rage. This is to be too sore, or sorrowful, a loser. One must recognize that it's only a game, while nevertheless not shrugging off the whole experience as frivolous or not worth getting upset about, for playing a game means allowing and honoring the seriousness of one's opponent's intentions.

It is not surprising that the demands to lose well have begun themselves to be codified. Sam Weinman explains that "learning to lose is an acquired skill, like juggling or parallel parking. It contradicts our most basic nature because everything in our DNA has taught us to want to win and to hate to lose" (2016, 4). Not surprisingly, losing well has become a metaphor for growth and a recommended route to wisdom and happiness. Hence, "losing is not only something that we should tolerate but also that we *need*" (Weinman 2016, 10). Sport is taken to be important because of its capacity to confer immunity to the devastating pain of loss through measured doses. So it should be embraced: "It's a mistake to try to shield yourself from failure, for reasons that should be apparent: Unless you become the first person in the history of mankind to go through life without setbacks, you're better served having a sense of how to respond when things fall apart on you, because at some point they will" (10–11).

The new field of history and philosophy of sport has been very slow to pay attention to the experience of losing, but on the rare occasions when it has done so, tends to see losing as a necessary preliminary to long-term victory. Yunus Tuncel reads the experience of loss in terms of the different accounts of negativity to be found in Nietzsche, Bataille, and Heidegger, concluding that "sport creates arenas and possibilities for the athletic *Dasein* to face up to his or her death in the form of risk-taking, making mistakes, and defeat and thereby to attain an authentic way of being-in-the-world" (2015, 415). But there is a kind of bad faith rather than authenticity in this immunological ethic, precisely to the degree that it allows one to absent oneself from the humiliation of defeat: one discounts the present pain, as it were, into a future equanimity, murmuring, perhaps, "This too will pass," thereby distancing and derealizing the experience of loss. To lose well requires that one advance into the visible condition of one's reverse. Losing well does not involve standing back from one's place but rather standing one's ground in a space where one no longer has standing, from which one's own standing has retreated. It does not involve vacating a place so much as occupying the vacated place of one's set-aside hopes.

Formal competition not only ritualizes losing; it also, and for that reason, makes it something that is likely to be undergone in public and therefore to have an exemplary character. To lose well is to be seen to be losing well, this being made apparent in the various ways in which the losers of competition are typically kept on display following the end of the match. As the winning team cavorts and laps the pitch, the losers sit or stand around disconsolately in the middle, not speaking to one another; or, in the case of a tennis final, the loser must receive the runner-up medal, appear to be grateful for it, and then stand to watch and applaud as the victor receives the trophy.

The public nature of formalized losing both intensifies and mitigates the experience of loss. Losing well means being seen to lose and having one's capacity to lose well being put to the test. The ordeal of visibility, which requires one to demonstrate simultaneously humiliation and composure, resembles the experience of shame, which similarly imposes the burden of exposure. Yet that very formalized visibility is what allows for the possibility of a kind of retreat from shame into the dignity of suffering. There is nowhere to hide but in exposure itself, in the formality of the ritual, following the principle that symbolism functions as a sort of metaspace, or better perhaps, an infraspace, insinuated within or behind physical space.

The good loser acknowledges that she has lost, as though losing were somehow verified and even essentially occasioned by this admission of defeat rather than by its external constitution, in terms of the numbers of points or goals scored. To be a good loser means to make one's defeat one's own, which is to say, to accept, acknowledge, and inhabit it. One must not only undergo defeat; one must, as we say, "admit defeat," which is to say, in a certain sense, join with the victor in imposing defeat on oneself, even while preventing that from teetering over into masochism, which is in fact a cowardly retreat into factitious positivity from the real admission of defeat and the almost intolerable condition of tension that it seems to require.

Good losers must admit, allow, and acknowledge their defeat, to the point at which it becomes temporarily their habitat. Though one should for a time dwell in defeat, to lose well requires one not to dwell on it. For that too would be to magic out a sort of sovereignty from one's very brooding. To make defeat a principle of one's being is not really to admit it but to seek to harness it for the purpose of self-securing in negativity.

The conflicting demands of losing well are therefore balanced with exquisite subtlety. The ethic of losing well has continuities with the ethic of fortitude or forbearance under suffering, but is in fact far more complex because of the principle that one cannot merely be brave or cheerful in defeat, lest this seem like a mode of disrespectful abnegation. To be a good loser requires one to live out or exist one's loss, as a mode or expression of one's being, rather than as something simply to be nobly or cheerfully borne or merely got over.

Losing well is matched by winning graciously, which requires a visible holding back from rampant or tumultuous forms of triumph. In a certain sense, the symmetry of the demands made both of the winner and the loser is intended to enforce equivalence itself. When, at the end of a savagely grueling bout, boxers immediately fall into an embrace, it is as though they are finding reciprocal comfort and support in shielding each other from the greater and unredeemable savagery of the snarling crowd. Instantaneously, the principle of absolute adversity is converted into the principle of absolute interconvertibility. It is essential for both winner and loser to demonstrate the imposture of victory and defeat, playing the part of winner and loser well, in order to assert the victory of the game over both winning and losing. This embrace anticipates and sets aside in advance the announcement of the victor, which is yet to come, in the physical demonstration of the interchangeable equivalence of winning and losing.

We may perhaps suspect that losing well represents the most demanding and paradoxical blend of assertion and reserve, or standing forth and standing back, and that its function is to allow for the play with these opposite possibilities. This may be why it is operative principally in the circumstances of agonistic play, which seem designed to engineer a convergence of extreme seriousness and absolute arbitrariness that is hard to maintain in other circumstances. The demand to lose well in other ways—in battle, for instance, or in amorous rivalry—seems to require competitive circumstances in which a high degree of codification is present, a codification that similarly allows at once for intensification and neutralization of the conflict. We should not be surprised that Norbert Elias paid serious attention to sport as part of the civilizing process (Elias and Dunning 1986). Games allow for the playful simulation of action, action that holds back or stands aside from the action it appears to be.

The example of losing in law is instructive here. You may very well lose your life as a result of a judicial process, but we rarely refer to a condemned man as having lost his case. Rather, it is the lawyer who has acted on his behalf who is said to have lost (Hedin 2002). The exception is in cases where somebody brings a suit against another; but losing an action for libel does not usually imply any obvious threat to life or liberty, so this example seems to confirm the principle that you can yourself lose only if you do not in fact lose your self. This may seem to be the acknowledgment that losing implies the necessity of living on beyond and with the loss.

The requirements attached to losing are in fact so various and conflicting that they must be regarded as impossible to fulfill. The point at which one would fulfill the responsibilities both to suffer the loss and fully acknowledge that suffering and its justice must always also let in the suspicion that one had developed a self-protective routine to fulfill one's obligations. Losing resembles apology in this respect. Losing too well, like apologizing too cheerfully and proficiently, is a failure to lose sufficiently, to own up adequately to the fact of losing. It may be the function of games and sport precisely to create the possibility of meeting these impossible conditions through an intensified convergence of really performing and merely performing. Sport has often been seen as providing the means for the impulses to aggression to be expressed without damage, but it may perhaps be better understood as providing an arena in which the discipline of losing well may be produced and practiced.

Losing well in the artificial circumstances of sport or competition is certainly very different from other kinds of loss and the responses to it, and indeed the arts of losing well are designed to stand apart from ordinary, more contingent forms of losing. Yet there are parallels between competitive and noncompetitive loss. Human beings stage and style their experiences of loss, allowing for the subjectification of subjection, or the living out of losing, that is a feature of all giving way.

## Letting Go

The history of the word *lose* gives some warrant to the idea that losing may be regarded as the transformation of an involuntary occurrence into a voluntary action. One of the commonest errors in written English is the substitution of *loose* for *lose*, the first meaning to free, detach, or unloose, and the second meaning to become deprived of. *Loose* is closely related to *lease*, meaning to let or allow, usually with the idea of some conditional restriction, as in the lease given to summer in Shakespeare's Sonnet 18, which "hath all too short a date" (2010b, 147), or in Sonnet 124, the impermanence of policy "which works on leases of short-numbered hours" (361). But the careful distinction made with the doubled *o* of *loose* in fact emerges from a tangled history of crossing and confusion between passively letting slip and actively giving away, coming apart from, and parting with. Well into the nineteenth century, to lose could mean to ruin or destroy, and also to perish, as in the expression "lost at sea." The options are nicely juxtaposed when Estragon in Beckett's *Waiting for Godot* inquires, "We lost our rights?" and Vladimir replies firmly, "We got rid of them" (1986, 20). Australian "lose your dinner," vomit, has the same ambivalence. The word *lose* could also be used to convey the sense of being lost, as in Hester Lynch Piozzi's remark that "our authors plunder French comedies in vain; the humour loses and evaporates" (1794, 2.56). *Loose* is in fact common as a spelling of *lose*, as in Francis Bacon's observation that "the degree of nullitie and quidditie or act, seemeth larger then the degrees of increase and decrease, as to a monoculos it is more to loose one eye, then to a man that hath two eyes" (1597, sig. 30v).

This relation between fact and act works strangely and powerfully in the expression "to lose" a loved one, as used in bereavement. Many have been struck by the offensive absurdity of the suggestion made by the word that the dear departed may merely have been mislaid. Yet there is indeed a sense in which losing something is not just an accident, something that happens to us, but something we seem actively to do or are impelled to think of as having done. To lose something valuable is always to lay ourselves open to the suspicion that we have loosed it, or "let it go" as the employers' outrageous euphemism has it. Part of the difficulty of losing in the sense of letting go is that there can be an aggressive component in it. Perhaps, indeed, the pain of the loss of something loved will always seek to mitigate itself by borrowing some of the assertive destructiveness of discarding, getting rid of, or doing without. Anna Freud suggests that the feeling of privation in loss may be accompanied by feelings of guilt, "as if we had not lost the thing unintentionally but discarded it in full consciousness," a feeling perhaps in turn defended against when we say that something has "got lost" or "gone missing," in which "the loser seems to ascribe some independent action to the lost object" (1967, 13). Freud is followed in this by Adam Phillips, who suggests that "when we lose something we have unconsciously got rid of it; consciously we are the victim, unconsciously we are the aggressor. Losing means hating" (2009, 16). To lose is to run the risk of winning at losing, which is to let slip the chance of losing well.

Sigmund Freud's discussion of the work of mourning makes clear that it is in fact a task to be performed, in the usual double sense of that word, meaning it must both be done and seen to be done in some way or other (1953–74, 14.243–44). Mourning is a kind of manners in extremity, the assertion of modulation in the face of the brute indifference and nondifferentiating factuality of death. There is an *ars luctus* as there is an *ars moriendi*, a styling of the process of missing.

We refer regularly to actions and occasions of losing, not just in human life but in nature, as though it were a simple and straightforwardly existent thing. Fish have lost the legs they once had, humans have lost the hair that covered their ape ancestors, and words often lose letters or sounds that were once in evidence, for example, in the process whereby *esquire* becomes *squire*, and *episcopus* becomes *bishop*, a process for which J. A. H. Murray invented the word *aphesis*, from Greek ἄφεσις, a letting go, from ἀφ- off, away + ἱέναι, to send, let go (1881, 175). The importance of temporality in all these things should make it clear that losing is not an event that simply happens in the world but rather an epiphenomenon of memory. Some part of anything that has been lost must be retained in order for it to be known to be lost, and being known to be lost is an irreducible condition of something having been lost. Nothing can be completely lost, because being completely lost would mean being lost to memory as well, meaning the loss of the loss. The only way to lose something is not to lose it entirely, to retain at least a trace or memory of its having existed, of a piece with, if lacking the intensity of, what Sigmund Freud calls a "hallucinatory wishful psychosis" (1953–74, 14.244).

This is why the experience of losing something can indeed be generative, a kind of accession or acquisition rather than a loss, for it is often true that you do not know what you have until it is gone or, if it is still with you, until you can imagine it gone and your prospective ache at once having had it. There has been much concern recently about the theft of personal data. Most of this data is not in the category of secret or confidential information—passwords, shameful predilections, details of adulterous assignations, and the like—but is rather information about us to which we give rise in the course of mediated actions that leave some appropriable trace that is capable of being treated as data. That is, what I call "my" data, about the loss of which I may be tutored to panic or pang, is only mine and is indeed only something anyone could think of as data, insofar as it has been appropriated. And this appropriation is actually inaugural, for it is the act of taking from me that makes it mine, or once mine. *Appropriation* seems just the right word for this, since the movement of my property toward its new owner is actually what establishes my proprietary right in it. The idea of "my" data that arises from the feeling that I have been dispossessed of it is in fact not something that I am able to give before the donation to me of my power to lose it through dispossession. Peter Checkland and Sue Holwell propose an influential distinction between *data* and *capta*, facts created by selection and combination from the neutral field of data: "Data are a starting point in our mental processing. Capta are the result of selecting some for our attention, or creating some new category—such as 'the number of octogenarian widows living alone in Wigan' . . . —or being so surprised by some items of data that pass across our gaze that we begin to pay them attention" (1998, 89). But since there is nothing that can function as data, that is, material with the potential to be transformed through processing into capta, that has not already been preprocessed in some way, there is in fact no data that is not already capta, captured for the purposes of being made significant, prised loose in order to be able to have been lost.

Losing always gives rise to these kinds of temporal convolutions, in which the past of presence that has not become a presence until its absence lingers on, both as a compensation for a loss and as the confirmation of it. Losing a prized possession, a loved one, or a social position gives rise to the minor mode of mourning known as *missing* someone or something. The word *miss* was used as a noun to signify a lack or absence until the eighteenth century, a usage that survives in the expression to "give something a miss." In the seventeenth century one could be said charmingly to "leave a miss" of oneself by leaving or being lost, as in the English translation of Pierre Gassendi's life of Nicolas Claude Fabri de Peiresc, which reports that "because he would depart sooner than was hoped, he left a great misse of himself, both in the Family of the Embassadour, and among his learned friends" (1657, 101). The miss here seems to be a ghostly facsimile, a vacancy possessing the precisely isomorphic contour of what is lacking, in the manner filled out by Constance, in Shakespeare's *King John*, speaking of the loss of her son:

> Grief fills the room up of my absent child,
> Lies in his bed, walks up and down with me,
> Puts on his pretty looks, repeats his words,
> Remembers me of all his gracious parts,
> Stuffs out his vacant garments with his form. (2018, 249)

The opposite of having is not having, but losing can never quite be not having anymore. A lost object is a positive thing, a positive absence or departure. Perhaps all lost objects are vicariates or avatars of that object that is loss itself. Is, then, the lost object the most absolute sort of object, objectness itself? You never know what you have till it's gone, and you cannot really have it unless you can imagine it going missing. Going missing is distributed between the object and the one who has lost it: when the object is missing, the one who has lost it misses it. To be the object of such a loss, by "leaving a miss" is a form of persistence rather than of passing away. "Did you miss me?" we sometimes ask, as though to acknowledge that being missed is an enhanced or doubled form of presence.

We keep things by us perhaps in part to maintain a certain kind of self-possession. I am self-possessed as long as I am not separated from my personal effects, a nice expression that allows us to see the convergence of the effect I have through my property, and the effect that property has in giving me my sense of personhood. As Anna Freud puts it, "It is the distribution of our libido between the animate and the inanimate world and the resulting positive cathexis of material objects which ensures that our possessions remain tied to us, or, rather, we to them" (1967, 12). Donald Winnicott's (1953) term "transitional object" suggests not just in-betweenness but also movement. All objects are transitional in that they are transportable, but they are also losable and so themselves perhaps on their way to being lost. We may define a precious object as an object capable of being lost, capable of inflicting the weight of its loss on us. It may be, as Alfred Tennyson writes in *In Memoriam*, that "'Tis better to have loved and lost / Than never to have loved at all" (2009, 220), but if so, this means that only the possibility, or prospect of loss, ever makes love possible. Indeed, one might say that the strange combination of possessiveness and self-loss, in the losing of the self to its imaginary possession of the loved one, that is thought to be characteristic of romantic or sexual love is an anticipation of the way in which one may build one's entire self around the fact of what has been lost to it in bereavement. We love things that are capable of being lost and the losing of which will cause us pain. We cannot love what cannot be lost and perhaps can love nothing as intensely as the phantom that the loved-lost object must be able to become.

I observed earlier that there are important differences between losing a game and losing an object or being deprived by death of a loved one. But there is one respect in which they are similar. Sigmund Freud's account of mourning requires the recognition that one loses a loved one twice, first passively and then actively. There is first of all the contingent fact of the loved one's death, an event that occurs to one, as a primary privation. This is then followed by the acceptance of this event, which Freud characterizes, not as a slow diminution of grief but as an active withdrawal of cathexis from the image of the loved one, the strange Freudian term *cathexis* (in fact devised by his translator James Strachey to render the homelier *Bestzung*) signifying both the energetic action of the subject's investment of love and the quantum of what it invests. It seems appropriate that this spectral term for the magical operation performed by a quasisubstance should be so central to the transactions with similarly absent yet quasi-present objects. So first one must adapt to the primary loss, and then one must find a way to lose, or, yes, *loose*, one's loss. Successful mourning, which most commentators seem, like Freud himself, to find less interesting than the incomplete mourning seen in what Freud calls melancholia, follows a strange logic whereby one both loses a loved object and reclaims the love one has invested in it, like Robinson Crusoe diving repeatedly to his sunken ship to retrieve the necessities for survival on his island. Cathexis is a kind of coin or currency, which must not be allowed to be lost along with the lost object in which it has been invested when it can be reeled back in to be spent on other things.

The distinctive feature of ordinary mourning, according to Freud, is that it is prolonged in time. In order to be able to attain a condition in which one can live with a loss, one has precisely to live for a time *in* loss, and even *on* it. The orders of the reality principle

> cannot be obeyed at once. They are carried out bit by bit, at great expense of time and cathectic energy, and in the meantime the existence of the lost object is psychically prolonged [wird . . . *die Existenz des verlorenen Objekts*

*psychisch fortgesetzt*]. Each single one of the memories and expectations in which the libido is bound to the object is brought up and hyper-cathected [*überbesetzt*], and detachment of the libido is accomplished in respect of it. (S. Freud 1953–74, 14.245; 1991, 10.430)

The paradox here, the perversity even, is that detachment is enabled by means of an apparent increase of attachment. At this point, we can begin to see a resemblance, which may at first have seemed unlikely, between the mourner and the good loser. Both are required not to retreat from the loss they have just suffered but to inhabit it for a period of time sufficient for them not to let slip altogether the experience of loss. They are perhaps in the position of the "lost soul," or unquiet spirit, haunting the living "for a certain time" (Shakespeare 2005, 211), which resembles the space of time required for the process of mourning. Losing and being lost seem here to be equivalent conditions. It is almost as though time itself, which is said to heal by erosion, were in fact a kind of countercurrency, in which the cathexis of the lost object can be paid off.

The work of mourning, as the work of losing well by consciously and purposively losing, has ritual embodiments that help formalize it, as game conditions formalize winning and losing. Formalizing works to actualize and even intensify the fact of losing, while also distancing it, or distancing oneself from it, thereby fulfilling something very like the dual process Freud described of simultaneously realizing and derealizing the loss of the loved one through hypercathexis.

Elegy is the literary mode that has often been adopted as the method for modulating the savagery of the deprivation of death. Elegy often has as its express purpose the stabilization of loss through its transformation into a monumental permanence. Perhaps the most uncompromising formulation of this view is to be found in Friedrich Schiller's *On Naïve and Sentimental Poetry*. The most important work performed by elegiac writing, according to Schiller, is to generalize a finite particular loss into an infinite condition, a process that might be regarded as equivalent to the hypercathexis that allows for the withdrawal of cathexis according to Freud: "The content of poetic lamentation can therefore never be an external object, it must always be only an ideal, inner one; even if it grieves over some loss in actuality, it must first be transformed into an ideal loss" (Schiller 1966, 127). Schiller's words allow us to understand "ideal loss" both as loss of an ideal object and a loss that is itself ideal, that is, both imaginary and a source of high value. This is never more the case than when the poet appears to be lamenting some external loss in nature:

> The external matter is, therefore, always indifferent in itself since the poetic art can never employ it as it occurs, but only by means of what poetry makes of it does it receive its poetic value. The elegiac poet seeks nature, but as an idea and in a perfection in which she has never existed, when he bemourns her at once as something as having existed and now lost. When Ossian tells us of the days which are no more, and of the heroes who have disappeared, his poetical power has long since transformed these images of recollection into ideals, and those heroes into gods. The experience of a particular loss has been broadened into the idea of universal evanescence and the bard, affected and pursued by the image of omnipresent ruin, elevates himself to the skies to find there, in the circle of the sun, an image of the immutable. (1966, 127–28)

In contrast with this idealized and idealizing mode of elegy, Schiller finds in the raw lamentation of Ovid's late works, written in exile on the Black Sea, an example of whinging untransfigured into poetry:

> I cannot consider the lamentations of Ovid when he chanted from his place of exile on the Black Sea, moving as they are and containing so much that is poetic in individual passages, as being as a whole a poetic work. There is far too little energy, far too little spirit and nobility in his pain. Necessity, not inspiration, utters those laments; in them breathes, if not actually a vulgar soul, yet the vulgar mood of a finer spirit that has been crushed by its fate. (127)

Having "too little spirit and nobility in his pain" amounts in Schiller to the charge that Ovid fails to be the kind of good loser that the elegiac poet must strive to be. I think it may be possible to defend Ovid against this charge, and in a way that highlights the bad faith involved into simply gearing up personal loss into abstract conceptions of the universal loss of things that have never in fact existed. The epilogue to Book III of Ovid's *Tristia*, addressed to an unnamed friend, reflects on Ovid's loss of what is most important to him, the writing life that he has previously lived in Rome. He asks his friend to take care of his works, which have not been sentenced to exile as he has been, speaking as though they were in fact bereaved of him, in particular the "thrice five books on changing forms, verses snatched from the funeral of their master"—the unfinished *Metamorphoses*:

> That work, had I not perished beforehand [*si non prius ipse perissem*], might have gained a more secure name from my finishing hand: but now unrevised it has come upon men's lips—if anything of mine is on their lips. (Ovid 1939, 154–55)

How might a book of changes be brought to completeness except by remaining open to change, even and especially the bitterest change of all suffered by Ovid? He speaks as though from some grim and Stygian afterlife, bereaved of those he imagines he has left bereft. Schiller may be right that this predicament does not seem capable of being transformed into uplifting and noble sentiment, precisely because Ovid's theme is the loss of a theme amid the rough and warlike Scythians of the town of Tomis: "Not here have I an abundance of books to stimulate and nourish me: in their stead is the rattle of bows and arms [*pro libris arcus at arma sonant*]" (154–55), the last phrase perhaps a glum spoiling of the sonorous *arma virumque cano* of the opening lines of Virgil's *Aeneid*. And yet Ovid is obviously continuing to write poetry, in the ghostly here and now of his unliterary life: "There is nobody in this land, should I read my verse, of whose intelligent ear I might avail myself, there is no place to which I may withdraw [*non quo secedam locus est*]" (1545–45). Language itself seems to be slipping away from him, a social aphasia that he nevertheless turns into its own faltering poetry: "Often I am at a loss for a word, a name, a place, and there is none who can inform me. Oft when I attempt some utterance—shameful confession!—words fail me: I have unlearned my power of speech [*verba mihi desunt dedidicique loqui*] (154–55). Not only is Ovid losing his grip on his precious Latin; he feels himself being unnaturalized in and by the language amid which he is exiled: Scythian tongues chatter on almost every side, and I think I could write in Getic measure [*videor Geticis scriber posse modis*]. O believe me, I fear that there may be mingled with the Latin in my writings the language of the Pontus" (156–57). In fact, in the later poem *Epistulae ex Ponto*, he admits to writing, or claims to have written, a poem in praise of Caesar in the local language and to have been acclaimed as a poet:

> Nor should you wonder if my verse prove faulty, for I am almost a Getic poet. Ah! It brings me shame! I have even written a poem in the Getic tongue, setting barbarian words to our measures: I even found favour—congratulate me! And began to achieve among the uncivilized Getae the name of poet. (476–77)

With the gritted skill of bitterness, Ovid uses the syncopation of word order to sandwich together the two languages and perspectives in which he finds himself writing: "setting barbarian words to our measures" is "structaque nostris barbara verba modis," a construction in which the barbarian words are literally insinuated into "our measures" and "began to achieve among the uncivilized Getae the name of poet" is "coepique poëtae / inter inhumanos nomen habere Getas," which shuffles together the names of poet and the inhuman name of the Getae.

None of this snooty squealing seems particularly adult or edifying, and there seems to be no doubt that Ovid exaggerated the degree of the deep, dark, and backward conditions in the town of Tomis in which he was marooned, which, despite the presence of the Thracian Getae, probably still had a cultured Greek presence. Ovid's self-dramatization has encouraged some critics to believe that the whole story of his exile may in fact have been a fabrication and that he never in fact went near the Black Sea (Fitton Brown 1985). But even were that true, it would only really add a layer to the laminations of self-projection that are part of the ostensible process of writing loss. Ovid's mode of grieving for his lost tongue is conducted in that very tongue, thereby hallucinating the return of the object of his loss in its very enunciation and putting him in the position of the one who loses well by inhabiting his own absence, visibly dwelling in the fine and private place of his own privation. The hint that he might even be able to write in the local language, giving way immediately to the fear that he may already have in fact started involuntarily to do so, is similarly paradoxical, since the Scythians were notably an oral people. To give that language in writing or give writing to that language would be to write the very abeyance of writing that is Ovid's predicament and predication. At the same time, he shows signs of beginning to pass beyond the stage of hypercathexis of his own language, opening up the strange, restitutive possibility that there might be a new Ovid, in a second home and language, writing the inaugural text of Scythian literature.

One can understand why Schiller should regret the absence of ennobling poetic transfiguration of suffering here, and Ovid's misery even at attaining accomplishment and admiration in the Getic language might seem to make him the very embodiment of a sore loser. But he anticipates many writers of and in the condition of exile, sometimes, as in the case of Beckett, Nabokov, or Celan, a perversely and stubbornly willed exile, who have existed their state of loss and made of it a wounded way of being, as in the closing words of Ovid's *Epistulae ex Ponto*:

> Omnia perdidimus: tantummodo vita relicta est
> praebat ut sensum materiamque mali
> I have lost all; life alone remains, to give me the consciousness and
> the substance of sorrow. (1939, 488–89)

There are other ways of writing one's condition of loss, that being the point—that there must always be modulation, some way or other in which to be at one's loss, or get oneself off the stage. It was sometimes said that to live one day of Charles Dickens's furiously energetic life would be enough to kill most people. But Dickens's writing life was one founded on, and drawing seemingly endless nourishment from, a kind of mourning for his own lost self. In the "Fragment of Autobiography" that John Forster quoted in his biography of the period during which Dickens's father was imprisoned for debt in the Marshalsea, and he was compelled to work in a shoe-polish factory to earn his keep, Dickens wrote:

> It is wonderful to me how I could have been so easily cast away at such an age. It is wonderful to me, that, even after my descent into the poor little drudge I had been since we came to London, no one had compassion enough on me—a child of singular abilities, quick, eager, delicate, and soon hurt, bodily or mentally—to suggest that something might have been spared, as certainly it might have been, to place me at any common school. Our friends, I take it, were tired out. No one made any sign. My father and mother were quite satisfied. They could hardly have been more so, if I had been twenty years of age, distinguished at a grammar-school, and going to Cambridge. (Forster 1876, I.25)

Dickens in fact escaped the exile from fame and greatness that he feared as a child or, more likely, imagined from his later rescued condition that he should have feared, would be his. But in his escape, he carried his period of exile with him and made his writing a work of mourning for the loser life that, in becoming a successful gentleman, he had lost. The young Dickens felt himself to have lost a future of gentility and eminence, but in attaining that fantasy future, he necessarily abandoned another future, the future that might have been his, as one of the abandoned of Victorian life. Dickens's writing life would be at once a redemption of and a revenge upon the life that he feared would be his. The further he drew away from the condition of the lost soul that he later surmised he must precociously have believed himself to be, the more he was drawn back in writing to the world of deprivations that he had survived but could only live on in continuing imaginatively to inhabit.

There are moments in Dickens's writing that indicate his strange, compulsive suspicion that perhaps he never did come back, that young abandoned Charlie never did in fact get to become "Charles Dickens." One of these is narrated in *An Uncommercial Traveller*, in which Dickens comes upon "a very queer small boy" on the road and takes him into his coach. The young boy is nine years old, lives and goes to school in Chatham, as Dickens did from the age of five to nine, and is an avid reader, as the young Dickens was, recognizing Gad's Hill as the scene of Falstaff's robbery and cowardly flight, about which the corpulent knight will later so fatly and magnificently fib. And then, they come upon a large house, and the young boy asks if they can stop the coach at the top of the hill to admire it:

> "Bless you, sir," said the very queer small boy, "when I was not more than half as old as nine, it used to be a treat for me to be brought to look at it. And now I am nine, I come by myself to look at it. And ever since I can recollect, my father, seeing me so fond of it, has often said to me, 'If you were to be very persevering, and were to work hard, you might some day come to live in it.' Though that's impossible!" said the very queer small boy, drawing a low breath, and now staring at the house out of window with all his might.
>
> I was rather amazed to be told this by the very queer small boy; for that house happens to be *my* house, and I have reason to believe that what he said was true. (Dickens 2000, 86)

The spectral young boy is like an image of what Dickens might have been if he had not been lost. Yet it is only through being lost, and the desperate labor of self-fabrication that has been his life, like Falstaff's, that Dickens can come to fulfill the imagined future of the very queer small boy that he is because he isn't. Dickens seems to recognize his collusion in his own abandonment, in the brutality of the phrase that abruptly chops off the reverie: "Well! I made no halt there, and I soon dropped the very queer small boy and went on" (86). So it is the little boy who has not yet been lost, the image of what Dickens's own life might have been if he had not been abandoned, who is in fact "dropped," let go to, or left to remain in, a history without a future, even though it consists of nothing but the yearning prospect of one, indeed, nothing but the prospect of the future that can come about it seems only if the boy is lost in the way Dickens was himself. It is as though Dickens has here usurped himself, fulfilled the boy's dream at the cost of no longer being able to be him, except in some very queer small sense.

Dickens's entire oeuvre will be driven by these lost-and-found dynamics, in which finding, keeping, and losing will often be caught up in complex fluctuations. The either-or orphan ur-story rarely in Dickens follows the curve of simple loss followed by restoration, or a simple finding of a lost inheritance: for what comes back to the lost child is usually the awareness of what is, at the very inauguration of their being, a loss. These orphaned characters move, at best, from their sense of a loss that cannot be named, that they may not even know they have lost, to the understanding of a life lived in, and as, having lost and been lost. One telling example occurs in *Bleak House* when Esther Summerson meets with Lady Dedlock, who has revealed that, unknown previously to either of them, she is Esther's mother, through her scandalous adulterous liaison with Captain Hawdon, later the law writer "Nemo." The establishment of the filial bond is twinned immediately to the requirement that it be disavowed: "She put into my hands a letter she had written for my reading only and said when I had read it and destroyed it . . . I must evermore consider her as dead" (Dickens 2003, 580). Their interchange about the investigations of the lawyer Tulkinghorn involves a strange alternation of different senses of saving and losing:

> "But is the secret safe so far?" I asked. "Is it safe now, dearest mother?"
>
> "No," replied my mother. "It has been very near discovery. It was saved by an accident. It may be lost by another accident—tomorrow, any day." (580)

One keeps oneself safe by keeping the secret knowledge of the loss that is one's essential constitution and continuing precondition. A secret is the name for a loss that protects itself and protects against itself by never deigning to speak its name.

Freud's account of melancholia suggests that it is the result of a kind of scrambling of losing, forsaking and preserving, in which, rather than successfully retrieving the libido invested in a lost object, the ego identifies itself with an object that has not been lost but actually abandoned, because of some offense or disappointment:

> But the free libido was not displaced on to another object; it was withdrawn into the ego. There, however, it was not employed in any unspecified way, but served to establish an *identification* of the ego with the abandoned object.

Thus the shadow of the object fell upon the ego, and the latter could henceforth be judged by a special agency, as though it were an object, the forsaken object. [*Der Schatten des Objekts fiel so auf das Ich, welches nun von einer besonderen Instanz wie ein Objekt, wie das verlassene Objekt, beurteilt werden konnte.*] In this way an object-loss was transformed into an ego-loss. (1953–74, 14.248; 1991, 10.435)

One might easily imagine how Dickens's own abandonment could be understandable in two senses—both the fact of having been abandoned and the aggressive act in his own literary self-making of abandoning those who abandoned him. Like the little boy lost in a store mentioned by Anna Freud who, when reunited with his mother, tearfully reproached her: "You losted me!" (1967, 16), Dickens found his place in the world by convincing himself that it had losted him. This simultaneously passive and active abandonment might have become a preservative, even a generative sense of the literary potency of loss. But my aim here is not to certify the Freudian account by nudging or shoving the case of Dickens into alignment with it. We would probably do better to regard Freudian melancholia and the Dickensian self-securing and self-investment in loss as parallel fantasy formations, testifying to the powerful and positive work the imago of loss can do in the symbolic imagination. What mediates the play of these questions of loss, of preserving and abandoning, saving and giving over, for Ovid, Freud, and Dickens is the ultimate fort-da fantasy of writing itself, which both preserves and is given up, and enables oneself to keep oneself in reserve while giving oneself away.

## Playing Out

All human life involves the experience of loss, until the loss that life has become itself begins to slip away. Ageing, one grows in fact ever more opulent in deficit, watching one's profit in the loss column grow ever more comfortable. The process of learning to accommodate oneself to the loss of one's self and its putatively indispensable attachments in age, and then the only end of age, has been regarded in many religious and philosophical traditions as a progressive divestment or discarding of inessentials by the soul, or on its behalf. But the examples considered in this chapter indicate that it may also be regarded as a kind of assumption of loss, a joining of oneself to the losing of what falls away and the cadence of one's own consequent declining. It is too easy to think of this as a simple fading out, when in fact the intensity of what has been lost, whether suppleness of limb or sharpness of mind, is more than matched by the undimmed intensity of one's sense of the loss, Ovid's *sensum materiamque*, sense and the substance of the losing itself. At Barbara Hardy's ninetieth birthday party, she told me of the vivid dreams she still had of climbing the cliffs above her cottage in Wales and of the strange desolation of being reeled back into the aches of her waking body, as day brought back her night. Shakespeare's Jacques describes extreme old age as "mere oblivion, / Sans teeth, sans eyes, sans taste, sans everything" (2006, 229). But this remorseless and unidirectional subtraction doesn't seem completely right. For in fact, the older we grow (unless and until we outgrow even this), the more thickly these other, earlier dream bodies will teem in us. Somewhere at large in the shuffling old geezer holding up the bus a boy is still teetering on the top board.

Dimming down garish August, autumn can often outdo it in ardency. This is the final or ultimate giving way, though one of which there will perforce have been many prior performances. It is to be distinguished from the ecstatic, hyperegotistic self-sacrifice of martyrdom, the burning and raving at close of day demanded by the young, as abdication is distinguished from dedication. Martyrdom forces the indifference of death into meaning: dying well does not scorn or defeat death, or even aim to. It does not decline to die, though it can divert it into declension.

The extension of life will very likely, it seems, mean an augmentation of the experience of Beckettian lessness, not just the losing of life but the living in losing. Denied the last freedom, to "play and lose and have done with losing" (Beckett 1986, 132), as Hamm says in *Endgame*, more and more human beings will be living in the sustained and progressive condition of self-losing, most terrifyingly for many not in the form of incurable forms of physical degeneration but in the form of cognitive degeneration brought by Alzheimer's and allied conditions. There is a grim absurdity in the predicament set out in Lisa Genova's *Still Alice*, in which a woman diagnosed with dementia sets up a test procedure to be followed each day, in which she provides the instructions for taking her own life should she be unable to answer a number of simple questions about who she is (2009, 119). When the time comes, however, the instructions for committing suicide seem confusing and frightening, leading the no-longer-quite-Alice to wonder who could be wanting her to kill herself. When you are not quite yourself, it is hard to put paid to yourself. Many people form and even articulate the resolve to embrace the ultimate loss, the loss of the self capable of feeling loss, but far from taking (or rather, surely, standing aside from) one's own life because there is nothing left to lose, it seems that, as Norman L. Cantor (2015) makes clear, you can meaningfully abandon your life only if you still have something left to lose.

Those in the ravening noon of life find it much easier to imagine taking arms against this kind of trouble ("Do not go gentle into that good night"; Thomas 1998, 148), but even Hamlet seems to have an intimation of the absurdity of armed conflict with, of all things, the sea. The narrator of Conrad's *Heart of Darkness* suggests the absurdity of such pseudo-martial understandings:

> I have wrestled with death. It is the most unexciting contest you can imagine. It takes place in an impalpable greyness, with nothing underfoot, with nothing around, without spectators, without clamour, without glory, without the great desire of victory, without the great fear of defeat, in a sickly atmosphere of tepid scepticism, without much belief in your own right, and still less in that of your adversary. If such is the form of ultimate wisdom, then life is a greater riddle than some of us think it to be. (2008a, 178)

Perhaps the abstention from the life-affirming drama of contest is the hardest form of losing well. I myself cherish the dream of ceasing and desisting under circumstances that would allow my obituarist to write that I eventually succumbed after losing a long battle against military-medical metaphor.

"Dying / Is an art, like everything else," affirms the speaker of Sylvia Plath's poem "Lady Lazarus" (1981, 245). Her words allude to the tradition, inherited from the classical world and developed through medieval and early-modern Europe, of the *ars moriendi*, the art of dying. However, it has to be acknowledged that the speaker at this point in Plath's poem is in fact rather more concerned with getting dead than with the manner or style of her dying. We in the modern world spend so long guarding against the apparently ever-present danger of death—through food poisoning, plane crashes, electrocution in the bath—that when the time comes to seek it, we are puzzled and outraged by how tricky it can be to procure it at will. One's death in a certain sense is less than ever these days one's own.

Over the centuries, human beings have devoted a great deal of time to determining the manner of their deaths: the history of the *ars moriendi* reveals that there is an ethics of dying that is quite as demanding as the ethics of the good life. To style one's manner of dying is to take responsibility for, and even to assert a kind of authorship over, an event that we customarily think of as coming upon us. There have been peoples, Sigmund Freud assures us, for whom death is always regarded as an avoidable accident rather than a general necessity (1953–74, 18.45). For such peoples, since something or someone must always be regarded as responsible in every case of fatality, every death is the occasion for an inquest. By contrast, to fashion and perfect the way in which one lives out one's death is to refuse to regard death as a mere, vulgar accident, waiting lifelong to happen. But in either case, death is a matter of social concern: it must be accounted for.

The most economical way of converting the accident of one's death into an intention is through one's last words. Dying well is in large part a rhetorical matter. Of course, speaking and dying, like speaking and eating, cannot literally coincide, which gives the words spoken right up to the point of death a certain grandeur. Samuel Beckett's Malone, in *Malone Dies* (1973), attempts something like the exercise of carrying on writing right up to the point of death, while Edgar Allan Poe's story "The Facts in the Case of M. Valdemar" (1978) imagines a man mesmerized in order to enable him to keep speaking even after the point of death. Words delivered *in articulo mortis* were taken to be absolute truth and could not be doubted in a court of law.

George V's advisers are said to have tried to cheer him up during his last illness with the prospect of visiting the resort of Bognor, his frequent visits to which undistinguished town meant that it was later permitted the dignifying attachment "Regis" in its name. "Bugger Bognor" the dying king retorted and promptly expired. Born as I was and, a little, bred in Bognor, I know what he may have meant. Most of us though still feel the desire to try to take some kind of ownership of our death. For dying seems to bring with it still a kind of responsibility. Those who, like Roger McGough in "Let Me Die a Youngman's Death," seek a sudden blackout ("mown down at dawn / by a bright red sports car") that will leave us no time for reflection or fine words recognize this responsibility, that at this terminal stage in one's life, one is always on a kind of stage, required to act out a final scene without a script and with no opportunity for retakes (2003, 60). For some of us, like George V, death is a chance to tell the world to bugger off; but for many of us, there is still the more diffuse sense that dying is a ticklish proceeding that we are at some risk of buggering up, like bungling the punchline of a long-drawn-out joke. The octogenarian McGough's hilariously melancholy retraction of his melodramatic youngman's excitable vision of exit resigns itself to having lost once and for all the chance of prematurity, of a life glamorously cut off in its prime: "Not for me a youngman's death / . . . Not a slow-fade, razor blade / . . . Not a drunken binge, dirty syringe / 'What a waste of life' death" (2012, 74).

Ultimately, the art of dying well is an attempt to give meaning and significance to the thing that seems arbitrary and unpredictable. But it may also disclose the fact that our finitude is in fact the very thing that makes things meaningful. The hero of the final story in Julian Barnes's *A History of the World in 10½ Chapters* finds himself in a heaven of unobstructed bliss and gratification, in which beautiful women line up enthusiastically to sleep with him and his team Leicester City wins the League and FA Cup every year. But after a while, he begins to yearn for the variety and texture that only disappointment and pain can bring. At length, he inquires whether there is an option to die in or, so to speak, from heaven and discovers that there is:

> "And what percentage of people take up the option to die off?"
> 
> She looked at me levelly, her glance telling me to be calm. "Oh, a hundred per cent, of course. Over many thousands of years, calculated by old time, of course. But yes, everyone takes the option, sooner or later."
> 
> "So it's just like the first time round? You always die in the end?"
> 
> "Yes, except don't forget the quality of life here is much better. People die when they decide they've had enough, not before. The second time round it's altogether more satisfying because it's willed." She paused, then added, "As I say, we cater for what people want." (Barnes 1990, 303)

Nature programs us to see death as the greatest evil, to be feared and shunned at all costs, but, since ultimately it is death that gives purpose and preciousness to everything we are and do, it is immortality, a world without the possibility of death, that would be the only absolute evil.

Literary representations of dying show that there are many different ways of dying well. One can die humbly and submissively; one can die in gladness and with the serene hope of going to a better place; one can die absentmindedly (or at least have a mind to), taking no account of one's death. From the seventeenth century onward, literary representations of dying move from the idea of the exemplary death, the death that confirms us as an example of more general virtues, to dying as the assertion of the unexampled uniqueness of a particular life, asserted in the face of the vulgar common lot. If human beings are the animals who are most aware of the fact of their mortality, our continuous condition of "being-toward-death" makes the manner of our dying something about which we have no choice but to make some kind of choice. Death is in fact the mediator between the singular and the universal. My death is the sign and enactment of my unshareable uniqueness: others may die, as we say, in my stead, in order that I may live; but nobody else can die my death for me. At the same time, it is the necessity to undergo this absolutely private experience that is the one absolute and universal feature of human life. Since we have no reliable reports from those who have passed beyond dying into death, our dying depends very much on the good or ill report of others, which is very much a matter for us in that we bend toward it in anticipation, in the unripeness that is all. And this is perhaps a sign of the larger meaning of dying: in undergoing our own, allegedly absolutely solitary and unshareable personal dissolutions, we enter into the largest and least exclusive community of all, as we give ourselves over to others for whom we may continue to live on in the manner of our dying, precisely because it is a manner, meaning a means, that may be a medium for others.

And being done for must itself be done in some way or other. In the era we inhabit of expanding and accelerating engineering, especially symbolic engineering through manner and style, we should expect to see growing demands for revivals and extensions of the *artes moriendi* so common in other periods and civilizations. Even the wish to die any old how or, like Beckett's Malone, "tepid, without enthusiasm" (1973, 179), is an inflection of the action we sometimes call "bowing out." It seems to be difficult to exercise impotentiality nonparadoxically, meaning that, as Andrew Bennett observes, even the act of ending one's own life must often be regarded as an assertion of one's ultimate freedom of action, suicide being "a profound, unfathomable denial, destruction or negation of the self, and simultaneously . . . an ultimate assertion of identity and agency" (2017, 2).

We are all subject to this demand, which inquires quomodo of every action, even, and especially, the action of refraining or resigning from action. We must all accede to the twin exigencies of the actor on the stage. First of all, the actor must, in the sense that he cannot not, do something, even if that something is "doing nothing," or exiting the stage. But the actor also cannot take his leave from the stage except in some style or other, as indicated repeatedly in Richard Sheridan's farce of theatrical rehearsal *The Critic* (1789). One scene ends with a group of characters kneeling, wondering whether they are to shuffle off the stage on their knees (Sheridan 1999, 58). At the end of another, the heroine's confidante, finding herself stranded onstage, inquires of the author, "But pray, sir, how am *I* to get off here?," receiving the irritable reply, "You! pshaw! What the devil signifies how you get off! Edge away at the top, or where you will" (64). Every actor knows the existential aporia of being asked simply to perform an action, like walking to a door and exiting through it, and suddenly being unable to decide how to extract the action from the million other conceivable ways of doing it or, having decided, how to do it without overdoing it. The action of ceasing to be able to act, or seceding from action, demands to be acted out, and the path to quietus must pass through action. Beckett's *Waiting for Godot* recalls Sheridan in the embarrassment suffered by the pompous Pozzo, who finds himself with no way that seems sufficiently convincing of leaving the stage, this anticipating the general difficulty of "going" in the play:

> ESTRAGON Then adieu.
> POZZO Adieu.
> VLADIMIR Adieu.
> POZZO Adieu.
> *Silence. No one moves.*
> VLADIMIR Adieu.
> POZZO Adieu.
> ESTRAGON Adieu.
> *Silence.*
> . . .
> POZZO I don't seem to be able . . . (*long hesitation*) . . . to depart.
> ESTRAGON Such is life. (Beckett 1986, 45–46)

To take no interest in the process of becoming an un- or ex-being, slipping out of existence leaving no stone turned, may seem the most natural and untheatrical way of giving way to it. But there can seem to be a wastrel improvidence in such an action, which leaves the grieving widow to choose the hymns and wrangle with the insurance company. In a sense the way in which one chooses, or cannot choose not, to make any kind of choice about how to extricate oneself from being is the mark of one's embedding, up to and beyond the ultimate abstention from being, within a collectivity that makes enormously high demands on the ways in which such unactions are enacted, and vice, to be sure, versa.

It is not accidental that theater provides the most telling examples of the intertwining of action and the abstention or secession from it. For it is in the theater that one is forced to recognize the impossibility for a human being of simply acting. This is not because the theater is exceptional, but just the opposite: the theater frames off the essential theatricality of all human behaving. This is in contrast to the suggestion made by Giorgio Agamben that the fluidity of modern forms of labor oppressively rules out abstention:

> The definitive confusion in our time [is] between jobs and vocations, professional identities and social roles, each of which is impersonated by a walk-on actor whose arrogance is in inverse proportion to the instability and uncertainty of his or her performance. The idea that anyone can do or be anything . . . is nothing but the reflection of the awareness that everyone is simply bending him- or herself according to this flexibility that is today the primary quality that the market demands from each person. (2011, 44–45)

Arguing that "nothing makes us more impoverished and less free than this estrangement from impotentiality" (45), Agamben calls implicitly for a strike against this condition, or at least an honoring and harboring of the capacity to exercise "strike action," a phrase that might be regarded as a translation of "impotentiality."

> Those who are separated from their own impotentiality lose . . . first of all the capacity to resist. And just as it is only the burning awareness of what we cannot be that guarantees the truth of what we are, so it is only the lucid vision of what we cannot, or can not, do, that gives consistency to our actions. (45)

Agamben implicitly sets impotentiality against the theatricality of the modern confusion of vocation and labor. Impotentiality, abstention, finding a way to exit the stage is seen in implicitly Platonic terms, as an access to the originary incandescence that casts the shadows in the playhouse—the "burning awareness" and "lucid vision" that will sweep away the maddeningly indefinite chiaroscuro of our theatrical condition. But abstention, in the form of the ambivalent play of prohibition and license that belongs to the festival, has been caught up in, has indeed been the engine of, theatricality for too long to be swept away by this kind of gesture or by its promise. Nothing could embody, not just the sabbath capacity for impotentiality but the necessity of a measure of impotentiality, more than the stage of being that human beings can never simply exit. There is no kind of getting off that does not remain onstage, no striking of a set that is not another setting.

So the real meaning of the literary trope of the last words is the inescapability of theater and the impossibility of uniqueness that death gives. It should not be a surprise that Norbert Elias (2001), who spent so much of his life thinking about the ways in which humans contrived to live tolerably with each other, should have devoted one of his later books to the question of the loneliness of the dying. Yeats's sequence poem "Upon a Dying Lady" ends with the bringing in of a Christmas tree and a courtly little address to death, the "great enemy," asking pardon for the harmless frivolity of decorating a Christmas tree at such a time:

> And she may look from the bed
> On pretty things that may
> Please a fantastic head.
> Give her a little grace,
> What if a laughing eye
> Have looked into your face—
> It is about to die. (1956, 157)

Being about to die signifies the imminence of the great event for the dying lady but also allows the idea that she is about her dying, and able to be so because of those who are about her. This need not, and perhaps cannot be, a solitary work. If we no longer script our taking leave as a prescription for some renewed life to come, it may be, if we take enough care not to abandon each other to our leave taking, a way of living out in a shared and common arena of being the mode of one's withdrawal from it.

# 7 Taking Care

Under "juvenile correctives," Peter Opie and Iona Opie record the following threat-jingle from Hackney, for children who say they "don't care":

> Don't care was *made* to care
> Don't care was hung,
> Don't care was put in a pot
> And boiled till he was done. (1960, 50)

Occasionally a plausible first verse is supplied that rounds out the narrative, if also thereby somewhat flattening its cryptically exorbitant violence:

> Don't Care didn't care,
> Don't Care was wild:
> Don't Care stole plum and pear
> Like any beggar's child. (Graves 1927, 18)

This is a nursery rhyme of course, a little piece of human behavior that is closely associated with the principal practice of human care, the upbringing of children. The child in the rhyme is taught to care about things by being killed, boiled, and eaten, more like a chicken than a child, while the child hearing the rhyme is also taught that he or she is not really meant to care about such horrors when they are in the careless form of nursery rhymes.

Common handling has similarly rubbed at and rounded out the meanings of the word *care*. To care for something means to enjoy or value it, but this idea seems to have arisen late in the word's evolution. Old English *caru* and Old Saxon *cearu* mean grief or, in Old Norse *kör*, bed of trouble or sickness. It could also mean the utterance of lamentation. By the eleventh century a kind of reflexive sense had formed, to name an anxious attitude of mind toward possible suffering or affliction, in the sense of heed, watchful attention, or, as concern, the concentration of the mind and, from the late sixteenth century, the specific object of such care ("looking after" preserves this sense of "looking out for"). At this point, care developed the strong suggestion of caution, or watchful vigilance, and from there the sense of the exercise as well as an attitude of caring, along with the charge or responsibility of exercising such care, as in the care of children.

But by the middle of the sixteenth century, the word had wandered far enough away from the earliest meaning of sorrow to mean something like the contrary, in something that you may be said to "care for," meaning like, enjoy, or have a fondness for or, in the case of a person, attachment to. Despite the considerable overlap with the range of meanings stemming from Latin *cura*, having charge of (curing, curation, curiosity), the *OED* tells us emphatically that *care* is "in no way related to Latin *cura*." Nor is there any etymological relationship with Latin *carus*, dear, precious, or the Sanskrit *kan*, to be beloved, from which *caress* and the complex and powerful term *caritas* derive, though it is surely not possible for the words not to have affected each other in the course of their long sonic-semantic cousinage in English.

The contrary tugs of sorrow, suffering, duty, love, and pleasure on which the nursery rhyme darkly plays continue to urge in the word, providing it with one of the richest and most complex cooperations of self-abatement and self-fulfillment. In the lives of women especially, the tension has been at its greatest between the positive instinct for and emotional rewards of exercising care, especially over children, though also nowadays in Western countries for their increasingly long-lived elderly relatives, and the external demand to provide various kinds of care service. In most societies, women increasingly provide the majority of care in family contexts as a kind of booby trap for their continued greater longevity than men, provided by women in their sixties and beyond, who might recently have themselves been thought elderly, to relatives of an even more advanced age. Medical improvements that have improved survival rates from serious illness have also created more chronic patients needing intensive, long-term care.

The growing concern with the differential gendering of care provision has produced, not just an understandable and predictable focus on the obviously increased burdens on women but also an interest in men's "nurturing practices of coaching, fostering independence, mentoring, and sponsorship in the public and economic world as well as other more direct caregiving [that] are as hidden as the caring practices more closely associated with traditional women's work" (Gordon, Noddings, and Benner 1996, ix). This has produced a new concern for the care needs of carers themselves, with numerous books appearing that offer therapeutic advice and support for those with caregiving responsibilities (Navaie-Waliser et al. 2002; Rezek 2015). Though some evidence has been reported of cognitive benefit among caregivers older than sixty-five, it is not clear whether this benefit might equally be achieved through other kinds of occupation (Zwar, König, and Hajek 2018). A recent review of nearly four thousand research articles claimed to find more general positive effects among caregivers to dementia patients, including the sense of growth, accomplishment and purpose, and the increase in family cohesion (Yu, Cheng, and Wang 2018).

Caring has become increasingly institutionalized and professionalized—the words *care home*, *caregiver*, and *care worker* all appear from the 1960s onward—though an economy and public system of care provision creates growing ambivalence, as expressed in the paradoxical idea of the "caring professions" (members of which may be ones who care more about their work, but may also just be ones whose work is to provide care), especially since many depend on and exploit the supposedly heightened natural propensity to caring among females. Feminist social theory has highlighted the complex interdependence between formal and informal, paid and unpaid caring responsibilities (Bashevkin 2002). The fact that caring has been delegated and autonomized, or the expectation that it should be, seems to indicate that we wish to have to care less about most of the ways in which care functions, because of what has been "made to care," not in the sense of being forced into caring but in the sense of being constructed as a means of exercising care on our behalf. At the same time, what seems like an irrepressible need to have objects and channels of caring may indicate that caring remains part of how humans are made.

Care and caring therefore enjoin the same kind of complex mixture of subjectivity and objectivity, assertion and setting aside of self, as has been analyzed in preceding chapters. To experience care is both to be the object, repository, or afflicted victim of cares, to be "care worn" or "burdened with care," and also to experience an active feeling of concern or attachment, or to affirm oneself by providing "care." To be one who cares for some other being, or cares about some object or topic, is to devote or subject yourself to it; it is to concern yourself with what concerns you (Latin *concernere* literally means to sift or mingle together, as in a sieve). It is part of what Jean-Paul Sartre identifies as the projective structure of human existence, according to which being must always put itself ahead of itself (2007, 23). But insofar as projection must always leave the merely existent behind in order to project itself into some external object of concern, it must include a willingness for that existent self, with its currently existing aims, needs, and investments, to be withdrawn or forgone.

## Bearing

Care is focused for human beings primarily on children, and parental care provides the matrix, literally the maternal pattern, for many other forms of care. Almost all creatures have some degree of concern for their offspring, even when they seem to take no care at all beyond the action of propagating. The fact of being able to reproduce can reduce one's being to that potential to reproduce, suggesting that every creature must be thought of at the very least as having, or perhaps even in itself being the embodiment of, concern with that form of indirect persistence that consists in giving rise to other embodiments of one's species. To reproduce is simultaneously to perpetuate and to sacrifice oneself. But the prodigious length of time required for human beings to reach maturity, and the huge investment of material and informational resources required in every infant from all quarters, makes care and the concern with its different forms a permanent and powerful feature of human life.

It may appear that we are progressively freeing ourselves from the demands of producing, feeding, and teaching young, demands that may seem to monopolize the entire existence of other creatures. But if so, it seems we have delivered ourselves only to a reflexive imperative of the care of the self, of a concern for and purposive parenting of one's own existence, nursing or nurturing one's self as assiduously as other creatures, or other human beings once, devoted their lives to the nurture of others. We care for and cultivate the self as that which is directed or dedicated to the task of caring or caring for those things it cares about. In *The Care of the Self*, Michel Foucault provides a history of the growth of "a new stylistics of existence" in ancient Rome (1986, 71), meaning a reflexive concern, not just with right action but with the actuating springs of right action in the self. In *The Care of the Self*, we read of the justification given by Epictetus for the abstaining of the Cynic, or philosopher, from the customary cares and concerns of marriage:

> The reason for which the ideal Cynic should, according to Epictetus, forgo marriage is not the desire to reserve his attentions for himself and no one else. On the contrary, it is because he has the mission of caring for humans, of looking after them, of being their "benefactor." It is because, like a doctor, he must "make his rounds" and "feel men's pulses." Kept occupied by the responsibilities of a household (and perhaps especially by the household Epictetus describes) he would not have the leisure to go about a task that takes in the whole of humanity. (158)

The progressive freeing of human beings, or some of them, from the necessities of child care has resulted in the extension and diversification of caring into many other duties of concern, social, economic, and political, from which it seems impossible to escape. Sitting at the bedside of his father, Henry V, Prince Hal addresses the crown on his pillow as "polished perturbation, golden care" (Shakespeare 2016a, 371). Almost every other appearance of the word *care* in Shakespeare (and there are more than two hundred) in fact involves people saying they "care not," but it is a freedom that, however often it may be aspired to, not many in fact care to endure. Not caring, or the action of disclaiming it, is a powerful breaking of a bond, as indicated even in the lighthearted sparring between Viola disguised as Cesario and Feste the fool in *Twelfth Night*:

> Viola: I warrant thou art a merry fellow and car'st for nothing.
> Feste: Not so, sir, I do care for something; but in my conscience, sir, I do not care for you. If that be to care for nothing, sir, I would it would make you invisible. (Shakespeare 2008, 252)

We still wish each other the safety that comes from being cared for when we say "Goodbye," or "God be with you," but it is nowadays just as common to say "Take care," which may increasingly mean not just look after yourself, be on your guard against the manifold perils of the path, but also take care of business, apply yourself conscientiously to your projects. To be wholly unburdened, to be deprived of the carriage, import, or voluntary weight of the cares we take on ourselves, for ourselves, is to risk the leaden dread of lightness of being. To find yourself in that numb, flat, featureless condition we often misleadingly call depression is in fact literally, and appallingly, not to have a care in the world. If we often find ourselves wanting to be unburdened of care, it is not in order to be careless but to be relieved of the merely externally imposed cares that prevent us concerning ourselves with the things we care about. We wish to be free of cares in order to be free to care, to form and cultivate our caring. As Samuel Johnson remarks offhandedly in his *Journey to the Western Islands*, "Plantation is naturally the employment of a mind unburdened with care, and vacant to futurity, saturated with present good, and at leisure to derive gratification from the prospect of posterity. He that pines with hunger, is in little care how others shall be fed" (Johnson and Boswell 1984, 134).

Philosophers have paid attention to many of the objects of human care and attention, but Martin Heidegger is unusual in the centrality he gives to the condition of care itself and as such. More than a mood, outlook, or phase of existence, the condition of care (*Sorge*) is, for Heidegger, identical with being in the world itself:

> Dasein's Being reveals itself as *care*. If we are to work out this basic existential phenomenon, we must distinguish it from phenomena which might be proximally identified with care, such as will, wish, addiction, and urge. Care cannot be derived from these, since they themselves are founded upon it. (1962, 227)

Care is closely related to anxiety for Heidegger, defined as a curious kind of fear without an identifiable object. The anxious unease of care derives from the always incomplete or unsettled condition of Dasein, characterized by Heidegger as "an entity for which, in its Being, that Being is an issue" (236); hence "'Being-in-the-world' has the stamp of 'care,' which accords with its Being" (243). The characteristically hyper-hyphenated chain gang of a concept Heidegger offers for the constitution of care is "ahead-of-itself-Being-already-in-the-world as Being-alongside entities encountered within-the-world" (237), in which each hyphen signals an incapacity for apartness. Heidegger sees the structure of care as always putting Being ahead of itself, meaning that it must always in a sense also be forced to hang back or hold back from itself.

But the structure of care is always apparently oriented to itself for Heidegger, never to those entities it may be "alongside." This dimension of

*Fürsorge*, caring for (entities other than oneself), seems to be absent from, or at least inactive in, Heideggerian care. He says explicitly, "Man's *perfectio*—his transformation into that which he can be in Being-free for his ownmost possibilities (projection)—is 'accomplished' by 'care'" (243). Dorothea Frede explicates this as care for one's own self-making:

> The decisive characteristic in our relation to the world as such, which includes ourselves as our ultimate point of reference, is conditioned by the care that allows us to treat everything as part of our *project* in the largest sense of the word. This feature leads to the temporal interpretation of the structure of our being-in-the-world. We project ourselves, our whole existence, into the world and understand ourselves as well as everything in the world in terms of the *possibilities* within the design or "projection" that we make of ourselves. (2006, 63)

It appears that one might therefore often use the word *ambition* in place of Heidegger's *care*. *Sorge* and its many derivatives in German seem not to have the same duality as English *care*, not having acquired so many of the positive emotional tonalities as English *caring*. The central idea of being concerned with (as opposed to being "concerned for," as we might sometimes say in English) is emphasized in *besorgen*, which is used to mean to obtain, provide, procure, manage, see to. It includes some of the more crudely instrumental ways of referring to sexual activity, broadly equivalent to the English *service* or *see to* somebody (or indeed to oneself, as *sich besorgen* means to masturbate). Heidegger's emphasis is always on Dasein's aim of fulfilling itself through care, not on its capacity to put itself in abeyance in order to fulfill the demands of care, which one imagines could never count as primary or fundamental. Concern with things or beings in the world is often in Heidegger seen as an attempt to dim down or demote the more essential authentic anxiety of Being-in-the-world. All this remains true even in the face of Heidegger's fierce and repeated refusals to allow Being, or the kind of being-there he calls Dasein, to be identified with the "self." Even as she acknowledges Heidegger's cautions, Annie Larivée can still find in his work the thought of "a certain way of human being coming to herself, a certain 'birth' of the human being through the care she may have for her authentic Self" (2014, 141). Alan Bass observes that "paradoxically, being-*in*-the-world as care immediately places Da-sein outside itself, as always together with things" (2006, 39). Heidegger similarly assures us that care requires a reaching forward to "entities encountered in-the-world" (1962, 237), but he seems far from sure that there could in fact be a real world or any entities in it that would not depend on Dasein's concerned self-projection into them: "In the order of the ways in which things are connected in their ontological foundations and in the order of any possible categorial and existential demonstration, *Reality is referred back to the phenomenon of care*" (255).

But if care is always part of Being's being ahead of itself, then it may always have to be in some sense separated from the being-for-itself of being. Indeed, even in what is thought of as caring (only) for oneself, there is an abeyance of self, an interior exteriority, as it were, a giving way of the self before or in relation to itself. There is a strange kind of self-sacrifice in the ways in which truly self-centered people can follow their vocation, sternly denying themselves a response to the call of concern for others. More than the condition of self-concern of a being finding itself in, if not fully at home in, the world, care must always in part be for that world.

As social creatures we abhor selfishness, even as we find it hard to imagine any kind of self-centeredness that is not in fact eccentric to itself, that is, does not involve a surrender of the self to things external to it, for example, in the obsession with possession. The compulsive form taken by so many pleasures, so compulsively examined and exemplified in David Foster Wallace's *Infinite Jest* (1996), is a sign of how hard we find it to resist the discipline of self-subjection in what we believe to be self-indulgence. Addiction is not for sissies. *Homo addictus*, whether mystically pledged to heroin, hamburgers, or hill running, must exercise a certain devotion in every dissipation. We require the force of some requirement we give ourselves when we give ourselves up to anything. We can never wholly abandon the ascetology at work in every abandonment. The care we devote to our addictions evidences our addiction to caring, our *dedication* (etymologically almost the same word as *addiction*) to being dedicated. "It is the cause, it is the cause, my soul," says Othello (Shakespeare 2016b, 309), madly deluded of course about the specific nature of the cause in his case, but also for that reason taking care not to name it to himself. His words exemplify and ensure the workings of an abstract will to be taken up in a necessity about which there could be no reasoning, an unspecific and unspecifiable "it" that "the cause" is said to be, and said to be able to do, while not in fact being said at all—"it is the cause that . . ." what? It is a lethal form of the lullaby hinted at by Wallace Stevens in writing "It is a child that sings itself to sleep, / The mind" (2015, 461). By giving ourselves to a cause, we cause it to be causative for us, putting us in its charge. And we crave the cost of a cause as much as any rewards it could conceivably bring.

Often the duty of self-care is signaled by the use of the word *soul* rather than *self*. The Christian idea, a development of late classical understandings, was that one had one's soul in one's keeping rather than simply being it (there are few dialogues between poets and their selves, while dialogues with one's own soul are common). This suggests that the soul, though immortal and beyond price, needed to be conserved and nurtured, with suicide being soul murder. An afterglow of this idea is the value accorded to the principle of "self-esteem" in liberal conceptions of the subject: the idea, not just that you learn to value yourself through the action of valuing and respecting others but that you cannot care for others unless you have a sufficient complement of self-care.

To turn outward is to turn inward, giving oneself the principle of solicitude, in the sense of the potential to be solicited, or made subject to disturbance or incitement, seeking out that which seeks you out. This reversible elasticity, of *reculer pour mieux sauter*, and also *sauter pour mieux reculer*, makes not just for a relation of care to the world outside but a necessary relation of care to the conditions, occasions, and possibilities of one's own caring. In his final lectures at the Collège de France in 1982–83, Foucault turns to Plato's discussions of philosophy with Dionysius the Younger, ruler of Syracuse, to articulate the relations between philosophy and politics. For Plato and, it seems, for Foucault too, philosophy must be concerned, cannot even be philosophy unless it is so concerned, with itself:

> The seriousness of philosophy does not consist in giving men laws and telling them what the ideal city is in which they must live, but in constantly reminding them (those at least who wish to listen, since philosophy's reality comes only from it being listened to), that the reality of philosophy is to be found in its practices, which are the practices of self on self and, at the same time, those practices of knowledge by which all the modes of knowledge, through which one rises and descends and which one rubs against each other, finally bring one face to face with the reality of Being itself. (2010, 255)

Yet this does not separate philosophy from political life, for it replicates exactly the relation between internal and external exercises of care that motivates the political questions of the period that concerns Foucault: "What then is the type of discourse which is such that the Prince will be able to take charge of himself, to take care of himself as well as those he governs? How can one govern the Prince in such a way that he will be able to govern himself and others?" (47). Indeed, this care of oneself is no mere self-indulgence; rather than preserving oneself in the inertia of equanimity, caring philosophically for the self involves solicitously subjecting its assumptions to scrutiny, making self-coincidence a charge, ardor, and task. The philosopher exhorts those he meets

> not to care about honor, wealth, or glory, but to care about themselves—this is the *epimeleia heautōn* as you know. And caring about oneself consists first and foremost in knowing whether or not one does know what one knows. Philosophical *parrēsia*, which is identified not just with a mode or technique of justice but with life itself, consists in practicing philosophy, caring about oneself, exhorting others to care about themselves, and doing this by examining, testing, putting what others do and do not know to the test. (326)

Care is a labor, but a labor that involves devoting one's care to helping impart to others the ordeal and ongoing concern of self-making and care. Socrates, who disturbed the sleep of the city of Athens so much he had to be put down, refused to speak publicly in the Assembly but spoke everyday language "so as to be able to look after himself by visibly and manifestly refusing the injustices that may be done to him, but also by encouraging others, questioning them casually [so as to] take care of them by showing them that, knowing nothing, they really should take care of themselves" (Foucault 2010, 351).

Many people have been impelled by the notion that human beings are, compared with other creatures, essentially immature, reaped before their time and, perhaps, for those persuaded that the earth is what John Keats in a letter of April 21, 1819, called "a vale of Soul-making" (2012, 2.102), for almost the whole of their lives unborn or in preparation, so requiring parental care (parent and preparation both come from *parere*, to make ready). As Peter Sloterdijk describes it:

> In the long period of prehuman development, a type of creature born immature developed out of the species of live-born mammalian humans. These, to speak paradoxically, entered their world with an ever-increasing excess of animalian unpreparedness. This led to an anthropogenic revolution—the transformation of biological birth into the act of coming into the world. (2009b, 20)

We still live and think with a distinction between the born and the made, with nature being literally that which has been born, *natus*. *Poeta nascitur, non fit*, runs the old saw: poets are born, one does not make them. Most of the variations on this formula seem to have been prompted by Horace's mocking remark in his *Ars Poetica* that poets all believe with Democritus that "native talent is a greater boon than wretched art" (*ingenium misera quia fortunatius arte*) (Horace 1926, 474–75), so assume that they should subject themselves to the sanctifying privation of leaving their nails and beards untended if they wish to drink the waters of Helicon (Ringler 1941, 498). Of course, poetry literally means making, meaning that the power of engendering embodied in genius has to have generated of itself, or even have generated itself. So the problem immediately connects to the question of Creation viewed in the largest possible perspective, whether anything can be regarded as existing without having been made, whether it is possible, in the Scholastic formulation, for there to be a distinction between a *natura naturans*, nature naturing, or giving rise to, itself, and *natura naturata*, nature natured, as it were passively, from some outside or some prior creative principle. The Latin word *nascitur* is a third-person-plural passive: *nasco*, the first-person present indicative active, has only a formal grammatical existence (*natura grammata*). As observed in the discussion of giving birth in Chapter 3, there is no immediate reflexivity: nothing can bear, bear on, or give birth to itself without the mediation of some other to bear it. Being born is the action of being acted on, being brought to action. *Nasco* is derived theoretically from *nascor*, not, as we would expect and often prefer to think, the inverse. One is able to beget only because and after one has been begotten. Even the idea of the deity, the uncreated creator, impersonating the assumption that there must be some indicative doing from which all the passive being done to must derive, must be the back-projected offspring of this condition. So the principle said to be self-born cannot be, in that being born is not an action one can perform for oneself. In English, being born depends not just on the care but also, in the poetic confusion of being born (as a child) and being borne (as a load), literally the carriage, of another. Everything depends on being tended.

The principle of care requires us to subordinate what might seem to be our immediate interests, to put ourselves out, as we say, from the course we might otherwise wish to follow, in order to help some other thing into being. Existing is essentially auxiliary; authority is essentially augmented. Not to care is to withdraw from involvement in the world; but any form of caring must always involve the partial retraction or digression from self, the suspension or standing down of one's primary care for oneself.

All living species, and perhaps all forms of being, exhibit care and concern for their world, if only in being selectively responsive to it, as trees, rocks, and proteins also are. Indeed, the kinds of selective attention that particular beings have toward their environments may be a sufficient definition of what they are: a species does not merely inhabit an environmental niche; it in some sense is that niche, since it can pay no attention to anything else and it forms the niche it fills. A species is a span of attention; it is coextensive with the world it cares about. Human beings inhabit, or similarly are, a much larger and much less selective economy of cares, which must be managed relative to each other. We can say that human beings must be attentive, not just to certain things in the world but to their structures of attention themselves. They must tend, or have a care for, their own forms of attentive care.

If everything depends on tending, if every tendency needs to be tended, then care is essentially temporal, for it will involve a care for the way in which time will unfold. For Heidegger, time is of the essence of care: "Because it is primordially constituted by care, any Dasein is already ahead of itself. . . . *The primordial unity of the structure of care lies in temporality*" (1962, 363, 375). We are today frequently enjoined by shop assistants and call-center workers to "bear with me." The relationship of subordination or following involved in caring or attention is preserved vestigially in a phrase like "look after," which implies a kind of following in time or space. The relation of care involves a work of watching and waiting that requires one to know what one is waiting for.

Most important, perhaps, being able to wait involves the most fundamental kind of self-curbing of all in the development both of individual humans and the species, in the capacity to defer gratification. The child taking Walter Mischel's famous Stanford marshmallow test— offered the choice of eating a marshmallow straight away or being given two to eat if as a reward for waiting fifteen minutes—recapitulates the discovery of the multiplicative power of planting seed rather than eating it, along with the advantages of keeping animals rather than merely hunting them (Mischel, Ebbesen, and Raskoff Zeiss 1972). The relation of care not only occurs in time; it perhaps brings about a new time awareness, an absorption of and in rhythms of opportunity, anticipation, growth, and fruition. The word *keep* derives from Old English *cēpan*, of which the etymology is unknown and which has no related terms in cognate languages. But it was used to translate many of the senses of Latin *servare, conservare, praeservare, reservare*, all of which include the idea of keeping safe, keeping watch over, or reserving from the effects of time. Caretaking, it seems, is timekeeping. Care invents time as projection, as the condition, not of data, being given in and as one is, but of dativity, or being-*for*.

We "take care" of business, but we "care for" only those entities that appear to us to have a capacity to care about what happens to them, that is, the kinds of thing we think of as beings rather than things. Indeed, by exercising care for abstract ideas, like "academic freedom" or "architectural heritage," we promote them into the status of beings who have a being-for-themselves, lifting them into the life we commit to preserve. That such beings can be cared for implies that they are mortal, vulnerable as well as merely frangible. To care for means to protect from danger, especially the danger of erosion or extinction in time. But if caring for means guarding against mortality, it also means assuming and maintaining the mortality, the loseability, in the terms suggested in Chapter 6, of what we care for. It is to promote what we care for into the possibility of being at risk from the very things from which we seek to protect them. Surprisingly often, that is the risk that we ourselves may pose to them. As shown by the efforts of conservationists to rescue works of art from the damage caused by the well-intentioned efforts at protection of previous conservators, we need to be careful about the ways in which we care for things. Perhaps all care must have a care regarding itself. Hence, perhaps, the special preciousness of fragile things, and the specially reflexive vigilance of the care we exercise over them.

Among these fragile things are the bodies of other living beings. The special kind of touch that is known as a "caress" derives much of its character from the quality it conveys of holding back, what in *The Book of Skin* I called "the tact of a tactility that retracts itself" (Connor 2004a, 262). Jean-Paul Sartre evokes the inductive power of this kind of touch, which, in abstaining from grasping or holding its object without letting it go, "is a *shaping*. In caressing the Other I cause her flesh to be born beneath my caress, under my fingers" (1984, 390). The caress therefore seems to enact the nonpossessive possession, responsibility without appropriation, of the action and relation of caring:

> Thus the revelation of the Other's flesh is made through my Own flesh; in desire and in the caress which expresses desire, I incarnate myself in order to realize the incarnation of the Other. The caress by realizing the Other's incarnation reveals to me my own incarnation; that is, I make myself flesh in order to impel the Other to realize for-herself and for me her own flesh, and my caresses cause my flesh to be born for me in so far as it is for the Other *flesh*

causing her to be born as *flesh*. I make her enjoy my flesh through her flesh in order to compel her to feel herself flesh. And so possession truly appears as a double reciprocal incarnation. (391)

We should not be misled by the palpable eroticism of this passage. Though it is the vehicle of erotic desire, the caress is that desire holding back from its sadistic or assumptive appetites. The caress is careful desire.

In the "Letter on 'Humanism'" of 1946 Heidegger introduces a new inflection of the idea of care, which had not previously been to the fore in his treatment of care in *Being and Time*:

> Of course the essential worth of the human being does not consist in his being the substance of beings, as the "subject" among them, so that as the tyrant of being he may deign to release the beingness of beings, into an all too loudly glorified "objectivity."
>
> The human being is rather "thrown" by being itself into the truth of being, so that ek-sisting in this fashion he might guard the truth of being, in order that beings might appear in the light of being as the beings they are.... The human being is the shepherd of being. It is in this direction alone that Being and Time is thinking when ecstatic existence is experienced as "care." (1999, 251–52)

The emphasis here is now not on "Man's *perfectio*—his transformation into that which he can be in Being-free for his ownmost possibilities" (Heidegger 1962, 243), but on his preservation of the possibility of other things coming into their being. This is the harbinger of the turn toward the mystical principle of "letting be," or *Gelassenheit*, in Heidegger's later work, a way of relating to the natural world that gives up the tyrannous desire to see the world as a collection of available objects:

> YOUNGER MAN: The human chases things around in an unrest that is foreign to them by making them into mere resources for his needs and items in his calculations, and into mere opportunities for advancing and maintaining his manipulations.
>
> OLDER MAN: By not letting things be in their restful repose, but rather—infatuated by his progress—stepping over and away from them, the human becomes the pacesetter of the devastation, which has for a long time now become the tumultuous confusion of the world. (Heidegger 2010, 149)

Although the term *care* is no longer so central in Heidegger's later thought, the idea of caring seems to have developed from the busy preoccupation with purposes and projects that is part of *Sorge* into a quieter, even quietist, attitude of careful attentiveness, a letting be that lets things come into their being. Human beings are necessary to this process, but it is also necessary that they do not intervene officiously in or seek to master it: "Thus man is originally and differently claimed by the truth of be-ing (for that is the allotted clearing). By this claim of be-ing itself, man is claimed as the guardian of the truth of be-ing (humanness as 'care,' founded in Da-sein)" (Heidegger 2000, 170).

Perhaps the most remarkable fact about Heidegger's philosophy of care is that it is a matter for beings: indeed, it may be said to be the way in which the world seems to matter for the creatures who live in it. But care is more than an attitude or outlook on existence: it is a practice, not just how the world seems to the entity known as a Being-in-the-world, but itself a mode of being in the world, a set of practices or ways of being that themselves come to constitute the social world. Even as Heidegger's work becomes even more allusively introverted, it has seemed to many to have an almost painfully direct reference to the growing problem of the human relation to the natural world, especially as it is mediated by technology. This is given focus not by the obvious kinds of technological intervention in the natural world—plows, automobiles, industrial production, electricity generation—but by newly emerging understandings of the most ancient and abiding process whereby humans have changed their environments, through the process of domestication.

## Taming

Perhaps all creatures have a relation of care to their environments. But in no other creature about which we have knowledge does it appear that caring about is so joined to caring for as in humans. Pat Shipman has suggested that the principal and overwhelming objects of human care are animals. It is so easy to be amazed and overwhelmed by the fact and the magnificence of ancient cave paintings such as those at Lascaux that one may fail to see the significance of what they largely represent: animals. As Shipman explains,

> Animals are what our ancestors were talking about through the external recording devices (paintings, sculptures, etchings, drawings, and carvings) that they devised. Animals and their anatomy and their habits—the fruits of their observations spawned by our ancient ties to animals—are what was so important to record and share that people created these artworks. (2011, 164–65)

This is the more striking given the many things we assume must have been important to prehistoric humans that are not depicted, especially human powers or relationships, and humans themselves, who are represented if at all as casual or abstract stick figures, in contrast with the careful realistic detail of animal representations. Even tools and weapons, "those magically transforming inventions of the first stage of human evolution," are nevertheless "hardly ever depicted" (165). Perhaps, however, we might discern or register an indirect depiction of tools in the very technique of depicting itself, the *techne* that is withdrawn from view in what it makes visible. Whatever the impulse to depict animals is for, instruction, pleasure, magical power, the primary purpose is identified exactly and entirely with the action of the depicting itself: it is to pay attention to them, a tending that is at work as much in their representation as in their breeding and keeping. The one tool that is often represented in such paintings, in an Escher-like handshake of implement and object, is the hand itself. If there is, as is often suggested, a magical purpose in the depictions, the promise of success in hunting through the proleptic capture of the image, for example, then what the art and its object have in common is that they involve the investment of time and the "opportunity cost" of withdrawing from other pleasures and necessities. Cave paintings depict animals, the objects of human care and concern, and in the process also make the caring for and about them itself their object.

Following the discovery by Iégor Reznikoff and Michel Dauvois (1988) that cave paintings were executed in caves characterized by high resonance, it has often been assumed that the paintings may have formed part of an audiovisual magical ritual. Steven J. Waller suggests, for example, that "Palaeolithic ungulate art was produced in response to percussive sound reflections perceived as hoofbeats. The production of hoofbeats via sound reflection could have been part of a ritual intended to summon up game" (1993, 501). We have no way of knowing whether prehistoric hominids experienced the same sense of fascinated awe at the fact of echo as modern humans. Whether or not this was the case, echo and image double each other in that both represent a return to its origin of what has been given up or given out. The image is the echo of a visual conception that comes back to the one who externalizes it on the wall; the echo is an image in sound of that reflection. As such, both are images of the essentially reflexive relation of the loss that turns to gain in the looping relation of care, in which giving and taking care in fact come to the same thing.

Many animals exploit the capacities of other animals, but human beings seem to be unique in the kind and extent of their domestication of other living creatures. All forms of domestication require close attention to the nature of the plant or animal being used as a resource. Certain animals, dogs and horses in particular, must have come to seem much more useful if they were kept alive than if they were consumed as food or for animal products like fur, because this allowed for the harnessing of their capacities for hunting and carriage. It was necessary for there to be a relationship of partial identification for humans to recognize that they could make use of animals in the way in which they made use of their own capacities. Animals acted as what Pat Shipman calls an *"extrasomatic adaptation"* (2011, 255), or living tool. All tools require forms of attention, but animals require much more intimate and continuous attention, especially if they are being bred or kept from a young age—and the domestication of a dangerous animal like the wolf would surely have started with the selection of the more docile infants. Keeping animals, both in the sense of keeping them apart from their life in the wild and in the sense of keeping them safe or sustaining them, makes for the distinctive relation of care, in which emotional bonds are likely to have grown up and been perpetuated in breeding. And, as Shipman suggests, the selective breeding may have gone in two directions: "Because humans who were more successful at handling and living with animals accrued a selective advantage, the animals undergoing domestication were effectively selecting for particular traits in humans" (2011, 258). In this close relation, animals could only be made into exploitable objects if they were in fact understood as subjective centers of existence: the exploiting subjects needed to train themselves to be carefully responsive to the animal's way of existing in the world, needed to bring it into a condition of subjecthood in order to be able to subject it to training. In Michel Serres's words, "To know, one must imitate; to train, one must know; to bring the animal into the farmyard, one must enter oneself as the counterfeit of the animal" (2001, 110; my translation).

It is only recently that we have begun to write the history of humanity in terms of its close and continuous relation to the thing it knows as nature, the realm of the merely born, and therefore of the to-be-made. It is common to represent that relation as an objectification, with the natural world thought of first as a threat to be defended against, then as a resource to be exploited through techniques of mastery. But a more encompassing understanding of this process might be that evoked in the word *domestication*, a process of making the whole of nature the concern of humanity, not to say, through economic exploitation, a going concern.

We are by no means the only creatures who exploit the capacities of other animals. But we seem to be the only animals who systematically establish practices and relations of care in our relation to animals for their own sake, or apparently so, since we are so unlikely to know what anything might turn out to be for in the long run. Very few of us now use dogs to perform work, in any traditional sense, and the thought of using cats for any kind of organized instrumental purpose beyond catching mice is proverbially comic (we say that an impossibly complex task is "like herding cats," that is, a job for which you would probably need a dog). But there are more than seventy million dogs in the United States, whose instrumental purpose, if it is to be thought of in these terms, is to perform a kind of emotional labor, as well as provide the occasion for that labor in ourselves.

There is a striking correlation between the degree of economic development of a country and the number of its domesticated dogs and cats. It is not the numbers that matter: there are many dogs in Africa, but they are much harder to count because they are, as we tellingly say, *stray*, a word that comes into English through Romance *estragare*, from Latin *extra vagari*, to wander outside. But perhaps the real extravagance in the unfolding history of human-animal relations is in the degree of domestication, forming a kind of explosion of enclosure, in which we no longer care for animals in order to have them at our disposal but keep them at our disposal in order to be able to care for them. As a result, through the process of domesticating animals, we domesticate ourselves, our feelings, and deepest impulses, generating, for example, the feeling of disgust for the idea of eating any of the animals we keep in our homes as pets rather than provender (Leach 1964, 32–33, 44).

Domestication is nowadays understood as a cooperative, coevolutionary, and reciprocally transforming process. There are many kinds and degrees of domestication, which were effected gradually, discontinuously, and variously across long periods of time. By bringing animals and plants into a new "domestic" space of care, human beings were also themselves domesticated, with different kinds of cognitive and practical capacity being "cultivated" by their charges, or by the charge itself.

More and more, we feel the need to train ourselves and each other in order to optimize our care relations with animals. Thus, we may read in a recent article on the "intervention strategies and behavior-change techniques" needed to help cat owners improve their management of domestic and stray cats, that "as the demand for better management practices of domestic cats has intensified, there has been pressure on cat owners and carers to change their behavior" (McLeod et al. 2017, 636, 637). Psychologists, social scientists, philosophers, and others interested in human-animal interactions are no longer solely concerned with the care and management of animals but are concerned also with the intellectual care and management of human-animal interactions themselves. By some way the most important concern in the management of the human menagerie seems to be the role of pets in providing therapy or increasing well-being in response to various kinds of human anxiety, ailment, and distress, followed closely by the issue of the management of human distress over pet ailment and death.

In the opening words of her study of eighteenth-century pet keeping, Ingrid Tague identifies what she sees as its central paradox: "a deep emotional attachment to individuals who provide the great gifts of 'love, happiness, and companionship' and whose loss means loneliness and, simultaneously, an awareness that those individuals are 'possessions'" (2015, 1). From the perspective of the cultivation of care, or caring for the act of care, this need not be regarded as paradoxical. One cares for that which one is assigned to provide care, as a charge or requirement. It is precisely the fact that animals are possessions, things that one has in one's keeping, that brings this responsibility. The depth of the responsibility can often make pet ownership deeply taxing rather than rewarding, even if the tax is part of the payout (Simon 1984).

In observing that "living with an animal forces a rethinking of some of the most important issues involved in what it means to live," Erica Fudge pushes us toward a recognition that our very interest in our interest in pets gives rise to a reduplicating circle of care investment (2008, 3). Part of the problem of pets is that their care is expensive, if also lucrative for some: a large industry tends to the work of tending to animals, with toys, medicine, and lifestyle accessories as well as food. To this can perhaps be added books about pets and even, if only in the smallest degree, reflections like this one. Pets occupy a central place in the human carescape, escape from this being precisely what we guard against. Donna Haraway emphasizes the many demands that training and interacting with a dog makes:

> The major demand on the human is precisely what most of us don't even know we don't know how to do—to wit, how to see who the dogs are and hear

what they are telling us, not in bloodless abstraction, but in one-on-one relationship, in other-ness-in-connection. (2003, 45)

Pets are characterized, among other things, by the fact that they have names. The naming of a pet seems to be a defining part of the relationship that is established with it. If the word *animal* signifies in part a creature without language, the expectation is that a pet will learn at least one human word, a word that will in the process become in part animalized, the sound of its name. To have a name means to have certain entitlements as an individual being, which include being "petted," caressed, fondled, or stroked. Such treatments are not limited to nonhuman animals, but in the case of a pet such treatment is part of the entitlement and part of the expectation. One is required to pet a pet, and a pet is expected to submit to being petted. That is, both parties in the pet relationship incur responsibilities, even if they are understood and nameable by only one party. The fact that such physical actions of petting among humans has become restricted to erotic or infantile relations gives a special potency to this kind of animating touch, which may be thought of in Sartrean terms as a reciprocal act of pseudo-shaping caress.

Such relationships can seem gratuitous, even grotesquely so, to those who are not of a pet-keeping disposition. But the gratuity is of the essence in the pet relation, which seems to furnish the utility of the unneeded. This relation may be related to the forms of symbolic atonement that James Serpell points to among hunting peoples, who, dependent on animals whom they have to kill, will often surround their killing and eating with complex propitiation rituals that mediate human guilt, stylizing and so holding back the simple exercise of human will (1986, 141–49). Modern pet keeping may have elements of this symbolic self-limitation of human dominance over animals, turning prerogatives into duties like paying for pet insurance and buying cats presents of play-mice at Christmas.

Peter Sloterdijk similarly suggests the parallel between the domestication of animals and the self-domestication of the human species. He reads the humanism inherited from Rome as the legacy of a struggle against the "bestialization" both of violence and of the mass media of the arena:

> Ancient humanism can be understood only when it is grasped as one opponent in a media contest: that is, as the resistance of the books against the amphitheater, and the opposition of the humanizing, patient-making, sensitizing philosophical reading against the dehumanizing, impatient, unrestrained,

sensation-mongering and excitement-mongering of the stadium. What the educated Romans called *humanitas* would have been unthinkable without the need to abstain from the mass culture of the theaters of cruelty. Should the humanist himself occasionally stray into the roaring crowd it is only to assure himself that he is also a human being and can thus be infected by bestialization. He returns from the theater to his house, shamed by his involuntary participation in the contagious sensations, and can now claim that nothing human is foreign to him. But, thereby, it is affirmed that humanity itself consists in choosing to develop one's nature through the media of taming, and to forswear bestialization. (2009b, 16)

Sloterdijk believes that this struggle for self-taming continues in the present and that "a titanic battle is being waged in our contemporary culture between the civilizing and the bestializing impulses and their associated media" (24). Just as the amphitheater was a mass medium for the Romans, so the mass media in their generality are our amphitheater, with their insatiable hunger for suffering and sadistic revenge; only now we can no longer count on the alternative source of value represented by the book and the library. Sloterdijk is not hopeful in the face of this: "Certainly any great success in taming would be surprising in the face of an unparalleled wave of social developments that seems to be irresistibly eroding inhibitions" (24).

The odd history of the word *humane* in English reflects this sense that becoming properly human requires the abnegation of the animalistic, specifically in relation to animals themselves. Originally *humane* was used as a simple alternative to *human*, rendered in different forms in Middle English as *humain, humayn, humayne, hewmayne, humaine*, and so on. But gradually the terminal *e*, perhaps with a slight suggestion of the French feminine form, and a corresponding lengthening of the vowel and shift of stress from the first to the second syllable, began to indicate not just the category of the human but also a certain ideal of human behavior, as civil, courteous, or thoughtfully obliging toward others. The earliest use of the word in this form in English may well be in an English translation from around 1500 of Jean d'Arras's prose romance *Melusine*, in which the fairy Melusine sends off her two sons on a voyage with various encouragements to behave generously and honorably, including the injunction "be meke, humble, swete, curtoys & humayne, both vnto grete & lesse" (1895, 111). During the sixteenth century, the word started to be applied to classical works imparting civilized values, *humane* here corresponding to the later *humanistic*. *Humane* came to signify the enlargement of the human in the self-limiting concern with other humans or *humanity*, the latter a word that could be used both as the name for humans in general and a name for the concern with them. The Society for the Recovery of Persons Apparently Drowned, which was founded in 1774, changed its name two years later to the Royal Humane Society. During the nineteenth century, the word *humane* began to be used specifically for measures designed to reduce or alleviate physical suffering, especially in judicial or martial contexts, where force might be applied in a mitigated form. With the rise of the antivivisection and animal-care movements of the 1890s, the word came to have a specific relation to the treatment of animals. The care for animal welfare provides the mediating, and moderating, self-supplementation necessary to be a civilized human, not just by belonging to humanity but by showing or exercising the virtue of "humanity."

## Cute

Domestication is a practice that colonizes animals twice over. First of all, it removes the animal from its natural environment. Simply keeping animals as convenient sources of fresh food need not require anything more than this relocation. But in many cases, physical relocation is followed or accompanied by a process of behavior modification to make it easier for the animal to inhabit the space of human culture without stress or difficulty to either party. The most important feature of this ethological rehabilitation is the reduction of fear and the aggression that it provokes. This requires a fundamental reorientation of the animal in relation to its environment, which Helmut Hemmer describes as "a general attenuation" in the creature's responsiveness: "Put broadly, domestic animals live less intensely than wild ones. . . . [There is] a general reduction in the significance of factors from the animate and inanimate environment including the social environment for domestic animals" (1990, 91, 92). This requires a reduction of attentiveness to the physical environment and a corresponding increase of attentiveness to the human environment. This process has two outcomes: human keepers gain an animal that is *tractable*, a word that suggests able to be led or drawn, as domesticated animals must be; and animals gain a degree of security from want, predation, and injury compared with life outside the human *domus*. They trade submission and aggression for care.

This is the same bargain that humans themselves needed to make in order to be able to sustain their large and complex communities. The process is assisted by the phenomenon known as *neoteny*, or extended youth (from Greek νέος, young + τείνειν, to extend). Indeed, the process often involves not only retention of infant behavior but a kind of regressive infantilization. Our family cat Leila came to us as many cats must have done in the course of human history; having lived wild for some months, she began to visit us in the hope of food and was eventually taken in, as we also were. But her behavior was nothing like that of other cats we knew: she was silent, easily alarmed, and could not stand to be touched in any way. Eventually, she began to enjoy being stroked, as noted in Chapter 4, started to meow when she began to have success with it as a social signal, and when particularly content while being stroked or scratched, would "knead" the air with her paws, in a recapitulation of the gentle beckoning scratch that kittens use on their mother to stimulate milk flow. Domesticating Leila meant teaching her how to be a "cat," habituating her to a life of play rather than aggression, and substituting behaviors characteristic of kittens for those of adult cats. To be a pet is to live in petition. Not only is the animal's behavior thereby more dependable; it becomes as a consequence able to depend on its owners for its care and upkeep.

Behavior is reinforced by appearance, as captive animals are modified by breeding and environment to acquire less aggressive skull and facial features that make them resemble the young of their own species. Konrad Lorenz first drew attention in 1943 to the phenomenon of what he called the *Kindchenschema* or "infant schema" in triggering reactions of caring and tenderness toward young (274–77). In human babies, this means a round head that is much larger in relation to the body than that of adults, a domed forehead, large round eyes, and a small nose. Lorenz's work has triggered a large number of investigations of how and why humans find such features "cute." It is intriguing that this quality, which is widely recognized across cultures, with terms like *kawaii* in Japanese, *mignon* in French, *sudara* in Punjabi, and *ke ai* in Chinese, should not have had a name in English until the mid-1800s, and that, as Ralf C. Buckley (2016) observes, there is no word for the sensation induced by cuteness.

The cute is the infrared of the nonthreatening, the intensification of non-aggression into helplessness. Not only are you safe from something that looks cute; you are strongly aware that it is defenseless against you. It is striking that many of the cutest animals are the young of what as adults may be large and physically threatening—puppies, piglets, bear and tiger cubs, elephant calves. This signal seems to be strongly associated with the instinct to care, which may be regarded as a kind of active inhibition of aggression.

The facial changes in domesticated species correspond to those that have taken place in humans, whose protruding muzzles and eye ridges have been softened and rounded in ways that mirror those in our domesticated animals. Modern humans showing anger or aggression are likely to compress the face, making it wider by baring the teeth, but also emphasizing the protrusion of the nose and eyebrows by drawing them together. The view that joined eyebrows signal a brutish nature or lack of intelligence indicates a strong responsiveness in particular to the eyebrow, which in modern anatomical humans is highly mobile and, of course, in women in particular, subject to extensive secondary symbolic modification. Since the late nineteenth century, the height or lowness of the brow has been thought to be a measure of cultural or intellectual refinement. In particular, the flattening of the forehead in modern humans means that they are able to move their eyebrows vertically, which widens the eyes and "opens" the face. Drivers and pedestrians wishing to signal appeal, acquiescence, and acceptance silently and at a distance, can do so effectively by raising and arching their eyebrows, which makes of the face an open palm. Digital modeling of the brow ridge in an archaic hominin known as Kabwe 1, a specimen of *Homo heidelbergensis*, has recently suggested that the large mass of bone in this area does not have structural or mechanical functions. Its diminishment in modern humans accompanies the development of "capacities to dynamically express affiliative prosocial emotions through highly mobile eyebrows" (Godinho, Spikins, and O'Higgins 2018, 959). The most important factor here is the replacement of permanent with mobile features, fixed bone becoming malleable flesh. "Animality" is therefore not replaced by a more "human appearance," since human appearance implies a variability that can include the animal as part of its repertoire—so that Darwin could propose that sneering and snarling would expose the canine teeth and that "the mouth being closed, a lowering brow and a slight frown" would give rise to "a dogged or obstinate expression" (1998, 23).

In fact, in evolving away from aggression into communication, human beings have evolved themselves into the direction of the cute. Ironically, where the openness of human facial features suggests the capacity for variation, the cute face may be regarded as a kind of mask of openness, the face frozen in a permanent startle: babies and young animals have no option but to look cute, unlike starlets or certain annoyingly self-aware children (indeed, not realizing you are cute is a particularly winning aspect of it). This may help account for the otherwise peculiar evolution of the word *cute* from *acute*, the primary meaning of which is sharp, from Latin *acus*, a needle, and which is then transferred to qualities of being sharp-witted, keen, subtle, discriminating. During the middle of the nineteenth century, the word *cute* started to be extended to neatly or prettily contrived objects. One may catch the word in course of evolution in Nathaniel Parker Willis's *Rural Letters*, where one character says that a "patent corn-sheller" is a "'purty cute tool," though the speaker disapproves of the device, remarking that "there aint no other hard work they haint economized" (1849, 158). The *OED* points, shrewdly enough, to a parallel American usage, of *cunning* to mean quaintly attractive: the word is both employed and explained in a novel of 1888 when introducing a young woman character as

> a rather petite figure, brunette in complexion, with a face that was interesting and intelligent, and that had an odd look hard to analyze, but which came perhaps from a slight lack of symmetry. As a child, she had been called "cunning," in the popular American use of the word when applied to children; that is to say, piquantly interesting; and this characteristic of quaint piquancy of appearance she retained, now that she was a young woman of eighteen. (Eggleston 1888, 9)

This usage matches *canny* in the Northern English sense of agreeable, attractive, or taking, a word that is itself often used of children and comfortably neat things. The evolution of *cute* also parallels that of *nice*, which has moved similarly from the idea of precision to pleasantness. So the cute involves a combination of nonthreatening smallness and dainty (a diminution of Latin *dignus*, worthy) contrivance. The cute appears comfortable and accommodating, even as it also suggests a certain fragility. Thus it attracts while also suggesting the need for a certain careful retraction, so as to avoid rough handling.

Dogs, cats, cubs, and calves are especially cute in photographs. This may be because being photographed redoubles their vulnerability and captive status: they are captive not just in being domesticated but also in being detained in the zoophotographic apparatus. One might even suggest that something that looks cute already looks like an image of itself. This is perhaps an extra dimension of the paradox of artifactual innocence. It is striking that many of the investigations of cuteness in academic studies of the phenomenon make use of techniques of digital morphing, which allow for the production of reliable gradients of more and less cute faces; there always appears to be craft, if not exactly craftiness, in cuteness. The idea that our pet animals are a kind of artifact is apparent, not just in the culture of dog shows but in the willingness of some owners to have their animals stuffed after their deaths. Representations of animals seem to evolve in parallel with the evolution we have encouraged in domesticated animals themselves. Stephen Jay Gould (1980) shows how the figure of Mickey Mouse evolved from the early 1930s, in which he appeared distinctly mouselike, with a protruding snout, to the pudgier, more wide-eyed and childishly flat-faced Mickey of later years. Robert A. Hinde and I. A. Barden found a parallel evolution in teddy bears from a 1903 example, which had a low forehead, long snout and muzzle, to larger foreheads and flatter faces, leading the authors to suggest that "we can thus picture the process involved in the evolution of such artefacts as a form of selection determined by human preferences" (1985, 1372).

Gary D. Sherman and Jonathan Haidt propose that cuteness should be understood not as activating impulses to care but to social involvement more generally, on the grounds that cuteness seems to increase the action of "mentalizing"—imputing human thoughts and feelings to the entity in question—thereby acting as "a mechanism that 'releases' sociality (e.g., play and other affiliative interactions" (2011, 246). They propose that "cuteness expands the moral circle and that it does so by motivating sociality, which in turn activates processes of mind perception" (248). Their argument seems to make an unnecessarily and implausibly sharp distinction between caretaking and socially affiliative actions. At the same time it helpfully focuses attention on the ways in which social affiliation, or "caring about" some other being, may be allied with "caring for." For creatures as highly socialized as humans, social affiliation is an essential form of care, and the refusal of affiliation is in itself a kind of abandonment. So the play relation may be already a relation of care. Playing almost always involves playing at and playing with threat, competition, and conflict, often in animals as a way of rehearsing skills that may be needed for attack and defense. Play is not just one form of social affiliation among others: it is the principal means whereby creatures learn the difference between real and symbolic violence, in the process learning the principles of reciprocal care.

This should help make sense of the fact that children should spend so much time playing games of care and should themselves seem so susceptible to the care solicitations of the cute. To care for somebody is always to invite that person into the sanctuary of the symbolic, the arena and possibility of play, a space of action held aside from the dangerous reality of the actual. As

Sherman and Haidt suggestively note, "Cuteness is as much an elicitor of play as it is of care. It is as likely to trigger a childlike state as a parental one" (2011, 248). Care and play are reciprocally mediating ways of keeping threats at bay. One study, however, did find a distinction between play and care: younger children were more likely both to prefer adult-featured teddy bears and to want to play with them, while older children preferred baby-faced bears that they liked to cuddle and sleep with. The authors conclude that "teddy bears are now better at being bought by adults, not better at being cuddled by the young children they are usually bought for" (Morris, Reddy and Bunting 1995, 1699).

The care reaction induced by cuteness can often, however, appear to be mingled with its contrary. A group of psychologists at Yale University found that babies with more obviously cute characteristics induced not only higher positive emotions but also higher feelings of aggression (Aragón et al. 2015). In another study, designed to investigate the desire to squeeze the care-inducing object, subjects shown pictures of appealing babies were invited to handle bubble wrap and pop as many bubbles as they felt like: increasing the cuteness seemed to increase the number of bubbles popped (Arnold 2013). Such studies may measure the common ludic ravening response, in which the baby may be pinched or the toes mock-munched. The authors of this study hypothesize that, far from being the sign of a dangerous ambivalence in our relations to the young and helpless, this kind of dimorphic play is a way of taming or tamping down the overflow of categories that is often a feature of strong emotions (weeping for joy). Adults are (usually) as skilled in holding back the instinct to tear and consume to which they seem to be giving expression as cats who keep their claws retracted in playing with their kittens.

Sianne Ngai finds this ambivalence embodied in the physical design of cute objects, like sponge bath toys, which sometimes seem to invite us to squeeze or squash them out of shape:

> The epitome of the cute would be an undifferentiated blob of soft doughy matter. Since cuteness is an aestheticization of powerlessness ("what we love because it submits to us"), and since soft contours suggest pliancy or responsiveness to the will of others, the less formally articulated the commodity, the cuter. The bath sponge makes this especially clear because its purpose is to be pressed against a baby's body and squished in a way guaranteed to repeatedly crush and deform its already somewhat formless face. (2012, 64)

The enjoyability of this Barthesian evocation, which actually redoubles the effect its describes, by making it seem that there is no end to the forensic prodding and poking to which the object may be half-playfully subjected and no way for the object to resist it, helps disguise its wrongness, even in terms of some of the other examples that Ngai provides, which tend rather to emphasize the delicacy and fragility of cute things. Ngai generalizes her example into the claim that "in cuteness, it is crucial that the object has some sort of imposed-on mien—that is, that it bears the look of an object unusually responsive to and thus easily shaped or deformed by the subject's feeling or attitude toward it" (65). But if this is true of the bath toy, it is because it may seem exceptionally to allow it, perhaps because, like cartoon animations, it combines softness with a certain sluggish resilience, which allows it, really rather unlike dough, precisely to resist deformation and slowly to resume its contours.

By no means do all cute things have this kind of softness, though it may be that there is a certain permission given in such objects for the destructive aggression that has often been noticed in the child's relation to the toy. It is a permission that Daniel Harris gives himself in his caustic assault on the manipulative images of helplessness to be found in cute things, their "aura of motherlessness, ostracism and melancholy, the silent desperation of the lost puppy dog clamoring to be befriended—namely to be bought" (2001, 5). No revenge, it seems, can be too much, or can be too bad for something revealed to be appallingly purchasable (or, of course, by extension, somebody who offers us something for sale). Harris notes and enjoys the revenge of what he calls the "anti-cute" in a film like *Gremlins*, which, he tells us

> launches a frontal assault on fuzzy-wuzziness with a blitz of images of the child as the petulant and demanding brat who disdains all the sacrosanct laws of property ownership, gleefully annihilating cuisinarts and microwaves as he mows a broad swathe of destruction through the household's inner sanctum. (2001, 19)

Recent accounts of cuteness similarly emphasize its role in the intensified love of things characteristic of what is called commodity culture. As Sianne Ngai writes, "With its exaggerated passivity, there is a sense in which the cute thing is the most reified or thinglike of things, the most objectified of objects or even an 'object' par excellence" (2012, 93) The aggression buried in cuteness can be redirected into sharp-toothed critique at the expense of cuteness, thereby defending against the sentimental softening that cuteness seems to solicit and imply. The cultural critic must be on her guard against the melting effects of what she analyzes, like Lenin, who told Gorky,

> I can't listen to music very often, it affects my nerves. I want to say silly things and pat the heads of those who can create such beauty, although they live in a filthy hell. One can't pat anyone on the head nowadays, they might bite your hand off. They ought to be beaten on the head, beaten mercilessly, though we pursue ideals opposed to any violence against people. (Ulyanov and Peshkov 2003, 289)

The disinhibition of aggressive critique cooperates with the inhibition of analytic distance, which displays the immunity of intelligence from the factitious seductions of coochy-coo caring; so acuteness defends against the defenselessness of being made to care in cuteness. Given the familiarity of the sawtooth critical defense in academic writing about popular culture, it is hard to know whether to see this as the release of hostility in disinhibition or another round in the spiral of domestication. On the whole it seems safe to assume the latter, that is, that the cultic nature of academic critique is enough to render it charmingly and engagingly *cutique*. Ngai finds in the preoccupation of the artistic avant-garde with the cute an allegory of its own powerlessness, and it is hardly worth the trouble, which I nevertheless hereby decline to spare myself, of pointing to the way in which this implicates the critic as well:

> All the poetic explorations of cuteness . . . can be read as a way of grappling with oft-made observations about the literary avant-garde's social powerlessness, its practical ineffectualness in the "overadministered world" it nonetheless persists in imagining as other than what it is. (Ngai 2012, 97)

The idea that popular images of cuteness are a way of playing with and playing out the sheer silliness of cultural critique may provoke a stern determination to squeeze triggers rather than babies' toes. But another view would be that the work of symbolic play, and playing with symbols, whether in the avant-garde or in advanced cultural analysis, is indeed part of a process of rendering or keeping things harmless that, so far, has proved even more powerful than power, or the urge to urgency it embodies.

It is hard not to feel queasy about the extension of cuteness to the natural world, in what might be seen as a sort of Bambified ecology. (Bambi is a girl's name, short for "bambina.") But it is possible to see the emergence of a rather different, less purely sentimental, relation of care for the natural world. The human struggle to free itself from necessity, which has taken the form of a struggle against the shocks and privations of a natural condition, may be said not just to have had a historical form, but to have formed history itself. Nature is time and in a sense is nothing else but the pure succession and elapsing of events, without memory or recurrence. Nature records but does not remember or anticipate. Human actions have wrestled history out of the pure temporality of nature. Nature is and has history but is not historical; humans are historical in that they have a relation to the time that they live through and live out, living both in retrospect and prospect.

# Conclusion
## Ministering

IT IS A well-mannered gesture to one's readers to offer them at the end of a book a reminder of what they are nevertheless assumed to know already for themselves through having read it. It would be reasonable for an inquiry into the modes and manners of giving way to conclude with some reassuringly inclusive statement about the substantial unity of the subject under review. Put at its simplest, this book has concerned itself with the different forms taken by what Robin Fox argues should be regarded as a drive to inhibition (1994, 79). I have wanted to show that this is more than a tendency, or even a capacity, to give way self-preservingly in the face of threat or danger. I have wanted to show that the apparent action of withdrawing from action, or giving up one's capacity for it, is itself a complex, powerful, and purposive form of action.

In this case, however, there is a difficulty, announced in my opening chapter and scarcely resolved even at this late moment, which is that we are so unaccustomed to thinking of the ways of exercising this drive to inhibition as any kind of positive. This seems to me to be linked to the strange fact that there are few ways of designating the forms of this drive, faculty, or disposition inclusively. It seems to be the fate of the nonpositive to resist singularity and to be forced to exist in the condition of plurality and dispersal. So the chapters of this book are not to be thought of as a complete and integrated account of the workings of social inhibition. Rather, they are, as I suggested at the end of Chapter 1, an attempt to decline some of its cases, occasions, or dispositions, that is, ways of varying or adjusting position, a process that I have called modulation.

Yet, if the sign of a genuinely interesting question is the fact that it generates an open rather than an exhaustible set of instances and occasions, then, of all topics, this one might be expected to display this characteristic. For the attempt to count the ways in which giving way can manifest itself is intended not just to allow for the recognition of core or recurrent features but also to emphasize the generativity of those ways of giving way. There may not be an obvious limit to the number of modes in which giving way can come about because modularity is so intrinsic to it. Giving way can not only be discerned in different kinds of disposition; it may even be defined, and may perhaps not be definable in any other way, as the substitution of manner for the matter of fact and the letting of symbolic variability into whatever might otherwise appear to be rawly and invariantly the case. It is hard to be definitive about the nature of giving way, since definiteness is one of the things that must give way for it to happen. The way that giving way works is by giving a way for things to be. The claim and clemency of giving way therefore echo with what Wallace Stevens calls "the beauty of inflections," which leaves him undecided whether to prefer "The blackbird whistling / Or just after" (2015, 100).

Although its concern has been with minorizing modes, of dialing down and scaling back, the book may be seen as itself describing a series of ever-expanding circles. My starting point was with discussions of some of the more implicit and small-scale kinds of human interactions involved in codes and conventions of politeness, as these are manifest in the nuances of idiom and accentuation. In the next chapter, the linguistic dispositions of politeness are amplified in the discussions of gesture and bodily disposition. The socially cohering effects of these actions are the subject of the larger-scale "cohibitions," or collectivizing inhibitions to the fore in Chapter 4. If the discussion of the workings of apology in Chapter 5 may be regarded as in one sense a retraction from larger social structures to fix on a particular feature of local, person-to-person interactions, this is *reculer pour mieux sauter*, since the real point at issue in the chapter is on the telling interferences of the small and large when such actions are made to perform as part of a repertoire of grandly historical gestures of penitence and recantation, a political dramaturgy of how to undo things with words. In Chapter 6, the focus expands beyond the vicissitudes of winning and losing among the living to encompass the ways of living out the largest loss of all, the mortal loss of oneself to oneself in death.

Chapter 7 widens the aperture even further to consider the dimensions of care that extend beyond intrahuman to human-animal and finally human-inhuman relations and responsibilities.

In this sense, the variability in depth of focus that characterizes the investigation of the focus depth at which the investigation has been conducted matches the duality that is a feature of giving way itself. The question of scale is always at work in the operations of giving way. The possibility of enlargement seems to be secreted in every willing inhibition, the performing on oneself of a diminishment always allows the assuming of a dilation.

But, it may be objected, and may have been objected throughout the reading of this book (and if so, I must thank my readers for their courtesy in persisting this far), that possibility is not actuality, and the actuality of giving way remains, as it has been in most human times and most human places, the negative and thoroughly wretched experience of force and subjugation, against which the only remedy is empowerment and the generalization of agency. If this is the case, then the proponents of agency have little to complain of, for the assertion of agency, marching always arm in arm with the agency of assertion, remains everywhere in the ascendant. The unquestionability of the value of agency makes it difficult to see all the comportments I have been considering in this book as anything other than enforced or defeated passivity. Not to agree to the universal injunction to activism, not to assent to assertion, is, we seem to be warned, to perpetrate on oneself the ultimate *felo de se*, in the withering wrong of self-subjugation or self-silencing. I suggested at the beginning of this book that such universal bearing of arms, and the inevitably consequent view of human relations as nothing other than this kind of war of every kind of agency against every other, could be regarded as the generalization into a universal principle of the kind of phallic assertion and patterns of aggression previously identified exclusively with male behavior.

That kind of thinking would make it easy to see the arguments I have assembled here for the assertion of nonassertion, in the arts and actions of modulation, withdrawal, and standing aside, as essentially female, with female experience as a rich reservoir of such possibilities. If, as Peter Sloterdijk counsels, the path of civilization is the only one that remains open, that may seem to point to the active cultivation of self-limitation as an essentially female disposition and to amount to an assertion of the need for cooperative female values to replace male ones. Such a view would have the virtue of a kind of clarity, even if the cultivation of the instincts and actions of self-limit as distinctively female virtues is unlikely to recommend itself to many feminists, given that it seems to require assent to all the many ways in which girls and women have historically been pressured to limit their own potential and ambition in order to leave the way rampagingly clear for males to fulfill theirs. If females have developed, or been encouraged to assume, certain kinds of expertise in these areas, becoming skilled, as we are often urged to believe, in the other-directed skills of caring and cooperation, it is becoming clear how very easily these dispositions can be reassigned or simply abandoned. It would not be hard, however, to point to the many ways in which boys and men have been encouraged to form their ideas of themselves through modes of inhibition and restraint, albeit often exercised for the purpose of self-fulfillment rather than to allow for the fulfillment of others. This is not to say that feminists, and others, would not be glad to see statutes of self-limitation applied in many more areas of male behavior.

In any case, the question of whether women or men have more resources with regard to the capacity for standing aside, and whether the values of giving way and standing back are congenitally female or must necessarily remain so, should not really have much bearing here, since this book is not intended as an assertion of the values of self-limit against the values of aggressive self-augmentation, in any kind of militant irenism. It has been written as and intended to be not so much an urging to action as an invitation to attention, in the recognition of all the many different forms of inhibitive routines, rituals, and behaviors that seem irresistibly to arise in human social arrangements. I hope I have managed sufficiently to insist that the arts of inhibition are not in fact the opposite of action but rather the modulation of action and, therefore, the action of modulation. If I have not succeeded, I think it will have to be allowed that it is not for want of trying.

Gender arrangements, which so often seem to depend on the formalized distribution of activity and passivity, as though they were opposites, and perhaps in order to ensure that they remain so, seem often to be the expression of these systems of inhibition or modulation. But I think it would be unwise to come to rest on gender arrangements as their occasioning cause or governing frame, and therefore to assume that inhibition exists in order to secure gender differences rather than that gender differences fulfill an accessory if powerful function in accomplishing the work of inhibition. Gender may be regarded as one of the most prominent ways of effecting the work of modulation. That is, it may modulate or give a variable form and form of variation to the abstract work of modulation itself. Theorists of gender and activists concerned with challenging and changing the distributions of activity and passivity are understandably less concerned with the grammar of these social relations than with the local conditions of their enactment. But the striking transformability of those relations is an indication that gender relations, though apparently ubiquitous and everywhere dominant, are ultimately only a local and contingent vehicle of that grammar of dynamisms. Naturally enough, to say that something is not all important is very far from saying it has no importance at all. This is why gender relations feature throughout this book as an unignorable part of the staging of relations of aggression and submission, even though gender has not been presented, any more than any other systems of unequal dominion, exercised through class, wealth, the thing we persist in calling "race," or beauty, as the ultimately containing frame or determining instance of these dynamisms. If the growth of civilization, which has already helped make us the only species in which the young routinely know their grandparents, continues to extend the average age of humans, we may well start to see the standoff between aggression and its modulations not primarily in terms of male and female but in terms of young and old.

*Grammar* can be a somewhat intimidating word, but if a grammar may be said to have a point, even a grammar of human comportments, it is not primarily to constrain possibilities but to release them. The rules of a game are ultimately what permit it to be played. We should not assume that if modesty, deference, and self-restraint have indeed been used to implant obedience, credulity, and servility or thereby to create and sustain relations of human misery and subordination, as they assuredly have, that this is all they have ever been used for or the only use they could ever have.

At the same time, and demurring from the apparently regnant assumption among readers of academic books that only absolute and greedily reductive claims can have any reckonable force, I would prefer not to have fathered on me the suggestion that the inhibitive drive or the capacity to give way provides everything we need to dispose of want, danger, injustice, and violence. One reader of a version of this book objected, in the face of what he or she took to be its urging, as a governing political principle and objective, of courtesy and consideration, that such milksop values are of little use in standing up to tyranny. After all, my reader scolded me, we can be sure that many imperialists and Nazis had exquisite manners. This is a variation of the showstopping *also-sprach-Hitler* gambit, which proclaims that the sentiments voiced by one's opponent are just what the Nazis would have said, at which point no further rational discussion is possible. But no such general claims for the omnipotence of the impotential will be found by a fair-minded reader of this book. Be it known that I am not suggesting that a "return" to civility will save us. Since this aims to be primarily a work of description rather than a campaign of redemption, I am not suggesting that anything will necessarily save us, in the grandiose sense of redeeming us or delivering us whole.

But there may be a more modulated, vernacular understanding of saving that has less to do with the perilous drive to salvation than with the pragmatic aim of keeping safe and holding back. For it does seem that, although human beings, young, old, male, female, are unlikely any time soon to give up their attachment to striving and thymotic self-assertion, they are nevertheless going to have to recognize, perhaps for the first time in their history, that, if they are to have any further history to be looked back on, and if there is to be anyone to perform the retrospect, getting bigger can no longer be regarded as identical with staying in being. If we are serious about developing a flipped version of the trick evoked in my opening pages, in "being forward in going backward" with regard to environmental degradation, thereby effecting an astonishing and historically unprecedented reversal in our dispositions toward ourselves and the world, it may turn out to be helpful to recognize that we are not entirely without resources in that immoderate undertaking.

All beings defend themselves against the contingencies of their environment and attempt to ensure their survival through reproduction. In all other organisms of which we have knowledge, this involves carving or transacting a habitat, an island of negentropic exception from a more general and more threatening environment. For most of their history, human beings have been subject to this law of habitat that decrees one can live only in one place or one kind of place. Human beings, like saxifrage, termites, swallows, and beavers, have always needed spaces of apartness—caves, houses, cities, localized habitats—within which to shelter and survive. But human beings have gradually lost their agoraphobia, making themselves an exception from the law of exception in the natural world by borrowing from it the principle of portable immunology, first of all by means of clothes, and the supplies and equipment we carry with us, and then within the artificial environments of ships, cars, trains, and airplanes, encapsulated spaces that allow us to traverse the seas, skies, and even space itself while never leaving home. Human beings have become ectopic, epidemic. In part this is because human beings have also constructed virtual spaces, of communication and information, that constitute new forms of immunity and shelter. I need razor and toothbrush when I travel, but a large proportion of my remaining personal and professional needs are supplied by the eduroam computing network that coddles me wherever I go. The two words that summarize this development are the words that first became familiar during the 1970s: "Mission Control." The sending out, or physical emission, of humans to unimaginable distances was governed by a fragile web of transmissions that made it possible to exist in previously uninhabitable habitats.

Spaces of apartness become and bring about temporal differentials: the hibernating bear slows time within its den. So to occupy all of space means to occupy all of time, or to inhabit different times at the same time. But under conditions of total occupation, it no longer makes any sense to speak of occupancy. Total occupation becomes a kind of exposure, to limit in every direction. Under such circumstances, the power to control one's environment becomes the responsibility to maintain it. Human beings need to be the caretakers of time. That is, human beings must take charge of historical time in order precisely to abolish irreversibility. Never again can there be a Never Again.

This represents the compounding of expedition and inhibition on the very largest scale. Remote sensing of forest growth, sea levels and currents, and animal movements are required in order to ensure the continuing noninterference of humans with their environments. In one sense, the creation of what, since the 1970s, has increasingly been known as *sustainability*, in economics, architecture, and energy use, is focused on the ambition of continuing to be able to make use of what we call a renewable resource. But the earlier history of the word, from Latin *sub-* + *tenire*, thus uphold or underpin, implies the sustenance that sustains us. Michel Serres's formulation, that "we end up depending on that which has recently ended up depending on us" (2008a, 177; my translation), captures the percolation of positions that implicates the subject's care for itself in the care for its objects.

In a sense the era of sustainability has been anticipated in a necessity that had become a familiar, but unnoticed part of social life since the industrial revolutions of the seventeenth century onward. Technology comes into being as a means of labor saving, a way of economizing on effort and thereby increasing human power. But there was always a secret cost, which has become ever more unignorable over the centuries. For every item of equipment deteriorates or malfunctions. When the fabricator of an object is also its user, the blunting of a blade or the slackening of a bowstring can quickly be made good. But as technologies become more complex and specialized, the skills of maintenance and repair become more remote and specialized. It was not perhaps until the late nineteenth century that maintenance became an extended, permanent necessity: the tinker's van grew into the Maintenance Department, and later the "administration."

Nowadays, when our technologies are black boxes made up of black boxes connected together, nobody knows how to mend any of the most important pieces of electronic equipment, such as cars, computers, and televisions, on which we depend. Repair consists simply of sending away for a replacement component. "Mission Control" now means something like the process of intensive care, the process of maintaining a continuous state of remission from the state of collapse or disrepair. T. S. Eliot evokes something like this condition in his blending of the theological and the medical in *East Coker*:

> The whole earth is our hospital
> Endowed by the ruined millionaire,
> Wherein, if we do well, we shall
> Die of the absolute paternal care
> That will not leave us, but prevents us everywhere. (1969, 181)

The advent of ongoing prevention, in such a dispensation, is not only better than cure; it displaces the very idea of it.

Peter Sloterdijk has unfolded in the final volume of his Spheres trilogy the great paradox of what T. W. Adorno following Max Weber called, with horror, the "administered world." Modernity, Sloterdijk writes, is to be understood not as secularization, imperialism, the cult of progress, the abandonment of traditional forms of privilege, or any of the other candidate definitions previously advanced, but as the extension of the principle of "explicitation" (2004, 87; my translation). The modern world is a world in which what had previously been implicit has to become explicit, as everything is subject to the imperative of design and therefore modifiability: not just consumer goods, but different aspects of the physical environment and, through more and more means of monitoring, the body itself. Chris Otter has shown that the development of technologies of artificial light, through gas and then electricity, not only made it possible to extend the possibilities of inspection, for example, into underground sewers, but also created new necessities for the continuous care of infrastructure, through metering, monitoring, and maintenance. If a literal work of bringing to light was essential to the extension to the project of nineteenth-century social and statistical surveillance, it also created the necessity for what Otter calls the "government of the eye," or sociotechnical ophthalmology. Maintenance became "a permanent and large-scale endeavor" (Otter 2008, 146). *Infrastructure*, a word that enters English in the 1920s, is the making and, more important, the keeping conscious of the unconscious. The three great conflicts of the twentieth century, the First, Second and Cold Wars, were all won by efficiency rather than force, by the side that was best able to mobilize its entire population to maximize economic output, so much so that the Cold War could be won through economic mobilization alone. Rosalind Franklin, who did so much in her photographic work literally to bring the structure of DNA to light, began her scientific career during the war investigating the porosity of coal (Maddox 2002, 83–84).

"O, I have ta'en / Too little care of this," says King Lear on the heath, confronted with the evidence of human wretchedness (Shakespeare 1997, 273), and the demand for government to exercise government over every aspect of its citizens' lives, not least in keeping them safe from the state itself, is maintained at a maximum. The twin demands of the media are first that nothing should be neglected, so that a government minister must be personally aware of every single sentence and statistic that is communicated in her department, lest she be guilty of not knowing about something said or done "on her watch," and second that the chokehold of self-serving administrators and bureaucracy be kept to a minimum.

Perhaps all empires are condemned to decay into administration. Every blitzkrieg of the lightning-fast race across empty and unresisting territory must be followed by the laying of cables, the putting down of resistance, the installation of civil servants, the building of new churches, or modification of the old. As the invading soldier Lieutenant Tonder in John Steinbeck's *The Moon Is Down* (1942) moans hysterically: "Conquest after conquest, deeper and deeper into molasses. . . . Flies capture two hundred miles of new flypaper" (1995, 68). Every invasion is a similarly glorious victory for Flykind. Revolutions and invasions are defeated not by resistance or counterrevolutions but by the autoresistance of implementation. The desire for *Lebensraum* is always a lust to escape reflexivity: we may feel we assert or establish ourselves as we advance into empty space, or a space we evacuate by our very advance, but in fact we find ourselves longing to escape the ordure of things, the stale latrines of self-habituation. Wherever there is settlement, there is the problem of waste disposal, hence the periodic spasms of resurgent nomadism, of which the most recent is the prospect of colonizing voyages to other planets to escape the self-poisoning of the earth. Rather than cleaning up, we have always assumed, we can clear out.

But the alternative to an administered world in the dominative Adornian sense is a religious and medical sense of *ministering*, a word that, in Latin, matches the twin sense of caring: *ministrare* means to manage, govern, direct, but also, via the swivel of having charge of, that is, being charged with a charge, means to attend, wait on, or serve. The word *minister* is formed as the minor form of *magister*, a master, and connects with a family of words signifying minority, diminution, and diminishment, for example, Greek μειόω, to lessen, and Sanskrit *mī-, minā-*, to reduce, diminish, destroy, as enlargements of two Indo-European roots, *mei-* and *men-*, indicating smallness (Ernout and Meillet 2001, 405).

But pending the development of plausible ways of finding alternative interstellar habitats for human beings and the various other terrene organisms we would need to take with us, it looks as though the only alternative may be a radically modified relation to our planet. Michel Serres offers an unusually positive and expansive view of this relation in his *Hominescence* (2001). The second section of the book begins by describing the dramatic decline in the human involvement with agriculture, which Serres, himself the product of a rural upbringing in the Garonne region of Southwest France, sees as the most dramatic event of recent human history. He reads this development as the replacement of one kind of shared home—that of the domestication of animals, in which human beings brought certain species in from the condition of wildness—to a second, shared habitat, in which human technology and knowledge create a kind of global home of knowledge, encompassing—and having responsibility for—all species. Being in charge of must change to being charged with. Serres calls this new interspecific collective body the Biosoma (2001, 106). He argues that, while the relation with other animals has always been at the root of human knowledge, glossing "conscience" as "knowledge-with" (127), now in the "second domestication" (115), human beings will take into protective custody all the species of the earth: "Technologies and the extension of the town will affect all wild species, situated between extinction and protection by the second wave of captivity as the universe has recently become the farm of knowledge" (115). With this "codomestication" (153), which is inevitably also a kind of "code-domestication," in which technology and technique effect a blending and coproduction of senses and faculties, the human will become, in a term that Serres borrows from genomic biology, *totipotent*, able to turn and be turned to anything.

This means that, in a certain sense, we have gone beyond the condition of habitation, as this has traditionally been understood, meaning the necessity of belonging to a particular place, habitat, or niche. We are in the process, Serres believes, of constructing a global new domain that is the integral of all particular niches, taking us decisively beyond the Heideggerian necessity of "being-there" that has always attached to embodied creatures. Such an expansion will disturb our traditional understanding of the subjects and objects of knowledge, even to the point of making us the mediators of a kind of "autocomprehension" of the world by itself (Serres 2001, 153).

But this huge enlargement of possibility creates anxiety, and the desire for disavowal:

> We hide ourselves from this totipotence, because it implies, not just a theodicy, but an anthropodicy, meaning the appearance before a tribunal of the one responsible, henceforth the human, for all the ills of the earth. For we have deposited this power in our own body, our own intelligence and our own capacities along with the atom bomb, genetic engineering, and population explosion, in short our integration into the becoming of the world. In producing or receiving totipotence, our metamorphic destiny converges today with omniresponsibility. (Serres 2001, 164)

A prospect like this may appear nightmarishly dystopian, compared with what seems like the alternative option of human self-limitation, a dramatic pulling back and stepping aside from human colonization of the earth. This latter option has been given articulation and encouragement by E. O. Wilson (2016), in his "half-earth" proposal that human beings resolve to vacate and give over to nonhuman species half of the available space of the earth by land and sea. Wilson's proposal, which is in fact given encouragement by the irresistible push to urban dwelling that is leading to the depopulation of rural landscapes in many parts of the world, has the rapturous attraction of all radicality, in its suggestion that the complex and diversified problem of diversity destruction requires and will respond to a simple and dramatic solution, a drastic and world-historical No applied to the catastrophic and aggrandizing Yes of human domination of the planet.

The strange thing about this proposal is that its attractiveness participates in the very logic of abandonment that is available only to a nomad able to move away from the space she has contaminated. In the half-earth proposal, instead of moving elsewhere, into free space, one moves back, away from space. Its strength lies in the proposition that time can be turned backward and, as long as we are able to let be and leave well alone, "nature" will regenerate itself. But the logic is still that everything can be left behind, even if the abandonment is now one of prudent retreat rather than reckless advance.

The idea also has the powerful perversity of the principle that the very difficulty of making small improvements may seem to make it easier to effect a complete transformation—so, rather than, following Aristotle, *qui peut le plus peut le moins* (1939, 108–9), one might cling to the hope, seemingly against hope, that *qui ne peut pas le moins, peut tout*. Thus, the addict who resists the day-by-day reduction of his dose, telling himself that such puny half-measures come nowhere near the heroic finality of total abstinence that he knows is necessary.

But the alternatives of reform and revolutionary abandonment may not in fact be such stark alternatives as they seem. In Joseph Conrad's novel *Under Western Eyes*, the young student Razumov, who has betrayed a revolutionary fellow-student to the authorities, is being interviewed by the policeman Councillor Mikulin, who suspects him of involvement in the crime. Razumov is determined to try to get back to his quiet, studious life:

> Razumov, with an impatient wave of his hand, went on headlong, "But, really, I must claim the right to be done once for all with that man. And in order to accomplish this I shall take the liberty...."
>
> Razumov on his side of the table bowed slightly to the seated bureaucrat.
>
> "... To retire—simply to retire," he finished with great resolution.
>
> He walked to the door, thinking, "Now he must show his hand. He must ring and have me arrested before I am out of the building, or he must let me go. And either way...."
>
> An unhurried voice said—
>
> "Kirylo Sidorovitch." Razumov at the door turned his head.
>
> "To retire," he repeated.
>
> "Where to?" asked Councillor Mikulin softly. (2008b, 73–74)

The point, for us, as for Razumov, is that there is no more free space, either outside or inside, either to retreat into or to allow us to accelerate away from trouble.

Retreats in any case, and as every military commander knows, must be orderly, and surrenders and divorces can be as costly and complex as the conflicts they bring to an end. Victory too often brings one to the brink of ruin, as Pyrrhus realized after routing the Romans at Asculum but losing six times as many men as the enemy in the process, prompting the remark "Another victory like that and we're done for" (Plutarch 1920, 417). A withdrawal such as the one Wilson proposes, and indeed any measures at all that might be large and sustained enough to result in a restoration of human-natural equilibrium, will require a globally coordinated mobilization of resources, technical, economic, political, computational, mediatic, and emotional, the like of which no previous conflict has ever achieved or needed. Many habitats will need to be repaired, as well as simply set aside (Maser 2009, 142–77), and even those that can simply be sequestered will need to be maintained, ensuring that human beings remain vigilantly present at their absence. Wherever we move, we must move out.

How do we nerve and instruct ourselves for this paradoxical task of *sauter pour mieux reculer*? Humans have an absurd and insatiable appetite for self-sacrifice: How do we bend that into the work of renouncing the lust for sacrifice in favor of rationally self-sustaining self-government? Such an enterprise will require a convergence and coordination of the two drives that have heretofore merely been kept in intricate uneasy balance: the drive shared with every other organism on the planet to maintain its existence through the principle of propagation in whatever direction it is possible, subject only to the limits imposed by its habitat; and the drive to mitigate that aggressive drive in order to maximize and maintain the social life that is necessary for human survival. In order to have a chance of being effective, the drive to a condition of global civility must be maintained as purposively and even aggressively as the drive for conquest and overcoming of adverse circumstances. We must inhibit ourselves as uninhibitedly as we have emancipated ourselves from necessity. There may at the very least be some utility in a confident awareness of the active power of holding back we possess, a power over power that is the only thing that makes civility or civilization possible for creatures as aggressive and appetitively ambitious as we show no signs of ceasing to be. Our best hope is that we will be able to extend what has historically been our greatest achievement, the deflection of our illimitable will-to-power into the power of limit.

# Works Cited

A. B. 1698. *The Mystery of Phanaticism. Or, The Artifices of Dissenters to Support Their Schism*. London: T. Leigh and R. Knaplock.
Ackerley, Chris. 2000. "Samuel Beckett and Thomas à Kempis: The Roots of Quietism." *Samuel Beckett Today/Aujourd'hui* 9:81–92.
Agamben, Giorgio. 1993. "Notes on Gesture." In *Infancy and History: The Destruction of Experience*, translated by Liz Heron, 133–40. London: Verso.
———. 1999. *Potentialities: Collected Essays in Philosophy*. Edited and translated by Daniel Heller-Roazen. Stanford, CA: Stanford University Press.
———. 2011. *Nudities*. Translated by David Kishik and Stefan Pedatella. Stanford, CA: Stanford University Press.0
Allen, Cynthia L. 1995. "On Doing as You Please." In *Historical Pragmatics: Pragmatic Developments in the History of English*, edited by Andreas H. Jucker, 275–308. Amsterdam: John Benjamins.
Aragón, Oriana R., Margaret S. Clark, Rebecca L. Dyer, and John A. Bargh. 2015. "Dimorphous Expressions of Positive Emotion: Displays of Both Care and Aggression in Response to Cute Stimuli." *Psychological Science* 26:259–73.
Aristotle. 1939. *On the Heavens*. Translated by W. K. C. Guthrie. Cambridge, MA: Harvard University Press.
Arnold, Carrie. 2013. "Cuteness Inspires Aggression." *Scientific American Mind* 24:18.
Arras, Jean d'. 1895. *Melusine: Compiled (1382–1394 A.D.) by Jean d'Arras; Englisht About 1500*. Edited by A. K. Donald. London: Kegan Paul, Trench, Trübner.
Austin, J. L. 1962. *How to Do Things with Words*. Oxford: Clarendon.
Bacon, Francis. 1597. *Essayes Religious Meditations. Places of Perswasion and Disswasion. Seene and Allowed*. London: Humfrey Hooper.
Barnes, Julian. 1990. *A History of the World in 10½ Chapters*. New York: Vintage.
Barthes, Roland. 1972. *Mythologies*. Translated by Annette Lavers. New York: Hill and Wang.

Bashevkin, Sylvia, ed. 2002. *Women's Work Is Never Done: Comparative Studies in Care-Giving, Employment, and Social Policy Reform*. New York: Routledge.

Bass, Alan. 2006. *Interpretation and Difference: The Strangeness of Care*. Stanford, CA: Stanford University Press.

Baumgarten, Britta, Dieter Gosewinkel, and Dieter Rucht. 2011. "Civility: Introductory Notes on the History and Systematic Analysis of a Concept." *European Review of History/Revue européenne d'histoire* 18:289–312.

Beckett, Samuel. 1973. *Molloy. Malone Dies. The Unnamable*. London: Calder and Boyars.

———. 1983. *Disjecta: Miscellaneous Writings and a Dramatic Fragment*. Edited by Ruby Cohn. London: John Calder.

———. 1986. *Complete Dramatic Works*. London: Faber and Faber.

———. 1995. *The Complete Short Prose, 1929–1989*. Edited by S. E. Gontarski. New York: Grove Press.

Becon, Thomas. 1542. *A Newe Pathway vnto Praier Ful of Much Godly Frute and Christe[n] Knowledge*. London: Iohn Gough.

Bennett, Andrew. 2017. *Suicide Century: Literature and Suicide from James Joyce to David Foster Wallace*. Cambridge: Cambridge University Press.

Bentham, Jeremy. 2002. *Rights, Representation, and Reform: Nonsense upon Stilts and Other Writings on the French Revolution. The Collected Works of Jeremy Bentham: Political Writings*. Edited by Philip Schofield, Catherine Pease-Watkin, and Cyprian Blamires. Oxford: Clarendon.

Benveniste, Émile. 1945. "La doctrine médicale des Indo-Européens." *Revue de l'histoire des religions* 130:5–12.

Bergler, Edmund. 1953. "Can the Writer 'Resign' from His Calling?" *International Journal of Psychoanalysis* 34:40–42.

Bergson, Henri. 2016. "Politeness." Translated by Leonard Lawlor. *Journal of French and Francophone Philosophy—Revue de la philosophie française et de langue française* 24:3–9.

Bolter, David Jay, and Richard Grusin. 1999. *Remediation: Understanding New Media*. Cambridge, MA: MIT Press.

Bradley, Henry. 1889. "The Etymology of the Word 'God.'" *Academy* 894 (June 22): 432.

Brand, Myles. 1971. "The Language of Not Doing." *American Philosophical Quarterly* 8:45–53.

Brooks, Roy L. 1999. *When Sorry Isn't Enough: The Controversy over Apologies and Reparations for Human Injustice*. New York: New York University Press.

Brown, George Spencer. 1969. *Laws of Form*. London: George Allen and Unwin.

Brown, Penelope, and Stephen C. Levinson. 1987. *Politeness: Some Universals in Language Usage*. Cambridge: Cambridge University Press.

Browning, Elizabeth Barrett. 1897. *Poetical Works*. London: Smith, Elder.

Buckley, Ralf C. 2016. "Aww: The Emotion of Perceiving Cuteness." *Frontiers in Psychology* 7:1740. https://doi.org/10.3389/fpsyg.2016.01740.

Bullinger, Heinrich. 1577. *Fiftie Godlie and Learned Sermons.* Translated by H. I. London: Ralphe Newberrie.

Bullokar, John. 1616. *An English Expositor: Teaching the Interpretation of the Hardest Words Used in Our Language.* London: Iohn Legatt.

Bulwer, John. 1644. *Chirologia, or, The Naturall Language of the Hand Composed of the Speaking Motions, and Discoursing Gestures Thereof: Whereunto Is Added Chironomia, or, The Art of Manuall Rhetoricke.* London: R. Whitaker.

Burton, Robert. 1989–2000. *The Anatomy of Melancholy.* Edited by Thomas C. Faulkner, Nicolas K. Kiessling, and Rhonda L. Blair. 6 vols. Oxford: Clarendon Press.

Bushrui, Suheil Badi, and Bernard Benstock, eds. 1982. *James Joyce: An International Perspective. Centenary Essays in Honour of the Late Sir Desmond Cochrane.* Gerrards Cross, UK: Colin Smythe.

Bynum, Caroline Walker. 1987. *Holy Feast and Holy Fast: The Religious Significance of Food to Medieval Women.* Berkeley: University of California Press.

Callahan, W. A. 2004. "National Insecurities: Humiliation, Salvation, and Chinese Nationalism." *Alternatives: Global, Local, Political* 29:199–218.

Cantor, Norman L. 2015. "My Plan to Avoid the Ravages of Extreme Dementia." *Bill of Health*, April 16. http://blog.petrieflom.law.harvard.edu/2015/04/16/my-plan-to-avoid-the-ravages-of-extreme-dementia/.

Cavarero, Adriana. 2016. *Inclinations: A Critique of Rectitude.* Translated by Amanda Minervini and Adam Sitze. Stanford, CA: Stanford University Press.

Chaucer, Geoffrey. 1988. *The Riverside Chaucer.* 3rd ed. Edited by F. N. Robinson and Larry D. Benson. Oxford: Oxford University Press.

Checkland, Peter, and Sue Holwell. 1998. *Information, Systems and Information Systems: Making Sense of the Field.* Chichester, UK: John Wiley and Sons.

Chesterton, G. K. 1901. "Humiliation." *The Speaker*, n.s., 5 (October 19): 67–68.

Cienki, Alan, and Cornelia Müller, eds. 2008. *Metaphor and Gesture.* Amsterdam: John Benjamins.

Clare, John. 1984. *The Later Poems of John Clare 1837–1864.* Edited by Eric Robinson and David Powell. 2 vols. Oxford: Clarendon.

Coffin, Edward. 1619. *A Refutation of M. Ioseph Hall His Apologeticall Discourse, for the Marriage of Ecclesiasticall Persons.* Saint-Omer, France: English College Press.

Connor, Steven. 1999. "CP: Or, A Few Don'ts by a Cultural Phenomenologist." *Parallax* 5:17–31.

———. 2000. *Dumbstruck: A Cultural History of Ventriloquism.* Oxford: Oxford University Press.

———. 2004a. *The Book of Skin.* London: Reaktion.

———. 2004b. "Windbags and Skinsongs." Preface to lecture at the Skin: Texture/Textuality/Word/Image conference, University of London Institute of English Studies, May 14. http://stevenconnor.com/windbags.html.

———. 2013. "Collective Emotions: Reasons to Feel Doubtful." The History of Emotions annual lecture given at Queen Mary, University of London, October 9. http://stevenconnor.com/collective/collective.pdf.

———. 2014. *Beyond Words: Sobs, Hums, Stutters and Other Vocalizations*. London: Reaktion.

———. 2019. *The Madness of Knowledge: On Wisdom, Ignorance and Fantasies of Knowing*. London: Reaktion.

Conrad, Joseph. 2008a. *Heart of Darkness and Other Tales*. Edited by Cedric Watts. Oxford: Oxford University Press.

———. 2008b. *Under Western Eyes*. Edited by Jeremy Hawthorn. Oxford: Oxford University Press.

Crozier, W. Ray, ed. 1990. *Shyness and Embarrassment: Perspectives from Social Psychology*. Cambridge: Cambridge University Press.

Cunningham, Michael. 2004. "Apologies in Irish Politics: A Commentary and Critique." *Contemporary British History* 18:80–92.

Daly, John A., and James McCroskey, eds. 2009. *Avoiding Communication: Shyness, Reticence, and Communication Apprehension*. 3rd ed. Cresskill, NJ: Hampton Press. ills, LOno

Darwin, Charles. 1998. *The Expression of the Emotions in Man and Animals*. Edited by Paul Ekman. New York: Oxford University Press.

Davetian, Benet. 2009. *Civility: A Cultural History*. Toronto: University of Toronto Press.

Deleuze, Gilles. 1993. *The Fold: Leibniz and the Baroque*. Translated by Tom Conley. London: Athlone Press.

Derrida, Jacques. 1995. "Ja, or the *Faux-Bond* II." In *Points . . . Interviews 1974–1994*, edited by Elisabeth Weber, translated by Peggy Kamuf, Christie V. McDonald, Verena Andermatt Conley, John P. Leavey Jr., Michael Israel, Peter Connor, Avital Ronell, Marian Hobson, and Christopher Johnson, 30–77. Stanford, CA: Stanford University Press.

———. 2002. "Declarations of Independence." Translated by Tom Keenan and Tom Pepper. In *Negotiations: Interventions and Interviews 1971–2001*, edited by Elizabeth Rottenberg, 46–54. Stanford, CA: Stanford University Press.

Diamond, Elizier. 2004. *Holy Men and Hunger Artists: Fasting and Asceticism in Rabbinic Culture*. Oxford: Oxford University Press.

Dickens, Charles. 1997. *Our Mutual Friend*. Edited by Adrian Poole. London: Penguin.

———. 2000. *The Dent Uniform Edition of Dickens's Journalism*. Vol. 4, The Uncommercial Traveller *and Other Papers 1859–70*, edited by Michael Slater and John Drew. London: J. M. Dent.

———. 2003. *Bleak House*. Edited by Nicola Bradbury. London: Penguin.

———. 2008. *Our Mutual Friend*. Edited by Michael Cotsell. Oxford: Oxford University Press.

Dickinson, Emily. 1975. *The Complete Poems*. Edited by Thomas H. Johnson. London: Faber and Faber.

Dumm, Thomas L. 1999. *The Politics of the Ordinary*. New York: New York University Press.

Dunbar, Robin. 1996. *Grooming, Gossip, and the Evolution of Language*. Cambridge, MA: Harvard University Press.

Durston, Christopher. 1972. "'For the Better Humiliation of the People': Public Days of Fasting and Thanksgiving During the English Revolution." *Seventeenth Century* 7:129–49.

Eagleton, Terry. 2018. *Radical Sacrifice*. New Haven, CT: Yale University Press.

Eggleston, Edward. 1888. *The Graysons: A Story of Illinois*. New York: Century.

Elias, Norbert. 1956. "Problems of Involvement and Detachment." *British Journal of Sociology* 7:226–52.

———. 1978. *The Civilizing Process: The History of Manners*. Translated by Edmund Jephcott. Oxford: Basil Blackwell.

———. 1994. "Notes on a Lifetime." In *Reflections on a Life*, translated by Edmund Jephcott, 81–154. Cambridge: Polity.

———. 2001. *The Loneliness of the Dying*. Translated by Edmund Jephcott. New York: Continuum.

———. 2017. "Essay on Laughter." Edited by Anca Parvulescu. *Critical Inquiry* 43:281–304.

Elias, Norbert, and Eric Dunning. 1986. *Quest for Excitement: Sport and Leisure in the Civilizing Process*. Oxford: Basil Blackwell.

Eliot, T. S. 1969. *Complete Poems and Plays*. London: Faber and Faber.

Elliott, Dyan. 1993. *Spiritual Marriage: Sexual Abstinence in Medieval Wedlock*. Princeton, NJ: Princeton University Press.

Ellmann, Maud. 1993. *The Hunger Artists: Starving, Writing, and Imprisonment*. Cambridge, MA: Harvard University Press.

Ellul, Jacques. 1985. *The Humiliation of the Word*. Translated by Joyce Main Hanks. Grand Rapids, MI: W. B. Eerdmans.

Erdozain, Dominic. 2016. *The Soul of Doubt: The Religious Roots of Unbelief from Luther to Marx*. Oxford: Oxford University Press.

Ernout, Alfred, and Alfred Meillet. 2001. *Dictionnaire étymologique de la langue latine: Histoire des mots*. Rev. 4th ed. Paris: Klincksieck.

Ferguson-Rayport, Shirley M., Richard M. Griffith, and Erwin W. Straus. 1955. "The Psychological Significance of Tattoos." *Psychiatric Quarterly* 29:112–31.

Fitton Brown, A. D. 1985. "The Unreality of Ovid's Tomitian Exile." *Liverpool Classical Monthly* 10:18–22.

Flusser, Vilém. 2014. *Gestures*. Translated by Nancy Ann Roth. Minneapolis: University of Minnesota Press.

Forster, John. 1876. *The Life of Charles Dickens*. 2 vols. London: Chapman and Hall.

Foucault, Michel. 1986. *The Care of the Self*. Translated by Robert Hurley. New York: Pantheon.

———. 2010. *The Government of the Self and Others: Lectures at the Collège de France,*

*1982–1983*. Edited by Frédéric Gross. Translated by Graham Burchell. Houndmills, UK: Palgrave Macmillan.

Fox, Robin. 1994. *The Challenge of Anthropology: Old Encounters and New Excursions*. New Brunswick, NJ: Transaction.

Frede, Dorothea. 2006. "The Question of Being: Heidegger's Project." In *The Cambridge Companion to Heidegger*, 2nd ed., edited by Charles B. Guignon, 42–69. New York: Cambridge University Press.

Freud, Anna. 1967. "About Losing and Being Lost." *Psychoanalytic Study of the Child* 22:9–19.

Freud, Sigmund. 1953–74. *The Standard Edition of the Complete Psychological Works of Sigmund Freud*. Edited and translated by James Strachey, Anna Freud, Alix Strachey, and Alan Tyson. 24 vols. London: Hogarth Press.

———. 1991. *Gesammelte Werke*. 18 vols. London: Imago.

Fudge, Erica. 2008. *Pets*. Stocksfield, UK: Acumen.

Fuller, Buckminster. 1961. "Tensegrity." *Portfolio and Art News Annual* 4:112–27, 144, 148.

Gassendi, Pierre. 1657. *The Mirrour of True Nobility and Gentility Being the Life of the Renowned Nicolaus Claudius Fabricius*. Translated by William Rand. London: Humphrey Moseley.

Genova, Lisa. 2009. *Still Alice*. New York: Gallery Books.

Gibney, Mark, Rhoda E. Howard-Hassmann, Jean-Marc Coicaud, and Niklaus Steiner, eds. 2008. *The Age of Apology: Facing Up to the Past*. Philadelphia: University of Pennsylvania Press.

Gilman, Sander L. 2018. *Stand Up Straight! A History of Posture*. London: Reaktion.

Godinho, Ricardo Miguel, Penny Spikins, and Paul O'Higgins. 2018. "Supraorbital Morphology and Social Dynamics in Human Evolution." *Nature Ecology and Evolution* 2:956–91.

Goethe, Johann Wolfgang. 1956. *Faust: Der Tragödie Erster Teil*. Stuttgart: Reclam-Verlag.

Goffman, Erving. 1955. "On Face-Work: An Analysis of Ritual Elements of Social Interaction." *Psychiatry: Journal for the Study of Interpersonal Processes* 18:213–31.

Goldin-Meadow, Susan. 2003. *Hearing Gesture: How Our Hands Help Us Think*. Cambridge, MA: Belknap Press of Harvard University Press.

Goody, Jack. 2006. *The Theft of History*. Cambridge: Cambridge University Press.

Gordon, Suzanne, Nel Noddings, and Patricia Benner, eds. 1996. *Caregiving: Readings in Knowledge, Practice, Ethics and Politics*. Philadelphia: University of Pennsylvania Press.

Gould, Stephen Jay. 1980. "A Biological Homage to Mickey Mouse." In *The Panda's Thumb: More Reflections in Natural History*, by Stephen Jay Gould, 95–107. New York: W. W. Norton.

Gourevitch, Anna. 1980. "Three Psychoanalytic Essays—Tension, Resignation, Self-Punishment." *Contemporary Psychoanalysis* 16:163–85.

Graves, Robert, ed. 1927. *The Less Familiar Nursery Rhymes*. London: E. Benn.

Graziano, Maria, Adam Kendon, and Carla Cristilli. 2011. "'Parallel Gesturing' in Adult-Child Conversations." In *Integrating Gestures: The Interdisciplinary Nature of Gesture*, edited by Gale Stam and Mika Ishino, 89–101. Amsterdam: John Benjamins.

Gruber, M. Catherine. 2014. *"I'm Sorry for What I've Done": The Language of Courtroom Apologies*. Oxford: Oxford University Press.

Habermas, Jürgen. 2001. *On the Pragmatics of Social Interaction: Preliminary Studies in the Theory of Communicative Action*. Translated by Barbara Fultner. Cambridge: Polity.

Hall, Edward. 1548. *The Union of the Two Noble and Illustrate Famelies of Lancastre [and] Yorke*. London: Richard Grafton.

Hall, Fitzedward. 1891. "The Verb *Demean*, 'Debase.'" *The Nation* 52:377–79.

Hallberg, Örjan, and Gerd Oberfeld. 2006. "Letter to the Editor: Will We All Become Electrosensitive?" *Electromagnetic Biology and Medicine* 25:189–91.

Haraway, Donna. 2003. *The Companion Species Manifesto: Dogs, People, and Significant Otherness*. Chicago: Prickly Paradigm Press.

Harris, Daniel. 2001. *Cute, Quaint, Hungry and Romantic: The Aesthetics of Consumerism*. Boston: Da Capo Press.

Heaney, Seamus. 1990. *New Selected Poems 1966-1987*. London: Faber and Faber.

Hedin, Douglas A. 2002. "On Losing." *American Journal of Trial Advocacy* 26:107–35.

Hegel, G. W. F. 2007. *Hegel's Philosophy of Mind*. Edited by Michael J. Inwood. Translated by W. Wallace and A. V. Miller. Revised by Michael J. Inwood. Oxford: Clarendon.

Heidegger, Martin. 1962. *Being and Time*. Translated by John Macquarrie and Edward Robinson. Oxford: Blackwell.

———. 1999. "Letter on 'Humanism.'" Translated by Frank A. Capuzzi. In *Pathmarks*, edited by William McNeill, 239–76. Cambridge: Cambridge University Press.

———. 2000. *Contributions to Philosophy (From Enowning)*. Translated by Parvis Emad and Kenneth Maly. Bloomington: Indiana University Press.

———. 2010. *Country Path Conversations*. Translated by Bret W. Davis. Bloomington: Indiana University Press.

Held, Gudrun. 1999. "Submission Strategies as an Expression of the Ideology of Politeness: Reflections on the Verbalisation of Social Power Relations." *Pragmatics* 9:21–36.

Hemans, Felicia Dorothea. 1808. *Poems*. Liverpool: T. Cadell and W. Davies.

Hemmer, Helmut. 1990. *Domestication: The Decline of Environmental Appreciation*. Translated by Neil Beckhaus. Cambridge: Cambridge University Press.

Henry, Michel. 2012. *Barbarism*. Translated by Scott Davidson. London: Continuum.

Herbert, R. K. 1986. "Say 'Thank You'—or Something." *American Speech* 61:76–88.

Herdt, Gilbert. 2011. "Talking About Sex: On the Relationship Between Discourse, Secrecy and Sexual Subjectivity in Melanesia." In *Echoes of the Tambaran: Masculinity, History and the Subject in the Work of Donald F. Tuzin*, edited by David Lipset and Paul Roscoe, 259–73. Canberra: ANU Press.

Hinde, Robert A., and L. A. Barden. 1985. "The Evolution of the Teddy Bear." *Animal Behaviour* 33:1371–73.
Hopkins, Gerard Manley. 1970. *The Poems of Gerard Manley Hopkins*. Edited by W. H. Gardner and N. H. MacKenzie. London: Oxford University Press.
Horace (Quintus Horatius Flaccus). 1926. *Satires. Epistles. The Art of Poetry*. Translated by H. Rushton Fairclough. Cambridge, MA: Harvard University Press.
Hostetter, Autumn B., and Martha W. Alibali. 2008. "Visible Embodiment: Gestures as Simulated Action." *Psychonomic Bulletin and Review* 15:495–514.
Johns, Brandon. 2009. "Refraining and the External." *Ratio*, n.s., 22:206–15.
Johnson, Samuel, and James Boswell. 1984. *A Journey to the Western Islands of Scotland and the Journal of a Tour to the Hebrides*. Edited by Peter Levi. London: Penguin.
Jolly, Alison. 2005. "Hair Signals." *Evolutionary Anthropology* 14:5.
Jones, Martin. 2007. *Feast: Why Humans Share Food*. Oxford: Oxford University Press.
Jonson, Ben. 1601. *The Fountaine of Selfe-Loue. Or Cynthias Reuels*. London: Walter Burre.
Joyce, James. 2008. *Ulysses: The 1922 Text*. Edited by Jeri Johnson. Oxford: Oxford University Press.
Kafka, Franz. 2007. *Metamorphosis and Other Stories*. Translated by Michael Hofmann. London: Penguin.
Kant, Immanuel. 1996. *The Metaphysics of Morals*. Edited and translated by Mary Gregor. Cambridge: Cambridge University Press.
Keats, John. 2012. *The Letters of John Keats 1814–1821*. 2 vols. Edited by Hyder Edward Rollins. Cambridge: Cambridge University Press.
Kendall, Timothy. 1577. *Flowers of Epigrammes*. London: Ihon Shepperd.
Kendon, Adam. 2004. *Gesture: Visible Action as Utterance*. Cambridge: Cambridge University Press.
Kimbara, Irene. 2006. "On Gestural Mimicry." *Gesture* 6:19–61.
Klein, Melanie. 1997. *Envy and Gratitude and Other Works 1946–1963*. London: Vintage.
Lakoff, George, and Mark Johnson. 2003. *Metaphors We Live By*. Chicago: University of Chicago Press.
Lakoff, Robin. 1973. "The Logic of Politeness: Or, Minding Your P's and Q's." In *Papers from the Ninth Regional Meeting of the Chicago Linguistic Society*, edited by Claudia Corum, T. Cedric Smith-Stark, and Ann Weiser, 292–305. Chicago: Chicago Linguistic Society.
Lamb, Charles. 1913. *The Last Essays of Elia*. Edited by A. Hamilton Thompson. Cambridge: Cambridge University Press.
Lane, Christopher. 2007. *Shyness: How Normal Behavior Became a Sickness*. New Haven, CT: Yale University Press.
Larivée, Annie. 2014. "*Being and Time* and the Ancient Philosophical Tradition of Care for the Self: A Tense or Harmonious Relationship?" *Philosophical Papers* 43:123–44.

Larkin, Philip. 1988. *Collected Poems*. Edited by Anthony Thwaite. London: Faber and Faber.
Lazare, Aaron. 2004. *On Apology*. New York: Oxford University Press.
Leach, Edmund. R. 1958. "Magical Hair." *Journal of the Royal Anthropological Institute of Great Britain and Ireland* 88:147–64.
———. 1964. "Anthropological Aspects of Language: Animal Categories and Verbal Abuse." In *New Directions in the Study of Language*, edited by E. H. Lenneberg, 23–63. Cambridge, MA: MIT Press.
Lemieux, Karl, and David Bryant, dirs. 2015. *The Quiet Zone*. National Film Board of Canada, September 15. https://www.youtube.com/watch?v=EUPQUP4QjxI.
Levy, Jacob T. 2000. *The Multiculturalism of Fear*. Oxford: Oxford University Press.
Liebersohn, Yosef Z., Yair Neuman, and Zvi Bekerman. 2004. "Oh Baby, It's Hard for Me to Say I'm Sorry: Public Apologetic Speech and Cultural Rhetorical Resources." *Journal of Pragmatics* 36:921–44.
Lind, Jennifer. 2008. *Sorry States: Apologies in International Politics*. Ithaca, NY: Cornell University Press.
Lorenz, Konrad. 1943. "Die angeborenen Formen Möglicher Erfahrung." *Zeitschrift für Tierpsychologie* 5:235–409.
Lucretius (Titus Lucretius Carus). 1975. *On the Nature of Things*. Translated by W. H. D. Rouse. Revised by Martin F. Smith. Cambridge, MA: Harvard University Press.
Luhmann, Niklas. 2013. *Introduction to Systems Theory*. Translated by Peter Gilgen. Cambridge: Polity Press.
Macdonald, George. 1867. *Annals of a Quiet Neighbourhood*. 3 vols. London: Hurst and Blackett.
Maddox, Brenda. 2002. *Rosalind Franklin: The Dark Lady of DNA*. London: HarperCollins.
Marcuse, Herbert. 2002. *One-Dimensional Man: Studies in the Ideology of Advanced Industrial Society*. Abingdon, UK: Routledge.
Marvell, Andrew. 2005. *Complete Poems*. Edited by Elizabeth Story Donno and Jonathan Bate. London: Penguin.
Maser, Chris. 2009. *Earth in Our Care: Ecology, Economy, and Sustainability*. New Brunswick, NJ: Rutgers University Press.
McAleer, Sean. 2012. "Propositional Gratitude." *American Philosophical Quarterly* 49:55–66.
McGough, Roger. 2003. *Collected Poems*. London: Viking.
———. 2012. *As Far as I Know*. London: Viking.
McGranahan, Carol. 2016. "Theorizing Refusal: An Introduction." *Cultural Anthropology* 31:319–25.
McLeod, Lynette J., Aaron B. Driver, Andrew J. Bengsen, and Donald W. Hine. 2017. "Refining Online Communication Strategies for Domestic Cat Management." *Anthrozoös* 30:635–49.
McNamara, Patrick. 1999. *Mind and Variability: Mental Darwinism, Memory, and Self*. Westport, CT: Praeger.

McNeill, David. 2012. *How Language Began: Gesture and Speech in Human Evolution*. Cambridge: Cambridge University Press.

———. 2016. *Why We Gesture: The Surprising Role of Hand Movements in Communication*. Cambridge: Cambridge University Press.

Mead, George Herbert. 1974. *Mind, Self, and Society from the Standpoint of a Social Behaviorist*. Edited by C. W. Morris. Chicago: University of Chicago Press.

Mendes, Kaitlynn. 2015. *SlutWalk: Feminism, Activism and Media*. Houndmills, UK: Palgrave Macmillan.

Merleau-Ponty, Maurice. 2007. *Phenomenology of Perception*. Translated by Colin Smith. London: Routledge.

Miller, J. Hillis. 2007. "'Don't Count Me In': Derrida's Refraining." *Textual Practice* 21:279–94.

Milner-Barry, Stuart. 1993. "Hut 6: Early Days." In *Codebreakers: The Inside Story of Bletchley Park*, edited by F. H. Hinsley and Alan Stripp, 89–99. Oxford: Oxford University Press.

Mischel, Walter, Ebbe B. Ebbesen, and Antonette Raskoff Zeiss. 1972. "Cognitive and Attentional Mechanisms in Delay of Gratification." *Journal of Personality and Social Psychology* 21:204–18.

Moore, Robert E. 1979. "Refraining." *Philosophical Studies* 36:407–24.

Morris, Desmond. 1977. *Manwatching: A Field Guide to Human Behaviour*. London: Jonathan Cape.

Morris, Desmond, Peter Collett, Peter Marsh, and Marie O'Shaughnessy. 1981. *Gestures: Their Origins and Distribution*. London: Triad Granada.

Morris, Paul, Vasu Reddy, and R. C. Bunting. 1995. "The Survival of the Cutest: Who's Responsible for the Evolution of the Teddy Bear?" *Animal Behaviour* 50:1697–1700.

Murphy, Jeffrie G. 1988. "Mercy and Legal Justice." In *Forgiveness and Mercy*, by Jeffrie G. Murphy and Jean Hampton, 162–86. Cambridge: Cambridge University Press.

Murphy, M. Lynne. 2016. "Minding Your Pleases and Thank-Yous in Britain and the USA." *English Today* 32:49–53.

Murray, J. A. H. 1881. "Ninth Annual Address of the President to the Philological Society, Delivered at the Anniversary Meeting, Friday, 21st of May, 1880." *Transactions of the Philological Society*, 18:117–76.

Najem, Gemma. 2018. "David Warner Defends Tearful Apology with Promise of More Revelations." *Stuff*, March 31. https://www.stuff.co.nz/sport/cricket/102745477/david-warner-defends-tearful-apology-with-promise-of-more-revelations.

Nanjundayya, H. V., and L. K. Ananthakrishna Iyer. 1928. *The Mysore Tribes and Castes*. Vol. 2. Mysore, India: Mysore University.

Navaie-Waliser, M., P. H. Feldman, D. A. Gould, C. L. Levine, A. N. Kuerbis, and K. Donelan. 2002. "When the Caregiver Needs Care: The Plight of Vulnerable Caregivers." *American Journal of Public Health* 92:409–13.

Negash, Girma. 2006. *Apologia Politica: States and Their Apologies by Proxy*. Lanham, MD: Lexington Books.

Ngai, Sianne. 2012. *Our Aesthetic Categories: Zany, Cute, Interesting*. Cambridge, MA: Harvard University Press.
Nobles, Melissa. 2008. *The Politics of Official Apologies*. New York: Cambridge University Press.
Noland, Carrie, and Sally Ann Ness, eds. 2008. *Migrations of Gesture*. Minneapolis: University of Minnesota Press.
Novack, Miriam A., and Susan Goldin-Meadow. 2017. "Gesture as Representational Action: A Paper About Function." *Psychonomic Bulletin and Review* 24:652–65.
O'Neill, Brendan. 2007. "Sorry to Say." *BBC News*, January 8. http://news.bbc.co.uk/1/hi/magazine/6241411.stm.
Ong, Walter J. 1967. *The Presence of the Word: Some Prolegomena for Cultural and Religious History*. New Haven, CT: Yale University Press.
———. 1989. *Fighting for Life: Contest, Sexuality, and Consciousness*. Amherst: University of Massachusetts Press.
Opie, Peter, and Iona Opie. 1960. *The Lore and Language of Schoolchildren*. Oxford: Clarendon.
Otter, Chris. 2008. *The Victorian Eye: A Political History of Light and Vision in Britain, 1800–1910*. Chicago: University of Chicago Press.
Ovid (Publius Ovidius Naso). 1939. *Tristia. Ex Ponto*. Translated by Arthur Leslie Wheeler. Cambridge, MA: Harvard University Press.
Owen, Marion. 1983. *Apologies and Remedial Interchanges: A Study of Language Use in Social Interaction*. Berlin: Mouton.
Pascal, Blaise. 1995. *Pensées, and Other Writings*. Edited by Anthony Levi. Translated by Honor Levi. Oxford: Oxford University Press.
Pererius, Benedictus. 1661. *The Astrologer Anatomiz'd, or, The Vanity of Star-Gazing Art*. Translated by Percy Enderbie. London: M. Wright.
Phillips, Adam. 2009. "On Losing and Being Lost Again." *AA Files* 59:12–14, 16–17.
Phillips, G. M. 1965. "The Problem of Reticence." *Pennsylvania Speech Annual* 22:22–38.
Piozzi, Hester Lynch. 1794. *British Synonymy: Or, An Attempt at Regulating the Choice of Words in Familiar Conversation*. 2 vols. London: G. G. and J. Robinson.
Plath, Sylvia. 1981. *Collected Poems*. Edited by Ted Hughes. London: Faber and Faber.
Pliny the Elder. 1601. *The Historie of the World: Commonly Called, The Naturall Historie of C. Plinius Secundus . . . The First Tome*. Translated by Philémon Holland. London: Adam Islip.
Plutarch. 1920. *Lives: Volume IX, Demetrius and Antony. Pyrrhus and Gaius Marius*. Translated by Bernadotte Perrin. London: William Heinemann.
Poe, Edgar Allan. 1978. "The Facts in the Case of M. Valdemar." In *The Collected Works of Edgar Allan Poe*, vol. 3, *Tales and Sketches*, edited by Thomas Ollive Mabbott, 1228–44. Cambridge, MA: Belknap Press of Harvard University Press.
Power, Henry, and Leonard W. Sedgwick. 1882. *The New Sydenham Society's Lexicon of Medicine and the Allied Sciences*. Vol. 2. London: New Sydenham Society.

Provine, Robert R. 2001. *Laughter: A Scientific Investigation*. London: Penguin.
Quintilian (Marcus Fabius Quintilianus). 2001. *The Orator's Education*. Vol. 3, *Books 3–5*, edited and translated by Donald A. Russell. Cambridge, MA: Harvard University Press.
———. 2002. *The Orator's Education*. Vol. 5, *Books 11–12*, edited and translated by Donald A. Russell. Cambridge, MA: Harvard University Press.
"Radio Quiet Zones Around Observatories." 2018. European Science Foundation, Committee on Radio Astronomy Frequencies. https://www.craf.eu/radio-quiet-zones-around-observatories/.
Ramachandran V. S., and S. Blakeslee. 1998. *Phantoms in the Brain: Probing the Mysteries of the Human Mind*. New York: William Morrow.
Raudive, Konstantin. 1971. *Breakthrough: An Amazing Experiment in Electronic Communication with the Dead*. Edited by Joyce Morton. Translated by Nadia Fowler. Gerrards Cross, UK: Smythe.
Réau, Louis. 1958. *Iconographie de l'art chrétien*. 3 vols. Paris: Presses universitaires de France.
Rezek, Cheryl. 2015. *Mindfulness for Carers: How to Manage the Demands of Caregiving While Finding a Place for Yourself*. London: Jessica Kingsley.
Reznikoff, Iégor, and Michel Dauvois. 1988. "La dimension sonore des grottes ornés." *Bulletin de la Société préhistorique française* 85:238–46.
Ringler, William. 1941. "Poeta Nascitur Non Fit: Some Notes on the History of an Aphorism." *Journal of the History of Ideas* 2:497–504.
Ruskin, John. 1905. *The Works of John Ruskin*. Vol. 7, *Modern Painters*, edited by Edward Tyas Cook and Alexander Wedderburn. London: George Allen.
Saint Francis of Assisi. 1906. *The Writings of Saint Francis of Assisi*. Edited and translated by Paschal Robinson. Philadelphia: Dolphin Press.
Sartre, Jean-Paul. 1984. *Being and Nothingness: An Essay on Phenomenological Ontology*. Translated by Hazel E. Barnes. London: Methuen.
———. 2007. *Existentialism Is a Humanism*. Edited by Arlette Elkaim-Sartre. Translated by Carole Macomber. New Haven, CT: Yale University Press.
Sax, Boria. 2000. *Animals in the Third Reich: Pets, Scapegoats, and the Holocaust*. New York: Continuum.
Schiller, Friedrich von. 1966. *Naïve and Sentimental Poetry and On the Sublime: Two Essays*. Translated by Julius A. Elias. New York: Frederick Ungar.
Schopenhauer, Arthur. 1913. *Studies in Pessimism: A Series of Essays*. Translated by Thomas Bailey Saunders. London: George Allen.
Schreber, Daniel Paul. 2000. *Memoirs of My Nervous Illness*. Edited and translated by Ida Macalpine and Richard A. Hunter. New York: New York Review of Books.
Serpell, James. 1986. *In the Company of Animals: A Study of Human-Animal Relationships*. Oxford: Basil Blackwell.
Serres, Michel. 1980. *Le parasite*. Paris: Grasset.
———. 1982a. *Hermes: Literature, Science, Philosophy*. Edited by Josué V. Harari and David F. Bell. Baltimore: Johns Hopkins University Press.

———. 1982b. *The Parasite*. Translated by Lawrence R. Schehr. Baltimore: Johns Hopkins University Press.
———. 1989. *Detachment*. Translated by Geneviève James and Raymond Federman. Athens: Ohio University Press.
———. 1995. *Genesis*. Translated by Geneviève James and James Nielson. Ann Arbor: University of Michigan Press.
———. 2001. *Hominescence*. Paris: Le Pommier.
———. 2008a. *La guerre mondiale*. Paris: Le Pommier.
———. 2008b. *Le mal propre: Polluer pour s'approprier?* Paris: Le Pommier.
———. 2011. *Malfeasance: Appropriation Through Pollution?* Translated by Anne-Marie Feenberg-Dibon. Stanford, CA: Stanford University Press.
Shakespeare, William. 1997. *King Lear*. Edited by R. A. Foakes. Walton-on-Thames, UK: Thomas Nelson.
———. 1999. *King Henry VI Part 2*. Edited by Ronald Knowles. London: Thomson.
———. 2000. *King Henry VI Part 1*. Edited by Edward Burns. London: Arden Shakespeare.
———. 2005. *Hamlet*. Edited by Ann Thompson and Neil Taylor. London: Arden Shakespeare.
———. 2006. *As You Like It*. Edited by Juliet Dusinberre. London: Arden Shakespeare.
———. 2008. *Twelfth Night, or What You Will*. Edited by Keir Elam. London: Arden Shakespeare.
———. 2010a. *The Merchant of Venice*. Edited by John Drakakis. London: Arden Shakespeare.
———. 2010b. *Sonnets*. Edited by Katherine Duncan-Jones. London: Arden Shakespeare.
———. 2011. *The Tempest*. Edited by Virginia Mason Vaughan and Alden T. Vaughan. London: Arden Shakespeare.
———. 2016a. *King Henry IV Part 2*. Edited by James C. Bulman. London: Bloomsbury Arden Shakespeare.
———. 2016b. *Othello*. Edited by E. A. J. Honigmann and Ayanna Thompson. London: Bloomsbury Arden Shakespeare.
———. 2017. *The Comedy of Errors*. Edited by Kent Cartwright. London: Bloomsbury Arden Shakespeare.
———. 2018. *King John*. Edited by Jesse M. Lander and J. J. M Tobin. London: Bloomsbury Arden Shakespeare.
Sheridan, Richard Brinsley. 1999. *The Critic; or, A Tragedy Rehearsed*. Edited by David Crane. London: Bloomsbury.
Sherman, Gary D., and Jonathan Haidt. 2011. "Cuteness and Disgust: The Humanizing and Dehumanizing Effects of Emotion." *Emotion Review* 3:245–51.
Shipman, Pat. 2011. *The Animal Connection: A New Perspective on What Makes Us Human*. New York: W. W. Norton.
Simmel, Georg. 1950. "Faithfulness and Gratitude." In *The Sociology of Georg Simmel*, edited and translated by Kurt H. Wolff, 379–95. Glencoe, IL: Free Press.

Simon, Leonard. 1984. "The Pet Trap: Negative Effects of Pet Ownership on Families and Individuals." In *The Pet Connection: Its Influence on Our Health and Quality of Life*, edited by Robert Anderson, Benjamin Hart and Lynette Hart, 226–40. Minneapolis: Center to Study Human-Animal Relationships and Environments.

Sloterdijk, Peter. 2004. *Sphären III: Schäume, Plurale Sphärologie*. Frankfurt am Main: Suhrkamp.

———. 2009a. *God's Zeal: The Battle of the Three Monotheisms*. Translated by Wieland Hoban. Cambridge: Polity.

———. 2009b. "Rules for the Human Zoo: A Response to the *Letter on Humanism*." Translated by Mary Varney Rorty. *Environment and Planning D: Society and Space* 27:12–28.

———. 2013. *You Must Change Your Life: On Anthropotechnics*. Translated by Wieland Hoban. Cambridge: Polity.

Sorel, Georges. 1999. *Reflections on Violence*. Edited by Jeremy Jennings. Translated by T. E. Hulme and Jeremy Jennings. Cambridge: Cambridge University Press.

Spiegel, James S. 2003. "The Moral Irony of Humility." *Logos: A Journal of Catholic Thought and Culture* 6:131–50.

Steinbeck, John. 1995. *The Moon Is Down*. Edited by Donald V. Coers. London: Penguin.

Stephenson, Peter H. 1980. "The Significance of Silence: On the Dialectical Evolution of Human Communication." *Dialectical Anthropology* 5:47–55.

Stern, Lesley. 2008. "Ghosting: The Performance and Migration of Cinematic Gesture, Focusing on Hou Hsiao-Hsien's *Good Men, Good Women*." In *Migrations of Gesture*, edited by Carrie Noland and Sally Ann Ness, 185–215. Minneapolis: University of Minnesota Press.

Stevens, Wallace. 2015. *The Collected Poems: The Corrected Edition*. Edited by John N. Serio and Chris Beyers. New York: Vintage.

Stone, Christopher D. 2010. *Should Trees Have Standing? Law, Morality, and the Environment*. Oxford: Oxford University Press.

Strate, Shane. 2015. *The Lost Territories: Thailand's History of National Humiliation*. Honolulu: University of Hawai'i Press.

Straus, Erwin W. 1952. "The Upright Posture." *Psychiatric Quarterly* 26:529–61.

Stubbs, Michael. 1983. *Discourse Analysis: The Sociolinguistic Analysis of Natural Language and Culture*. Oxford: Blackwell.

Tague, Ingrid H. 2015. *Animal Companions: Pets and Social Change in Eighteenth-Century Britain*. University Park: Pennsylvania State University Press.

Tausk, Viktor. 1933. "On the Origin of the 'Influencing Machine' in Schizophrenia." Translated by Dorian Feigenbaum. *Psychoanalytic Quarterly* 2:519–56.

Tavuchis, Nicholas. 1991. *Mea Culpa: A Sociology of Apology and Reconciliation*. Stanford, CA: Stanford University Press.

Tennyson, Alfred. 2009. *The Major Works*. Edited by Adam Roberts. Oxford: Oxford University Press.

"*This Week* Transcript 6-3-18: President Trump's Personal Attorney Rudy Giuliani."

2018. *ABC News*, June 3. https://abcnews.go.com/Politics/week-transcript-18-latest-us-north-korea-summit/story?id=55608126.

Thomas, Dylan. 1998. *Collected Poems 1934–1953*. Edited by Vernon Watkins and Ralph Maud. London: J. M. Dent.

Tuncel, Yunus. 2015. "Defeat, Loss, Death, and Sacrifice in Sports." *Journal of the Philosophy of Sport* 42:409–23.

Udall, Ephraim. 1642. *Noli Me Tangere; or, A Thing to Be Thought On*. London: I. S.

Ulyanov, Vladimir Ilyich (Lenin), and Alexei Maximovich Peshkov (Maxim Gorky). 2003. *Lenin and Gorky: Letters, Reminiscences, Articles*. Translated by Bernard Isaacs. Honolulu: University Press of the Pacific.

Vogel, Cyrille. 1963. "La signation dans l'église des premiers siècles." *La Maison-Dieu* 75:37–51.

Wallace, David Foster. 1996. *Infinite Jest: A Novel*. Boston: Little, Brown.

Waller, Steven J. 1993. "Sound and Rock Art." *Nature* 363:501.

Wang, Zheng. 2012. *Never Forget National Humiliation: Historical Memory in Chinese Politics and Foreign Relations*. New York: Columbia University Press.

Warner, Marina. 2002. "Sorry: The Present State of Apology." *Open Democracy*, November 7. https://www.opendemocracy.net/en/article_603jsp/.

———. 2003. "Who's Sorry Now? Personal Stories, Public Apologies." In *Signs and Wonders: Essays on Literature and Culture*, by Marina Warner, 459–80. London: Chatto and Windus.

Watkins, Calvin. 1995. *How to Kill a Dragon: Aspects of Indo-European Poetics*. New York: Oxford University Press.

Weinman, Sam. 2016. *Win at Losing: How Our Biggest Setbacks Can Lead to Our Greatest Gains*. New York: Tarcher Perigee.

White, Patricia. 2011. "On the Capacity for Gratitude." *Canadian Journal of Psychoanalysis* 19:229–51.

"Why Does This U.S. Town Ban WiFi and Cell Phones?" 2016. *DNews*, July 10. https://www.youtube.com/watch?v=VCPuufwOGMM

Willis, N. Parker. 1849. *Rural Letters and Other Records of Thought at Leisure: Written in the Intervals of More Hurried Literary Labor*. New York: Baker and Scribner.

Wilson, E. O. 2016. *Half-Earth: Our Planet's Fight for Life*. New York: Liveright.

Wimbush, Andy. 2014. "Humility, Self-Awareness, and Religious Ambivalence: Another Look at Beckett's 'Humanistic Quietism.'" *Journal of Beckett Studies* 23:202–21.

Winnicott, Donald. 1953. "Transitional Objects and Transitional Phenomena: A Study of the First Not-Me Possession." *International Journal of Psychoanalysis* 34:89–97.

Withers, Philip. 1789. *Aristarchus, or the Principles of Composition. Containing a Methodical Arrangement of the Improprieties Frequent in Writing and Conversation*. 2nd ed. London: R. and T. Turner.

Wordsworth, William. 1954. *Poetical Works: Volume 3*. 2nd ed. Edited by Helen Darbishire and Ernest de Selincourt. Oxford: Clarendon.

Yeats, W. B. 1956. *Collected Poems*. London: Macmillan.

Young, Edward. 1762. *Resignation in Two Parts. And a Postscript, To Mrs. B\*\*\*\*\*\*\**. London: N.p.

———. 1989. *Night Thoughts*. Edited by Stephen Cornford. Cambridge: Cambridge University Press.

Yu, Doris S. F., Sheung-Tak Cheng, and Jungfang Wang. 2018. "Unravelling Positive Aspects of Caregiving in Dementia: An Integrative Review of Research Literature." *International Journal of Nursing Studies* 79:1–26.

Zentall, Thomas R., and Rebecca A. Singer. 2008. "Required Pecking and Refraining from Pecking Alter Judgments of Time by Pigeons." *Learning and Behavior* 36:55–61.

Zwar, Larissa, Hans-Helmut König, and André Hajek. 2018. "The Impact of Different Types of Informal Caregiving on Cognitive Functioning of Older Caregivers: Evidence from a Longitudinal, Population-Based Study in Germany." *Social Science and Medicine* 218:12–19.

# Index

Abstention, 97–98, 100–102, 105, 120, 172
Abstinence, 100–107, 110; collective, 105–6, 112
Absurdity, 130–35
Addiction, 181
Adorno, T.W., 212
Adverbs, 36
Agamben, Giorgio, 3–4, 51–52, 84, 95, 112, 119–20, 172
Agency, 2, 9–10, 207
Aggression, 24, 28, 32, 64–65, 69, 76, 78, 92, 112–14, 126, 147, 152–54, 195–97, 200, 201–2, 217
Alibali, Martha W., 90
Allen, Cynthia L., 54
Allocutions, 125
Andrew, Saint, 73
Animals, 64–65, 188–98
Anorexia nervosa, 103, 113, 117, 120
Aphesis, 154
Apo-, 30–31, 74
Apology, 121–47, 152; theatricality of, 142–43
Apophasis, 110, 111
Aristotle, 3–4, 51–52, 216

*Ars moriendi*, 167, 170
Assertion, 89
Austin, J.L., 130

Bacon, Francis, 153
Barden, I. A., 199
Barnes, Julian, 169
Barthes, Roland, 70
Bass, Alan, 180
Baumgarten, Britta, 44
Bearing, 85–86, 177–88
Beat gestures, 80, 90–91
Beatles, The, 54
Beckett, Samuel, 8, 25, 26, 58, 68, 69, 70, 74, 105, 153, 166, 168, 170, 171
Becon, Thomas, 79
Behaving, 87
Bekerman, Zvi, 128
Bennett, Andrew, 170
Bentham, Jeremy, 66
Benveniste, Émile, 22–23
Bergler, Edmund, 14
Bergson, Henri, 48, 56–57
Blair, Tony, 131, 141
Bletchley Park, 27
Bolter David Jay, 22

235

Bowing, 70-1
Brandt, Willy, 131, 137-38
Brooks, Roy L., 139
Brown, George Spencer, 25
Brown, Penelope, 37
Browning, Elizabeth Barrett, 83, 85
Bryant, David, 21
Buckley, Ralf C., 196
Bulimia nervosa, 119-20
Bullinger, Heinrich, 78
Bullokar, John, 82
Bulwer, John, 80
Bynum, Caroline Walker, 73, 102, 118-19
Byrne, Gabriel, 131

Callahan, W.A., 108-9
Calvinism, 17
Cantor, Norman L., 167
Caravaggio, Michelangelo Merisi da, 73
#Care, 174-203; of the self, 177-78
Caress, 186-87, 193
Cathexis, 157, 158
Cavarero, Adriana, 86-87
Charles I, 108
Chaucer, Geoffrey, 87
Checkland, Peter, 155
Chesterton, G.K., 13, 109
Children, 86, 162-64, 174, 175, 177-78, 185, 198-201
Civility, 29, 31, 44, 64; global, 217
"Civilizing process" (Elias), 24, 29, 47, 106, 119, 152
Clare, John, 71
Coen, Joel and Ethan, 100
Cohibition, 95-96, 101, 206
Collectives, 132-36
Conrad, Joseph, 167, 216
Continence, 105-6
Copropriation, 93
Crucifixion, 72
Curtsey, 70, 90
Cuteness, 196-203

Dali, Salvador, 72
Dance, 30, 56-57
Darwin, Charles, 197
Data, 155
Dauvois, Michel, 189
Davetian, Benet, 31
Declaration of Independence, 129-30, 134
Delayed gratification, 113, 185
Deleuze, Gilles, 24
Demanding, 123-26, 128-29
Demeaning, 87-88
Democritus, 184
Demosthenes, 81
Derrida, Jacques, 24, 92, 105, 129-30, 134
Diagonals, 74-75
Diamond, Elizier, 98-99
Dickens, Charles, 59, 133, 162-65
Dickinson, Emily, 73
Dionysius the Younger, 182
Domestication, 190-96, 202, 214-15
Dumm, Thomas L., 14, 15
Dunbar, Robin, 53-54
Dying, 167-73

Eagleton, Terry, 31-32
Eating, 46-47, 103, 118-20
Echo, 189
Elegy, 158-59
Elias, Norbert, 24, 43, 44, 47-52, 119, 152, 173
Eliot, T.S., 71, 212
Ellmann, Maud, 117
Ellul, Jacques, 44-45
Erdozain, Dominic, 17
Esteem, 7. *See also* Self-esteem
Eucharist, 8, 41, 119, 134
"Explicitation" (Sloterdijk), 212

Face, 34-35, 37, 47-49, 50-51, 197
Face-threatening acts, 35, 38, 39
Fasting, 102-4, 107-8, 117-19

Index    237

Flusser, Vilém, 84
Formality, 52–53, 55
Forster, John, 162
Foucault, Michel, 117–18, 177–78, 182–83
Fox, Robin, 114–15, 205
Francis, Saint, 8
Franklin, Rosalind, 213
Frede, Dorothea, 180
Freud, Anna, 153–54, 156, 165
Freud, Sigmund, 15–16, 24, 93, 104, 114, 154, 157–58, 164–65, 168
Fudge, Erica, 192
Fuller, Richard Buckminster, 52

Gassendi, Pierre, 155
Gender, 140–41, 175–76, 207–9
Genova, Lisa, 166
George V, 168
Gesticulation, 79–80, 81–82
Gesture, 24, 39–40, 64, 69, 70, 71, 73–86, 88–93
Gibney, Mark, 135
Gilman, Sander, 66
Giuliani, Rudy, 18
"Giving way," 45–46, 74
God, 59–60, 110
Goethe, Johann Wolfgang von, 109
Goffman, Erving, 34–35, 36, 37
Goldin-Meadow, Susan, 89, 90, 91
Goody, Jack, 44
Gosewinkel, Dieter, 44
Gould, Stephen J., 199
Gratitude, 57–63
Groveling, 67–68
Gruber, M. Catherine, 125
Grusin, Richard, 22

Habermas, Jürgen, 63
Haidt, Jonathan, 199–200
Hair, 98–99
Hall, Fitzedward, 88
Hand, 80

Haraway, Donna, 192–93
Hardy, Barbara, 36, 143, 166
Harris, Daniel, 201
Heaney, Seamus, 116
Hegel, Georg Wilhelm Friedrich, 66–67, 72
Heidegger, Martin, 92, 93, 179–81, 185, 187–88, 215
Held, Gudrun, 44–45
Hemans, Felicia, 72
Hemmer, Helmut, 195
Henry IV, 131
Henry, Michel, 93
Herdt, Gilbert, 115
Hinde, Robert A., 199
Hobbes, Thomas, 49
Holding back, 94–95
Holland, Philémon, 67
Holwell, Sue, 155
*Homo heidelbergensis*, 197
Hopkins, Gerard Manley, 72, 74
Horace (Quintus Horatius Flaccus), 184
Hostetter, Autumn B., 90
Howard-Hassmann, Rhoda E., 135
Humane, 193–94
Humiliation, 5–6, 44–45, 107–8; National, 108–9
Humility, 5–10, 67
Humor, 15–16
Hussein, Saddam, 142

Impotential, 3–4, 14, 51–52, 95, 172
Incest, 104, 114
Inclination, 86–87
Inhibition, 112–15, 205–6, 208–9, 211
Inoperativity (Agamben), 112
Izzard, Eddie, 104

Johns, Brandon, 100–101
Johnson, Mark, 64–65, 81
Johnson, Samuel, 179
Jolly, Alison, 98
Jones, Martin, 41

238  Index

Jonson, Ben, 68
Joyce, James, 47, 68, 83
Judaism, 96–97, 98

Kafka, Franz, 102–3
Kant, Immanuel, 48, 62–63
Keats, John, 183
Kendall, Timothy, 56
Kendon, Adam, 74, 78, 88
Kempis, Thomas à, 8
Kissing, 75
Klein, Melanie, 60–1

Lakoff, George, 64–65, 81
Lakoff, Robin, 38
Lamb, Charles, 7
Larivée, Annie, 180
Larkin, Philip, 48
Laughter, 47–51, 53
Law, 152
Leach, Edmund, 99–100
Leila, my cat, 116, 196
Lemieux, Karl, 21
Lenin (Vladimir Ilyich Ulyanov), 202
Levinson, Stephen C., 37
Levy, Jacob T., 138, 143
Liebersohn, Yosef Z., 128
Lind, Jennifer, 143
Lorenz, Konrad, 196
Losing, 148–73
Lowliness, 71–72
Lucretius (Titus Lucretius Carus), 95–96
Luhmann, Niklas, 52–53
Lukardis, of Oberweimar, 73

McAleer, Sean, 59, 61
Macdonald, George, 5
McGough, Roger, 168–69
McGranahan, Carole, 104
Maclagan, William, 109
McNamara, Patrick, 113
McNeill, David, 90–93
Magic, 141

Maintenance, 212–13
Marcuse, Herbert, 113
Marshmallow test, 185
Martyrdom, 166
Marvell, Andrew, 66
Mead, G.H, 92
Media, 19–27
Melancholia, 164–65
Memory, 136, 154
Mercy, 16–19, 24–25
Merleau-Ponty, Maurice, 92
Mickey Mouse, 199
Miller, J. Hillis, 105
Ministering, 214
Mirror neurons, 92–93
Mischel, Walter, 185
Missing, 155–56
Modulation, 24, 25, 32–33, 36–37, 46, 206, 208–9
Moro reflex, 72–73
Morris, Desmond, 90, 115
Mourning, 154, 157–58
Mouth, 47, 49, 50, 80, 84, 85
Murphy, Jeffrie, 17
Murray, J. A. H., 154

Nature, 53, 96–98, 114, 154, 169, 183–84, 190–91, 203
Nazirites, 98–99
Negash, Girma, 143, 144
Neoteny, 196
Ness, Sally Ann, 91
Neuman, Yair, 128
Ngai, Sianne, 200–202
Nietzsche, Friedrich, 1
Nobles, Melissa, 135, 139, 143
Noise, 40–43
Noland, Carrie Ann, 91
Novack, Miriam A., 90

O'Neill, Brendan, 145
Ong, Walter, 24
Opie, Iona and Peter, 174

Orality, 24
Otter, Chris, 212–13
Ovid (Publius Ovidius Naso), 159–62, 165, 166
Owen, Marion, 125

Paravicino, Basilio, 48
Parting, 99–100
Parvulescu, Anca, 47
Pascal, Blaise, 6
Performatives, 130, 134
Peter, Saint,, 73
Pets, 192–96, 198–99
Phillips, Adam, 154
Philosophy, 182–83
Photography, 198
Piozzi, Hester Lynch, 153
Plath, Sylvia, 167
Plato, 182
Play, 199–200
Please, 54–6
Pliny, the Elder (Gaius Plinius Secundus), 67
Plutarch, 217
Poe, Edgar Allan, 168
Politeness, 34–63
Postulation, 77, 87
Posture, 66–77, 86–87
Prayer, 55–56, 79
Prohibition, 109
Provine, Robert, 53

Quiet zones, 20–21
Quintilian (Marcus Fabius Quintilianus), 30–1, 73, 81, 88

Raudive, Konstantine, 26
Refraining, 100–101, 105
Remediation, 22
"Repressive desublimation" (Marcuse), 113
Resignation, 11–16
Reznikoff, Iégor, 189

Ritualization, 114
Rucht, Dieter, 44
Ruskin, John, 67

Sacred, 104–5
Sacrifice, 31–2
Sartre, Jean-Paul, 177, 186–87, 193
Sax, Boria, 103
Scale, 207
Schiller, Friedrich, 158–59, 160, 161
Schopenhauer, Arthur, 41–2
Schreber, Daniel Paul, 21
Secrets, 115, 164
Self-esteem, 7, 182
Seriousness, 138–39
Serpell, James, 193
Serres, Michel, 22, 30, 37, 40, 42–43, 190, 211, 214–15
Sexuality, 115
Shakespeare, William, 11, 12, 16, 17, 31, 39, 72, 87, 138, 153, 156, 158, 166, 178, 181, 213
Shame, 127
Shaving 98, 99
Sheridan, Richard, 170–71
Sherman, Gary D., 199–200
Shipman, Pat, 188–89, 190
Shyness, 1
Signation, 12–13
Silence, 115–17
Simmel, Georg, 58
Sitting, 85
Sloterdijk, Peter, 28, 95, 103–4, 183, 193–94, 207, 211
Socrates, 183
Sorel, Georges, 111–12
Soul, 182
Sovereignty 126, 129
Space, 39–40, 43, 64–66, 70–71, 74, 75–76, 78, 86–87, 93, 147, 199, 210–11, 213–16
Speech acts, 44
Spiegel, James S., 8, 9

Spiritual marriage, 107
Sport, 149–52
Standing, 77–78
States 131–33
Steinbeck, John, 213
Stephenson, Peter H., 115–16
Stevens, Wallace, 181, 206
Stone, Christopher, 78
Strachey, James, 157
Strate, Shane, 108
Straus, Erwin W., 68–70
Strikes, 110–12, 117, 120, 172
Submission, 5, 10, 44, 65, 71
Suicide, 170
Surrender, 121
Sustainability, 211
Symbolism, 133

Tague, Ingrid, 192
Tattooing, 13
Tausk, Viktor, 21
Tavuchis, Nicholas, 126, 127, 128, 139–40, 142
Teddy bears, 199, 200
Teeth, 49, 50, 197
Tennyson, Alfred Lord, 156
Theater, 171–73
Thomas, Dylan, 167
Throne, 85
Time, 158, 185–86
Traffic signals, 76

"Transitional object" (Winnicott), 156
Trump, Donald, 18–19
Tuncel, Yunus, 149–50

Unsaying, 39, 44, 117
Uprightness, 66–67, 68–70, 77, 86

Vegetarianism, 103, 106
Ventriloquism, 41, 80
Victimage, 124
Virtue, 2
Visibility, 150

Wallace, David Foster, 181
Waller, Steven J., 189
Warner, David, 143
Warner, Marina, 128, 140–41, 142, 144–45
Watkins, Calvin, 23
Weber, Max, 212
Weinman, Sam, 149
Willis, Nathaniel Parker, 198
Wilson, E.O., 215, 217
Winnicott, Donald, 156
Wordsworth, William, 6–7

Yeats, W.B., 97, 173
Young, Edward, 11–12

Zero, 25
Žižek, Slavoj, 111

Lightning Source UK Ltd.
Milton Keynes UK
UKHW010718140720
366314UK00015B/403